Stump, Bar, and Pulpit

STUMP, BAR, AND PULPIT
SPEECHMAKING
ON THE MISSOURI FRONTIER

BY FRANCES LEA McCURDY

UNIVERSITY OF MISSOURI PRESS
COLUMBIA

Standard Book Number 8262-9112-X
Library of Congress Card Number 74-93050
Copyright © 1969 by The Curators of the University of Missouri
Printed and bound in the United States of America

"Stump Speaking" by George Caleb Bingham has
been reproduced, by permission, from the Collection
of The Boatmen's National Bank of St. Louis.

*To the frontiersmen who settled Missouri
and to the descendants of all frontiersmen,
this study is dedicated.*

Contents

"Some would add to Edmund Burke's pronouncement that no one should indict an entire people the far more limiting declaration that no one can depict an entire people. Others would go further and assert that national character does not exist and that even to employ the concept is to incarnate a defunct myth."

Walter Metzger, "Generalizations about National Character: An Analytical Essay," *Generalization in the Writing of History*, Louis Gottschalk, ed.

Preface

When we recall that Missouri was for many years the western outpost of the United States and for fifteen years after its admission the westernmost state in the Union, it seems justifiable to label the speechmaking of that place in those periods as *frontier rhetoric*.

Missouri's role as a frontier occurred midway in the nation's period of westward expansion. With the exception of Florida, the Atlantic seaboard had lost its frontier characteristics by the time of the Louisiana Purchase. Under the impact of the irregular advance of settlers, the frontier was disappearing even in the area west of the Appalachians. From the Atlantic Coast to the eastern bank of the Mississippi, westering Americans had taken up most of the land that could be bought cheaply or squatted on without payment. By 1800 the wilderness had given way to civilization in Kentucky and Tennessee. The herds of game had disappeared; fertile lands were no longer readily available to settlers. In the southern part of the Northwest Territory the pioneer era was also closing. Territorial governments had been established in Indiana and Illinois, and Ohio had already achieved statehood when Jefferson made the decision to add the vast area west of the Mississippi to the possessions of the United States.

In the first half of the nineteenth century, most of the settlements in Upper Louisiana shared common frontier characteristics. As on other frontiers, a surplus of land and mineral wealth exceeded the needs of the population. The population was on the move; social stratification was fluid; the economy was unspecialized and speculative; the institutions of law and government were in a state of evolution as the people in the area advanced from concern for primitive individual needs to social consciousness.

By 1850 the frontier had moved farther west. The population of Missouri, which had been formally admitted to the Union in 1821, had reached nearly 700,000 and averaged between ten and eleven persons to the square mile by the end of the first of the nineteenth century. By then three million acres of farm land were under cultivation, and one hundred of the eventual one hundred and fourteen counties had been organized. By 1850 Missourians were moving out toward Texas, Oregon, and California. New frontiers lured adventurers and held out hopes for improved fortunes.

Though the frontier period in Missouri was relatively brief, it has significance in the nation's history. Missouri, as a frontier, was an area where the advance of traders and farmers coalesced as in few other regions. In Missouri the French fur traders combined with American farmers to form political institutions and to develop a distinct social structure; in Missouri patterns for the development of all Upper Louisiana were tested. Missouri's frontier period ushered in the successive frontiers of the Great Plains and of the Pacific Coast. St. Louis became the gateway to the new West that opened with the explorations of Lewis and Clark. The town of Independence was for some years the starting point for the Santa Fe and Oregon trails. St. Joseph, Missouri, was the eastern terminus for the riders of the Pony Express on their race to California. At the same time that they were deeply involved in the development of the West, Missourians debated ideas that engrossed the nation. They rehearsed the slavery controversy in the struggle for statehood; they sent to the United States Senate Thomas Hart Benton, exponent of pre-emption, Western expansion, and nationalism; they divided into factions over hard and soft money; and throughout the state's pioneer era, Missourians tested Jacksonian democracy by experiment.

To the Missouri frontiersman, the phrase *Jacksonian democracy* represented no complex philosophy. It meant opportunity for the man born without special advantages to gain wealth and prestige. When a speaker in Missouri affirmed his belief in Jacksonian democracy, he was declaring his faith in the right of the common man to participate in government, his trust in the superiority of common sense over formal education, his dislike of special privilege, his impatience with forms or principles that seemed to offer no positive benefits. The phrase signified the beliefs that a man could rise in society as high as his abilities would allow him and that one who had not heretofore held power had an equal right and perhaps as much ability to govern as the next man.

Both Jacksonian democracy and the influences of the frontier have been described and interpreted extensively by historians and by literary and social critics. To these sources I acknowledge indebtedness for background materials. In bringing together these materials, I have worked with the thesis that the process of testing and popularizing frontier ideas of democracy is most clearly traced in the rhetoric of the frontier speaker. His assumptions, the reasoning he used, the stratagems he scorned to hide, and the language he chose to influence his hearers show *how* rather than *what* ideas came to be thought of as typical of the frontier.

Appreciation is due to many people for help in locating materials and for thoughtful criticism of the manuscript. The staff of the State Historical Society of Missouri, where the primary materials for this study are located, were unfailingly courteous and helpful through the more than ten years of my research there. Appreciation is due particularly to the editors of the *Missouri Historical Review* for permission to include material from two articles previously published by them. Interpretations of the frontier and of Jacksonian democracy that proved especially helpful include the essays on the Turner thesis edited by George Rogers Taylor and those in the volume entitled *The Frontier Perspective* edited by Walker Wyman and Clifton B. Kroeber. I am indebted to Arthur K. Moore's *The Frontier Mind*, John William Ward's *Andrew Jackson: Symbol for an Age*, Arthur Schlesinger, Jr.'s, *The Age of Jackson*, and Marvin Meyers' *Jacksonian Persuasion* for insights and interpretations.

I wish to express my gratitude to the Research Council of the University of Missouri for a modest grant that enabled me to employ clerical help. To Victor M. Powell, who read the manuscript, and to Bower Aly, who criticized the work out of their full knowledge of pioneer history and speechmaking in Missouri, I am much indebted. For the errors and omissions I take full responsibility. Not the least of my debts is one of gratitude for the patience and encouragement of my husband, William Edward McCurdy.

Columbia, Missouri   F.L.M.

May, 1969

Foreword

The American West has, since its opening, been a source of fascination to the speculator, the land hungry, the adventurer, the trader, and finally to the scholar. The processes of conquest, exploring, occupying, inhabiting, and developing went forward swiftly after the initial settlements were founded and firmly established; the scholars began their research and evaluation of the West after Frederick Jackson Turner published his seminal essay in 1893. Turner gave them purpose and an interpretation that released their creative powers, made potent by newly found research techniques. The result was an avalanche of scholarly articles and books on the West, which flowed from the presses for the next half century. The rapid growth of state and local historical societies has been due in part to the general awareness that the story of western development is highly significant and that sound interpretations depend upon rich and varied source material.

The focus of interest has shifted in recent decades from the formation of states and the taming of the wilderness to the various factors that promoted the evolution of social life, business activity, and culture from the raw conditions of the formative years. Historians in recent years have directed their attention to the development of the specializations that quickly emerged after the frontier had moved on. The place in society of the business and professional man and the rapid development of institutions have become the scholar's concern in the modern period.

The study of communications on the frontier has concentrated, in the main, on the history of newspapers and travel. Dr. McCurdy has opened the door to a more elusive art, that of speechmaking, or, to use the scholar's terminology, frontier rhetoric. The original materials for an accurate, critical, and exhaustive study of speechmaking do not exist; usually they disappeared the moment the speech was uttered. But the hearer and reporter sometimes recorded a speech and once in a great while a manuscript survived. Such materials, difficult to find, are the bases for Dr. McCurdy's study. There can be little doubt about the validity of her conclusions; her documentation is full and convincing. Hers is a significant study.

W. Francis English

Stump, Bar, and Pulpit

I

"*There is scarcely anything more difficult than correct delineation of character. This task is usually undertaken by friends or enemies, and the result is either panegyric or satire.*"

H. M. Brackenridge, *Views of Louisiana.* . . .

The Pioneer Missourian

In the bitter congressional debate of 1838 over the bill extending the right of purchase to actual settlers on public lands, Joseph F. Randolph of New Jersey spoke contemptuously of the ignorance and lawlessness of frontiersmen. Congressman Albert G. Harrison of Missouri defended the pioneers as the "best blood in the country": "Men who go into the deep solitudes of the wilderness, seeking a home for themselves and their families, risking their lives at every step, ready for any danger, and prepared for any difficulty . . . are not the men to be guilty of the foul charges that have been alleged against them," he declared. He added in their further defense, "If they are deficient in those accomplishments which a liberal education affords to others they make up for the loss in an . . . eloquence which burns upon the lip, because it comes warm from the heart."[1]

The Missouri congressman's reference to eloquence as a measure of worth was understandable in the light of his constituents' fondness for oratory. He knew their love for the rolling periods and figures that graced the speechmaking of the day. They thronged into courtrooms to hear lawyers plead, gathered in groves to listen to discourses on sin and church doctrine, applauded legislative debates from their seats in the galleries, and celebrated holidays with orations.

Speechmaking had not always flourished in the area. The French settlers, who had crossed to the western shore of the Mississippi after Americans occupied the Illinois side, made few public speeches. Their government did not encourage free expression of opinion. Nor did the transfer of Louisiana to Spain increase the freedom of the inhabitants. Spanish officials, like the French, governed

[1] Jefferson City *Jeffersonian Republican*, July 14, 1838, pp. 1-2.

paternalistically. They permitted no political debates, and when a controversy arose between settlers, the lieutenant governor or commandant acted as prosecutor, judge, and jury. The flood of Americans pouring into the territory after 1804 brought changes that were bewildering to these earlier settlers. Controversy, loud political declamation, and fevered litigation supplanted the authoritative pronouncements of officials. About them on every side, the old inhabitants now heard a spate of oratory from office seekers, lawyers, soul-savers, and celebrators of holidays.

The early settlers had no opportunity for gradual adjustment to these changes. American newcomers doubled the population in the eight years between 1804 and 1812, continued to arrive even during the war years, and flooded in by the hundreds when the threat of attack by Indians quieted.[2] Daily, the wagons, carriages, and carts rolled into the new frontier, bringing arrivals from Illinois and Indiana, from New England and the Middle States, from the Carolinas, and, most frequently of all, from Virginia, Kentucky, and Tennessee. Among those who turned their faces westward were men disappointed in political or professional hopes, Revolutionary veterans determined to profit from government grants of land, younger sons without inheritances, adventurers who loved the excitement of the frontier, and reckless desperadoes driven out of the more law-abiding regions. Some men came because they wished to be free of the duties and impositions of government or to rid themselves of the frictions of a settled society; many came because a new land held hope of a better life than they had known. A young man from Kentucky expressed a common hope when he wrote to a friend in Missouri, "I have no doubt but I could increase my property handsomely by moving to your state."[3]

Not all pioneers were poor. Some came in carriages, bringing

[2] The population increased from slightly over 10,000 in 1804 to more than 20,000 in 1810 and rose to more than 67,000 by 1820. Sister Chelidonia Ronnebaum, "Population and Settlement in Missouri 1804–1820" (microfilm; Master's thesis, University of Missouri, Columbia, Missouri, 1936), 23, 30, 50, 66, 77, 96, 105.

[3] William Broadwell to Jacob Payne, September 8, 1830, Moses Payne Papers and Account Books.

silver teaspoons and sugar tongs. Their Negroes drove herds of cattle and sheep before them; their wagons creaked under loads of furniture.[4] Others made the trip west on foot. When they arrived on the land they would settle, they built rough cabins and made rude beds by throwing piles of deerskins over poles laid across forked sticks driven into the ground.

Pioneer Missourians were as diverse as their households. In St. Louis, Robert Wash, graduate of William and Mary College, practiced the manners and amusements that he had known in his old home in Virginia. He joined the merchants, speculators, army officers, and government officials in a coterie of aristocrats who exchanged social amenities with the wealthy French residents and who included in their reading the works of Shakespeare, the essays of Hume, and Young's *Night Thoughts*. He had counterparts in Ste. Genevieve in John Scott, graduate of the College of New Jersey at Princeton, whose courtly manners charmed ladies on the frontier; in St. Charles where Rufus Easton, suave New Yorker, had settled in 1804; and in the vicinity of Franklin where John Hardeman had created a beautiful plantation in the wilderness. At the other extreme were the "branch water" men, so named because they were too lazy to dig a well on the land where they squatted. They built nondescript shelters and when they were ready to leave had only to whistle for the dog and put out the fire. To still more remote areas went men who hunted and fished for a livelihood, shunned civilization and its restraints, and moved on when they could hear the sound of a neighbor's axe. More usually, settlers were plain people who lived frugally, worked hard, and hoped to prosper with the advance of civilization.

The frontier was no place for weaklings. Indians burned outlying cabins and killed unwary travelers; lawless men roamed the area, and violence was commonplace. Missourians insisted, however, that the tales of brutality and bloodshed circulated in the East were

---

[4] Henry J. Brown, Papers and Account Books; J. Thomas Scharf, *History of St. Louis City and County, from the Earliest Periods to the Present Day: Including Biographical Sketches of Representative Men*, I, 298–99.

exaggerations. They admitted that danger existed, but they scoffed at the lurid tales of their country told in the more settled regions. They pointed out that the crimes, just as elsewhere, were committed by a small number of unprincipled and licentious men. Timothy Flint, sent out by the Connecticut Missionary Society in 1816 to Christianize Missourians, indignantly repudiated Dr. Timothy Dwight's charge that the West was a "grand reservoir of the scum of the Atlantic States." Flint conceded that worthless people did reside in the region — most of them, in his opinion, came from New England — but he declared that citizens generally, even backwoodsmen, possessed a substantial, though admittedly coarse, morality. Acknowledging that the frontiersman was not free from vice and barbarism, admitting that he habitually carried a knife or dirk in his bosom, Flint yet characterized him as sincere, hospitable, and upright in his dealings.[5]

The dirks and knives, so alarming to Easterners, were less deadly than the dueling pistols commonly brought into use by the more genteel citizens. The dueling code was as rigid on the frontier as in the settled regions. A real or fancied insult was sufficient cause for a challenge. A disparaging remark about a friend or relative, especially about a woman, had necessarily to be avenged. A gentleman was not required to meet on the field of honor a ruffian or a man he considered dishonorable, but he must show that he was not afraid. Frontier society rejected a coward and denied him political or professional advancement. The experience of young H. M. Brackenridge illustrates the frontiersman's attitude concerning personal valor. On his way to Missouri, where he hoped to practice law, Brackenridge angered the captain of the river boat on which he was a passenger. The captain demanded satisfaction, with butcher knives as weapons. Ignoring the challenge — a serious breach of the code duello — Brackenridge left the boat at New Madrid and prepared to

[5] Timothy Flint, *Recollections of the Last Ten Years, Passed in Occasional Residences and Journeyings in the Valley of the Mississippi, from Pittsburg and the Missouri to the Gulf of Mexico, and from Florida to the Spanish Frontier; in a Series of Letters to the Reverend James Flint, of Salem, Massachusetts,* 175–76.

continue his journey by land. He had not gone far when friends overtook him and told him that, if he expected to make his home in Missouri, he must return to New Madrid and show that he was not afraid of facing the captain in personal combat. A stroll through the streets of the town was all that was necessary on that occasion, but challenges rarely ended so tamely.[6]

Citizens attempted to legislate duels out of existence, but combatants merely retired to a secluded spot or held trysts outside the legal jurisdiction of officials. Duelists of St. Louis rowed to an island in the river between Missouri and Illinois and there, in sight of the shore, paced off the agreed distances and satisfied the demands of honor. On that spot of land known as Bloody Island, Thomas Hart Benton fired the pistol ball that took the life of young Charles Lucas and won him the relentless hatred of John B. C. Lucas, the duelist's father; and there in 1831 Congressman Spencer Pettis and Thomas Biddle, brother of Nicholas Biddle of the United States Bank, killed each other in a duel growing out of an election dispute. Editors deplored and ministers denounced the practice, but pioneer Missourians placed the code above legislation and clerical anathemas.

On the frontier, fighting was a sport as well as a means of defense or of satisfying one's honor. Unscheduled battles occurred when a frontiersman got "chock full of liquor" and the spirit of combat. "Hell's afloat and the river's risin'!" the belligerent one would cry. "I'm the yaller flower of the forest; a flash and a half of lightning; a perfect thunder gust. Who wants to fight?"[7] Wherever crowds gathered and liquor flowed, a fight was almost certain to erupt. Among the rougher element, combat was brutal and merciless. With their thumbs gladiators gouged out opponents' eyes; they bit off noses, ears, or chunks of flesh from their adversaries, who, in turn, tried to stomp them into submission. The best man in a community was the one who had whipped all the rest, and maimed faces testified to the fury of the fighting.

[6] H. M. Brackenridge, *Recollections of Persons and Places in the West*, 188–90.

[7] Such a scene is described in the Jefferson City *Jeffersonian Republican*, July 23, 1842, p. 1.

Physical strength and agility were much admired on the frontier, and the boisterous and disorderly amusements often revolved around individual or team feats of strength. In tugs of war men united their forces by locking arms around each others' waists and tugging with all their might to pull a similarly joined team across a designated line. Equally popular was gander pulling, a sport in which men riding at full speed attempted to snatch the greased head from a gander suspended from the limb of a tree. The feat was not easy, for a joker might station himself near the tree to whack the horse across the rump just before the rider reached for the prize.

Horsemanship was a necessary skill of the time, and Missourians took pride in their mounts, as did men in other parts of the world. The race track was a major attraction in a community, but men tested the speed of their horses off as well as on the track. In St. Louis, the city of greatest refinement in the region, the city fathers found it necessary to ban racing on main streets by either riders on horseback or drivers in carts.[8]

A favorite pastime of early settlers was the shooting match, a feature of military musters, political canvasses, Fourth of July celebrations, and Saturday night gatherings. Marksmanship was more than a sport in a region where a man's life might depend on his skill; the pioneer spoke of his rifle with affection, applying the names "blood-letter," "panther-cooler," and "hair-splitter" to his crude weapons. Target shooting had still another appeal; it offered an opportunity for laying wagers. Betting was second nature for many Missouri frontiersmen, who laid wagers on the speed of their horses, on the mettle of their gamecocks, and on their own abilities to outwrestle any other man in the settlement.

The frontiersman was notorious for his boastfulness, as witnesses the genre of "tall stories" of the era. The Missourian declared that the women of Missouri were the fairest, the men of the state the bravest, the soil the richest, the opportunities the greatest in the United States; the United States, in turn, was the greatest of coun-

[8] St. Louis *Missouri Republican*, May 21, 1823, p. 3.

tries, its heroes the noblest, its government the wisest, its ideals the highest, its leaders the ablest. Compared to the Missouri and the Mississippi rivers, Missourians said, the Nile was but a rill. The backwoodsman's boasts have become legendary. A typical braggart announced himself as "a real ring-tailed roarer of a jaw-breaker" who could "out eat, out work, out grin, out snort, out run, out jump, out lift, out sneeze, out sleep, out brag, or out lie anything in the shape of man or beast from Maine to Louisiana." [9] The last two claims should certainly have gone unchallenged.

The rowdiness of boatmen and trappers whose headquarters were in St. Louis disturbed the more sedate settlers. At intervals the editor of the *Missouri Gazette and Public Advertiser* called on the police to put a stop to the hallooing and shouting of "vagabonds" roaming the streets after "decent folk were abed." "While all our citizens were wrapt in sleep," the editor lamented, "a parcel of grown children amused themselves in parading our streets, whooping and yelling in a style similar to their brothers of the woods." [10]

Rowdiness was by no means limited to any one group. Contributing to the general high spirits was the almost universal use of intoxicants. A Methodist preacher of the day maintained that liquor was found everywhere — "on the sideboard of the wealthy and fashionable and in the cabin of the farmer and laborer." [11] A man was thought uncivil if he failed to offer his guest a drink, and refusal to accept a glass was considered churlish and unsociable. A general belief existed that the heat made consumption of water unmixed with some spirituous drink harmful, and Missourians were cautious of thus endangering their health. Virtually every settlement had its grocery where buyers could obtain liquor. A visitor reported that in St. Louis in 1838 the sales of wines and whiskeys dispensed from

[9] Columbia *Missouri Intelligencer and Boon's Lick Advertiser*, September 12, 1835, p. 2.

[10] St. Louis *Missouri Gazette and Illinois Advertiser*, May 6, 1815, p. 3; *Missouri Gazette and Public Advertiser*, January 2, 1822, p. 4.

[11] D. R. McAnally, *History of Methodism in Missouri; from the Date of Its Introduction in 1806, down to the Present Day; with an Appendix, Containing Full and Accurate Statistical Information, etc.*, 259.

9

fifty-eight houses amounted to two thousand dollars a day.[12] The black junk bottle filled with whiskey was an indispensable factor in the political aspirant's campaign for votes; it was a cheering companion to the lawyer on his rounds of the judicial circuit, and frontier preachers unselfconsciously took their turns when the bottle was passed round. Throughout the period some men and women strongly opposed any use of liquor, but the few advocates of temperance were a feeble force against entrenched custom.

John Mason Peck, a Baptist minister who came to preach in the territory soon after the cession, was horrified at the intemperance of the settlers and even more shocked by the blasphemous oaths. Profanity was unconscious and habitual for many of the most respected citizens, as well as for the boatmen and hunters. Swearing was such an integral part of the speech of John Scott, territorial representative from Missouri, that his enemies sneered that he was unable to make a speech on the floor of Congress without using profanity. His admirers rarely defended him against the charge; they were rather proud of his verbal prowess. Blasphemy was a mode of emphasis, and Missourians scarcely considered it irreverent. They laughed about the incident in which Peyton Hayden, a lawyer from central Missouri, was involved when he represented a client in a trial held in a church for want of a courthouse. A minister who was in attendance heard Hayden mutter as he listened to his opponent, "By God! he has traveled out of the record. By God! I will travel out of the record also." When the clergyman protested his use of profanity, Hayden indignantly denied the charge, saying, "If you hear any person say that I indulge in profane language, you are authorized to say for me that he is a damned liar."[13]

To some early visitors, the language of Missourians was less disturbing than their manners. Eager for news of the world outside and curious about the people he met, the frontiersman was given to ask-

---

[12] "The Journal of Henry B. Miller," *Missouri Historical Society Collections,* Thomas M. Marshall, ed., VI, 3 (1931), 270–71.

[13] W. V. N. Bay, *Reminiscences of the Bench and Bar of Missouri, with an Appendix, Containing Biographical Sketches of Nearly All of the Judges and Lawyers Who Have Passed Away . . . ,* 62.

ing personal questions and unabashedly investigating a stranger's be-longings. When Duke Paul Wilhelm of Württemberg traveled through Missouri, he was more than once annoyed by the forward-ness of the settlers. Generally irritated by the throngs of people who crowded about his boat, he was angered and frightened when towns-men at Franklin came on board and meddled with his papers. He be-lieved that his life was being threatened when two young men took hold of his arm and urged him to go with them to their boarding-house for dinner.[14] The youths probably had no intention of fright-ening the titled stranger; more likely, they wanted to hear about his travels and show their neighbors that they were associating with a duke on familiar terms.

Despite the pioneer's loud declarations of his belief in equality, he enjoyed association with aristocrats. His insistence that he was as good as the next fellow and would raise his cap to nobody carries a note of defensiveness. White persons who worked for others ob-jected to being called servants; they were the "help." Missourians re-peated approvingly the story of the domestic who answered a for-eign visitor's query as to whether her master was at home with the reply that she had no master.[15]

This concept of equality, however vehemently asserted, did not extend to Negroes. The relatively small number of Missourians who supported a restriction clause in the state constitution hastened to as-sure slaveholders in the region that they held no abolitionist senti-ments. Few Missourians held many slaves, but even the yeoman farmer who owned no slaves supported the institution, if not ac-tively, then by his silence. Thomas Hart Benton, leader of the Jack-sonian democrats in Missouri, owned slaves, as did many others who guided the political affairs in the state. Perhaps the resentment against the attempt to force restriction upon Missouri as a price for her admission to statehood, perhaps the dominance of citizens who had come from the South, perhaps the settlers' preoccupation with

[14] Paul Wilhelm, Duke of Württemberg, *First Journey to North America in the Years 1822 to 1824*, trans. by William G. Bek, 258–60.

[15] St. Louis *Missouri Gazette*, December 7, 1808, p. 4, quoting from C. W. Janson, *Stranger in America*.

their own problems in opening up the frontier quieted antislavery sentiments. Whatever the reason, slavery was not an issue in the political contests between the Whigs, generally made up of the wealthier and slaveholding groups, and the Jacksonian democracy, to whom laborers, mechanics, and yeoman farmers gave their allegiance. In this climate of thought, slaves did not figure in the concept of equality.

Those white men who had reached positions of leadership had little to say of equality unless they were attempting to influence their less fortunate white neighbors. Despite loud denials to the contrary, an aristocracy of wealth existed, and unless he was a candidate for office, an aristocrat did not generally associate with the "lower class" citizens. The brashness of "ignorant and uncouth" frontiersmen who did not seem to recognize the superiority of wealthy men occasionally caused trouble. For example, when General Lafayette visited St. Louis, a butcher "still greasy from handling meat" annoyed the official welcoming committee by pushing through the protective ring around the General and seizing the great man by the hand. The "impudent" man further irritated the aristocrats, when they commanded him to go away, by asserting that he was as good as they were.[16]

Those who assumed themselves to be aristocrats justified the distinction by holding that wealth was evidence of natural leadership and superior intelligence. They pointed out that any man who had the ability could rise on the frontier, and they frequently compared the fluidity of society in the thinly settled areas with the more rigid social classifications in the older settlements. Not all were pleased by the mobility. One observer complained that men who came to the area, ambitious to gain wealth and prestige, kept the elements in continual chaos. Men without distinction in their former homes had, he said, with the aid of the tailor and a few externals, set themselves up as gentlemen on the frontier.[17]

[16] John F. Darby, *Personal Recollections of Many Prominent People Whom I Have Known, and of Events — Especially of Those Relating to the History of St. Louis . . . .*, 59–60.

[17] Flint, 179–81.

Although an aristocracy of education and family, as well as wealth, controlled political offices in early territorial days, the old leaders lost control as the power of the common man increased. By his authority at the polls, the citizen without wealth or educational advantages retaliated for former slights, real or imagined, and a candidate's lack of formal education became a positive asset. Nevertheless, even while he boasted that he had received all his learning in the school of experience, the pioneer wanted his children to have an education, and as soon as possible he combined with his neighbors to provide some sort of schooling for his sons and daughters.

Despite these efforts illiteracy remained high. As late as 1840, 15 per cent of the total white population of Missouri over twenty years of age could neither read nor write, and the percentage had dropped only slightly by 1860.[18] Alfred Waugh, an artist of sorts who spent some time in Missouri in 1845 and 1846, ascribed the frontiersman's lack of interest in the refinements of society to the conditions of his life. He thought that the people, still laboring for necessities, had neither the wealth nor the leisure to bestow on mental culture. "The *utile* and not the *dulce* found favor with them," he said, and, perhaps justifying his failure to sell his own pictures, explained that frontiersmen thought a cow, a sheep, or a hog "more beautiful than the work of Raphael or Titian."[19]

Although the difficulty of obtaining necessities in primitive surroundings discouraged pursuit of culture, the pioneers who loved or respected books managed to bring a small library along with their coffee pots and Dutch ovens and to import an occasional volume. These books they loaned to neighbors. Perhaps it was this lending of treasured volumes that encouraged the early attempts to set up libraries. In 1819 members of the St. Louis Debating Society formed a corporation and sold shares to establish a city library.[20] A library had already been established in Franklin, down in the interior of the territory. Maintaining the libraries was often more difficult than start-

---

[18] David D. March, *The History of Missouri*, I, 730.
[19] Alfred S. Waugh, "Desultory Wanderings in the Years 1845–46," John F. McDermott, ed., *Bulletin of the Missouri Historical Society*, VI, 4 (July, 1950), 514–15.
[20] St. Louis *Missouri Gazette and Public Advertiser*, March 3, 1819, p. 3.

ing them. In 1819 private citizens of Franklin reported trouble with borrowers who failed to return library books, and town trustees, who were engaged in persuading citizens to furnish themselves with water buckets for fire fighting, had little time to attend to overdue books or to promote culture.[21] At Franklin, as elsewhere, libraries were supported by relatively small groups of interested townspeople.

Family libraries generally centered around biblical literature. Of the thirty-six books listed by a frontier settler who inventoried his property, four were Bibles and twenty others were on religious subjects.[22] But pioneers did not restrict their reading to the Bible. The western frontier consumed much contemporary English literature. Favorite authors were Scott and Byron, but Bacon and Hume's philosophical Works, Johnson's *Lives of the English Poets*, the plays of Shakespeare and Goldsmith, the poems of Robert Burns and of a now forgotten Hannah Moore were also popular. Practical and moral advice was offered for sale in books about law, medicine, and morality. In St. Louis merchants advertised — along with the best liquors, fresh medicine, and dressed skins — law books by Coke, Blackstone, Tidd, and Chitty. There and elsewhere settlers could purchase medical dictionaries: Wilson *On Fevers*, Desault's *Surgery*, Bell's *Anatomy*, and Lewes' *Midwifery*. Abbott's *Young Christian* and *Mother at Home* were equally available for a price. In the library of a frontiersman who expected to speak in public, a manual of oratory was quite likely to be found.

Speaking was educational, the pioneer believed. His almanac told him so. In 1848 the thought for the month of April admonished fathers, "Your children's scholarship depends more on what books you furnish them with, and on how much good public speaking they hear, than on how much schooling you give them."[23] The phi-

[21] Franklin *Missouri Intelligencer*, December 10, 1819, p. 3, and January 7, 1820, pp. 2 and 4. The situation had become so serious that on page 3 of the December 3, 1819, issue Dr. Lowry inserted a notice asking borrowers to return library books in order to permit the library to carry on its business.

[22] Brown Papers.

[23] *Chambers and Knapp's Missouri and Illinois Almanac for the Year of our Lord, 1848.*

losophy was comforting to a father whose conscience troubled him at the poor opportunity his way of life provided for his children, for even though subscription schools had been set up in the towns, many of the settlers could not raise the seven, or twelve, or fifteen dollars a term that the schoolmaster charged and could afford even less the cost of boarding the children in town.

Even if he could not send his children to school, however, the frontiersman could take them to speakings. Besides being educational for his offspring, the gatherings offered the parents diversion and an opportunity to meet with other people. For settlers on the frontier, life was often dull. All days were not made up of fleeing from the tomahawk, shooting for the beef, or dining upon wild turkeys and strawberries. On the contrary, most waking hours were filled with drudgery. Fathers and sons labored at clearing the fields and planting crops, and the women worked as hard as the men to provide food and clothing for their families, along with helping in the fields. Coffee was an almost unobtainable luxury, and in the intense heat of the summer months milk soured, meat spoiled, and vermin flourished. Wood ticks and flies were more than annoyances; they were actual hazards for men crossing the prairies. The mosquitoes did their work so thoroughly that almost every Missourian suffered from malarial chills and fever, the symptoms occurring with such regularity that frontier humorists said they had no use for timepieces. Scourges of cholera swept through the area so frequently that, in satiric spite, Illinoisans nicknamed their neighbors across the river "the pukes." The powerful medicines were sometimes less bearable than the diseases they were designed to cure. Worn out by poor food, hard work, and bodily discomforts, men and women looked old at forty and many died young.

Not the least of the hardships for many of the settlers was separation from the company of other men. The extreme isolation of some families resulted in almost unbelievable ignorance. Brackenridge reported that a frontiersman he met in 1811 had never heard of Jefferson, Madison, or Franklin. Few were the cabins that the circuit rider did not reach with the story of salvation, but some settlers in the remote interior were so isolated that they were missed by even these hardy itinerants. An early clergyman told of traveling all day in the rain without seeing any sign of habitation until he glimpsed at nightfall the light of a hearth fire through a half-shut cabin door. He hailed the cabin, and, though a bevy of children scattered like frightened partridges, a woman invited him to come in and placed a supper of bear beef and buttermilk before him. After supper, when the preacher questioned the children about their religious experiences, they told him that they had never seen a Bible and had heard prayer only once. The mother, at the close of his exhortation on sin and the Savior, answered, when asked if she knew that Jesus had died for her, that she "never knowed afore that Jesus was dead." [24]

Though the townsman could not plead lack of opportunity to hear sermons, his links with his national leaders and the outside world were limited. Mails often failed to arrive. In 1810 a citizen of St. Louis observed — and his capitalization expressed his attitude — "Public indignation has never been so strongly manifested, or so justly created since the american government took place, as at the present moment, occasioned by the repeated failure of the Mail. . . . We had but one solitary Mail from the Eastward, during a period of 11 or 12 weeks." [25] In 1808 a letter mailed in Washington, D. C., arrived in St. Louis forty-two days later; a writer in St. Louis had to wait over two months for an answer from the nation's capital.[26] By 1835 the more settled portions of the state enjoyed mail service twice a week, and the conditions of travel had so improved that the trip from Franklin to St. Louis, which had taken a month in 1819, required only three days.[27] Even with improved conditions, travel was perilous, mud was deep, roads were poorly marked, and high water was a hazard for travelers on horseback and in stage

[24] McAnally, 406–10.

[25] St. Louis *Louisiana Gazette*, March 1, 1810, p. 3.

[26] Meriwether Lewis to the Secretary of War, August 20, 1808, *The Territorial Papers of the United States, the Territory of Louisiana-Missouri 1806–1814*, Clarence Edwin Carter, ed., XIV, 212.

[27] Editorial, Columbia *Missouri Intelligencer and Boon's Lick Advertiser*, December 5, 1835, p. 2.

coaches. Crossing the streams by ferry was little safer. When overloaded boats sank, plunging passengers and cargo into the water, the passengers could save themselves, but mail and cargo were often lost.

Uneducated, isolated, lonely, the pioneer turned to speaking occasions for identification with public men and for information about issues. The speechmaking also provided an outlet for his repressed emotions: His neighbors would have scorned him if he had shown fear of Indians or wild animals; they expected him to bear sickness and death with fortitude; but he could be emotionally uninhibited at the public speakings without fear of ridicule. The weeping, falling, jerking, and other physical manifestations of repentance at frontier religious meetings were scarcely less violent than many of the reactions in a town meeting at which the Whig and Democratic faithful met to hear a speaker praise party candidates and tear into the opposition. When a member of the audience favored a man or measure, he showed his enthusiasm. He cried, "Yes, yes!" or "No, no!" to the speaker's questions; he stepped out on call and, with hand on heart, swore allegiance to a doctrine or leader. Speakers sometimes capitalized on this willingness to participate by moving to the edge of the platform to ask an old man in the audience to verify a statement or to give an account of his experiences to illustrate a point.

Such exuberance and lack of restraint could also be troublesome. Verbal exchanges between speaker and listeners were not always good natured. Unfriendly auditors embarrassed the speaker by unscheduled comments or answers to his rhetorically intended questions. Fights broke out and shouts, blows, and threats added to the confusion. Even well-disposed crowds became restless. Children wandered in and out of meetings, and dogs and stranger animals came to satisfy their curiosity as speaker and audience sparred.

Missourians of the time indulged in hero worship as avidly as other people in other places and other times. One evidence of their admiration was arrangement of a dinner in honor of a favorite. Such dinners provided opportunity to compose toasts, to drink to the sentiments offered by others, and to listen to speeches lauding the man of the hour. But these pleasures in honoring a favorite were equaled by the malicious glee to be derived from deflating a disliked, self-important figure. Puncturing the dignity of a pompous fellow might consist of playing rough and sometimes dangerous jokes on the victim.

The enjoyment of another's discomfort was one aspect of a macabre quality that flowed through much of the humor of the early settlers. In the Indians' attacks, the hangings, the epidemics of cholera, and even in his own financial ruin, the man who lived in crude and perilous conditions found subjects for humor. He opined gravely that an Indian met in the woods was apt to suffer from the falling sickness; when a prisoner received a last-minute reprieve from hanging, he commented that a great many people had to go home disappointed.

Language on the frontier took its color from the environment. Respect for the labor and industriousness demonstrated by cultivated fields was imaged in such expressions as, "We have some corn to tread out," meaning that the speaker faced a problem. An insincere man was "hollow as a polk stalk" or "rotten as a mushroom" and a homely one was "sallow as a dried cornstalk." A poor business was a "weedy concern" and an individual who refused to be drawn into another's quarrel "designed to attend to his own truckpatch." "He is only measuring my corn by his own standard," a speaker said contemptuously of a critic, and corn, the staple of life, recurred in the comment of a skeptical man who declared his unwillingness to be "fed on soft corn."

Scorn, when it rose to expression, was strong and vivid. Missourians wrote off a braggart with the remark, "How we apples swim," or predicted that he "would have to be burnt for the big head." They impugned the good sense of a fellow with the comment that he had "barely enough brains to keep his skull from caving in" and contemptuously remarked the stature of a small man as a "little fellow barely able to kick up a sapling." They derided a man who refused to take a stand as one who "could not be got to the scratch," was "crawfishing," "tucking his tail," or "trying to wear his coat the way the wind blows."

18

On the other hand, one complimented a fellow citizen by calling him a horse, a buster, a real painter [panther], an old fellow, or by declaring that he had "nine rings around his tail." A project that failed was said to fall stillborn; a deep subject was "swimming water"; a man taking a searching view of a subject said, borrowing from the experience of the frontiersman who climbed a tree to get his bearings, "It looked so to a man up a tree." A belligerent fellow wanted to "pick a crow" or was "hungry to fight." A cautious man "refused to be hooked"; a man unable to convince his audience was "whistling jigs to a millstone" even though what he said was "true as preaching."

The importance of animals in the life of the pioneer is evident in his metaphor. The meaning of an advocate of liberty of the press who declared that he did not wish his ox to be muzzled was as clearly understood as was another man's comment on the judgment of a fellow whom he advised to get the right pig by the ear. The neighbors of a man greedy for office characterized him as a "dog in the meathouse grasping for all and barking for more." A citizen present at an opposition political meeting confessed that he felt like a sheep at a barbecue; when Democrats quarreled among themselves, a Whig editor laughed that the fight was like a contest between a skunk and a snake.

A society for which the horse was so necessary, naturally based its metaphors on the animal and its management. A man who spoke without success was "singing songs to a dead horse"; a candidate who supported a popular bill was said to be running a "Gilpin race on a hobby horse"; a speaker who presented proof had "the documents in his saddle bags"; and a citizen who campaigned on a ticket with a more popular man was "trying to ride behind the old hunter." A telling bit of sarcasm was a "touch of the spur"; subservience to a party or leader marked a "collar man." When a man had taken an unsupportable position, he was said to be in a corner too short to turn in; when criticism roused an angry response, the critic might laugh that "a chafed horse is easy made to flinch."

Some terms had a special meaning on the frontier. *Plunder* referred to a man's personal belongings; a *grocery* was a store that sold liquor; *chance* was a synonym for quantity, and *right smart* was a large quantity. *Reckon* meant *suppose* to Missourians; to *let on* was to admit; *pert* was to be cheerful or in a state of well being; *slope* was the act of running away; and *raise* was a term used to mean propagation and nourishment of the species.

Both understatement and exaggeration were characteristic of speech on the frontier. The tall tale, with its straining at the bounds of truth, recalled feats of prowess in hunting, marksmanship, and fighting. The frontiersman enjoyed hearing the exploits of early settlers in combat with Indians, of which the story of Baptiste, or Louis, or Baptiste Louis Roi was one of the favorites. The name of the hero and the details varied with the teller, but the basic story was the same. Timothy Flint's version includes a brief description of an attack by savages on Roi's (Flint spelled the name Roy) garrison and the killing of Roi's companion. In Flint's story Roi and his wife withstood the siege for four days. During that time the trader's wife melted lead, molded bullets, and took her turn at shooting. On the fourth day the Indians increased the strength of their attack and set the roof of the fort on fire with flaming arrows. Flint's story ends with the account of Roi's knocking off the burning boards and saving himself and his wife from a fiery death.[28]

John Mason Peck's account of the incident includes some details that Flint omitted. The Baptist minister credited the story to Samuel Smith, who had reputedly heard it from his father-in-law. Peck, who set the date in 1814, repeated the story of the Indian attack and the blazing roof. In Peck's story, the Rois were saved from burning to death by Madame Roi's bringing the contents of a chamber pot to quench the flames. The minister stated that the young men of St. Louis honored Roi with the gift of a rifle for his bravery, but he added no further details.[29]

Alphonse Wetmore's account demonstrates the influence of a

[28] Flint, 161.
[29] Rufus Babcock, ed., *Forty Years of Pioneer Life, Memoir of John Mason Peck D. D. Edited from his Journals and Correspondence*, 130–31.

good storyteller upon a few details.[30] Wetmore called the hero Baptiste Louis Roi and placed the scene at Cote Sans Dessein some time after 1808. He described the attack more dramatically, telling how the wife and sister-in-law of Roi lent aid by repeatedly putting out the fires started by the burning arrows. In Wetmore's story, which reaches its climax more slowly than the other versions, the women dashed milk upon the fires when the water in the fort was exhausted. In his account, the fearless Roi was aghast when the arrows again hurtled through the air, until his wife, with "an angelic smile," produced "from the night vessel the fluid" that saved the garrison. Wetmore not only included conversation that supposedly took place during the attack, but added Roi's speech to the young men who presented the rifle. Roi was delighted with it, Wetmore wrote, until some thoughtless young man suggested the presentation of a silver chamber pot to Madame Roi, whereupon he angrily rejected the gun with the words:

> Gentlemen — it is a *fuzee* of beautiful proportions — containing very *much* gold in de pan, and silver *on his breeches*; he is a very *gentleman-gun for kill de game*. I *tank* you. I shall not take him. Some gentleman had consider to give *ma cherie ami* one *urinal silvaire*! I tell you, sare, I take care of dem tings myself — go to h–ll, anybody, by d—n sight! [31]

Despite his sense of humor the frontiersman was generally credulous and superstitious. An easy mark for the sellers of patent medicines, he gave testimonials to the miraculous cures resulting from the use of Jacob Albright's Columbian Syrup or Swain's Panacea. John Hinkle testified that his son John was cured of a cancerous ulcer of the throat by the use of Columbian Syrup; Mrs. Patterson said that, although she had been unable to lift her arm before taking the medicine, the syrup had completely cured her. William Baker declared

---

[30] Wetmore, who lived in Franklin for a time, published his *Gazetteer of Missouri*, in 1837. See note 31.

[31] Alphonse Wetmore, *Gazetteer of the State of Missouri with a Map of the State from the Office of the Surveyor-General, Including the Latest Additions and Surveys to Which Is Added an Appendix Containing Frontier Sketches, and Illustrations of Indian Character*, 48–51.

that two bottles of Columbian Syrup had cleared up his scrofulous eruption, although it had been unrelieved by over fifty bottles of other syrups.[32] Settlers placed their faith in the power of madstones to cure the victim of a mad dog's bite and believed that dreams were fraught with meaning. The slightest act might be filled with portent. To dream of blood meant that the dreamer would receive money; to eat a crowing hen would bring bad luck; to sweep the house after sundown would cause the loss of a friend; and to fail to turn a mirror to the wall after a death in the family would make the newly dead uneasy in his grave.[33]

Many pioneers believed in premonitions and prophecies. After the death of President William Henry Harrison they told how incidents had pointed to a coming disaster. They said that on the way to his inauguration, Harrison had narrowly escaped death when his horse stepped into a deep hole. To be sure, such an accident might have happened to any traveler on western trails, but Missourians believed that this event had special significance. Such portents were considered by many frontiersmen to be indisputable; others scoffed at the superstitions and scorned the patent medicines.

It should be stated here that any generalization about the pioneer Missourian can be disproved by pointing to exceptions; the frontiersman's character prevents easy categorizing. Although the new land attracted a wide variety of people, nevertheless, in their diversity, they held some ideas in common. In their personal ambitions, they were generally materialistic. Wealth was an obvious proof of success, and many of them had come to the frontier because they hoped to increase their property and to gain prestige. In their public beliefs they were inclined to be idealistic and to think in broad generalizations. They saw the present as a continuation of the past and looked toward the future with optimism. The frontiersman envisioned a continuing frontier. He believed that western expansion

[32] These particular testimonials appeared in the Fayette *Missouri Intelligencer and Boon's Lick Advertiser*, October 23, 1829, p. 4, although such statements are frequently found.

[33] "Boon's Lick Folk Tales," *Bulletin of the Missouri Historical Society*, VI, 4 (July, 1950), 489–90.

was morally right and inevitable and that settlers would find freedom and plenty in a new land. He believed that God had made the frontier rich and beautiful *for his use*, for to him virtue lay, not in the primitive wilderness, but in the cultivated earth. A visitor expressed the views of many settlers when he said that man's virtues, like the fruits of the earth, are excellent only when subjected to culture.[34] Far removed from his nation's capital, the frontiersman was a fervent patriot. He believed in the superiority of all things American over anything European and never tired of hearing speakers denounce the British and praise the blessings of republicanism.

Hearing speakers on any subject was one of his chief pleasures, for the spoken word was his primary source of information, inspiration, and entertainment. The public speech substituted in large measure for the absence of large collections of literature, either public or private, and the lack of education to take advantage of them, had they been available. For people who were living in crude circumstances and at remote distances that made social intercourse an occasional matter, the gathering to hear a speaker offered more than the knowledge and information the speaker communicated. A "speaking" held opportunities that satisfied many needs for the frontiersman and his family.

[34] Elias Pym Fordham, *Personal Narrative of Travels in Virginia, Maryland, Pennsylvania, Ohio, Indiana, Kentucky; and of a Residence in the Illinois Territory: 1817–1818*, Frederick Austin Ogg, ed., 225.

II

"*We aim to elevate the standard of public speaking among us, we admire eloquence, and we feebly try to imitate it. We know that ours is but a farthing candle in the sun, but we feel there is no harm in trying.*"

John H. Blue, Address before the Chariton Polemic Society.

The Young Idea

Leaving much of his past behind him as he moved westward, the frontiersman carried with him his faith in eloquence as a means of influence. Even though he was himself unschooled, he was concerned with "teaching the young idea how to shoot" and wanted his sons to learn to speak well.

Rhetorical training had not been available for children of the early French and Spanish settlers. It would have been useless for most of them to study an art so little practiced in their society. The few schools existing in Upper Louisiana before 1804 were generally church schools in which instruction was limited to reading, writing, arithmetic, and religion. Schools taught by lay teachers, notable more for their use of the rod than for their instilling of knowledge, did not differ much from those taught by the priests.[1]

The children of the Americans who came to the territory before 1804 had little opportunity for education of any kind. The parents, often illiterate, chose to live in isolated areas away from the villages and to avoid as much as possible any notice by officials. After the cession, although schools were woefully inadequate and illiteracy high, settlers, even in remote areas, generally contrived to employ a school-

---

[1] Typical of the lay schools was that conducted by John Baptiste Trudeau, who arrived in St. Louis in 1774 to teach the sons of the principal men of the city. Brought to the city by Governor Don Zenon Trudeau to educate his own family, he continued his school until 1827. Margaret McMillan and Monia Cook Morris, "Educational Opportunities in Early Missouri," *The Missouri Historical Review*, XXXIII, 3 (April, 1939), 320.

For a short time a school in Ste. Genevieve provided an exception to the general pattern of education. A French *émigré* operated a school there in which he taught courses in science and oratory as well as the usual religion and fundamentals. He further digressed by teaching English as well as French and Spanish languages, but since his school continued only two years, it could not have had much influence. Floyd C. Shoemaker, *Missouri and Missourians*, I, 319.

master of some sort to teach the children to read, write, and solve simple problems of arithmetic.[2]

Throughout the pioneer period, schools depended primarily for support upon the church or private citizens. The Act of 1812, which organized the Territory of Missouri, affirmed the belief that schools and the means of education should be encouraged and supported by revenue from the public lands, but the belief was not implemented by action. When the state constitution was being drawn up, citizens urged some plan of state aid for schools, and the document, when adopted, provided for one or more schools in each congressional township "as soon as practicable or necessary." [3] Unfortunately, legislators failed for a long time to consider that public schools were practicable or necessary. Not until 1839, when the Geyer Act was passed, did they provide for a system of public education. Even then, the adoption of a system stopped short of providing material support. As a result, education was generally limited to those who could pay for it. Even though schools permitted children to attend as paupers, some parents could not afford the expense of supplying their children's books in addition to losing the benefit of their labor.

From the earliest days the sons of wealthy families in the area had enjoyed opportunities for education. Some traveled to Europe to attend schools; others studied in the older states. Even in families for whom money was not a problem, the difficulty of travel and the unwillingness of parents to send their children far from home motivated a drive to establish higher education in the area. Missourians showed an interest in academies by chartering as early as 1808 a school designed to offer instruction beyond the fundamentals. By 1850 forty academies had been chartered in Missouri, along with several other unchartered schools that offered advanced study.[4]

Settlers chose teachers from men who advertised their willing-

[2] H. M. Brackenridge, *Views of Louisiana: Together with a Journal of a Voyage up the Missouri River in 1811*, 117.

[3] Typical of the citizens' concern is the comment by "Cape Girardeau Farmer," Jackson *Missouri Herald*, June 24, 1820, p. 2.

[4] Frank L. Barton, "History of the Academy in Missouri," (Master's thesis, University of Missouri, Columbia, Missouri, 1910).

ness to provide moral training and teach the common or more advanced branches of learning. American schools differed from those set up by the French and Spanish in two important ways: they offered instruction in the English language, and they gave training in speaking.

In offering rhetorical training, the schools followed the customs established in the older states, which were, in turn, following European practices. The restoration of the classical doctrines of rhetorical training in late seventeenth-century England influenced the curriculum in colonial colleges, and colonial teachers were often products of English schools. The seventeenth century's emphasis on the classics gave way to a more practical turn in education in eighteenth-century American schools. Benjamin Franklin, a leading spirit in the movement to give utilitarian studies a larger place in the curriculum, advocated emphasis upon practical sciences, English language and literature, and training in speaking. In Franklin's sketch of the enlarged intellectual life, ability to speak well was important, and he urged teachers to require students to declaim, repeat speeches, and deliver orations.[5]

Though Franklin's influence upon frontier schools was indirect — if it existed at all — Missourians wholeheartedly endorsed his emphasis upon public speaking. The debating society organized in St. Louis by George Tompkins, one of the earliest schoolmasters to arrive in the territory after the cession, became famous for the ability of its members and for the brilliance of its discussions.[6] James Sawyer listed rhetoric as one of the higher branches of the curriculum of his seminary, announced in the *Missouri Gazette* for July 22, 1815. When Mr. Sawyer combined forces the following year with the Reverend Timothy Flint, the teachers pledged that they would "strive to teach their pupils a correct elocution and to deliver with propriety."[7] Not only in St. Louis but throughout the area wherever higher branches of instruction were offered, elocution and rhetoric had a

[5] Albert Henry Smyth, ed., *The Writings of Benjamin Franklin*, II, 386–96.
[6] J. Thomas Scharf, *History of St. Louis, City and County*, I, 824.
[7] St. Louis *Missouri Gazette*, June 1, 1816, p. 2.

place in the curriculum. In Franklin in the Boon's Lick country, children attending the school of Grey Bynum studied *The Kentucky Preceptor* and *Lessons in Elocution*.[8] At Bowling Green in the Salt River country, S. P. Robinson advertised instruction in the English and Latin languages and listed as a text to be studied Jamieson's *Rhetoric*. Though nineteenth-century rhetorics emphasized written language, Jamieson stated in his *Rhetoric* that "spoken language has a great superiority over written language in point of energy and force" and further asserted that all the great and high efforts of eloquence must be made by means of spoken, not of written, language.[9] Some six miles southeast of Columbia the Little Bonne Femme Academy, charging twenty-five dollars per session for board— including washing, fuel, and candles—announced a curriculum that included rhetoric, logic, composition, and declamation.[10] At Jefferson City, Samuel Hart offered rhetoric, history, logic, and composition at a cost of twelve dollars for a five-month session; for only seven dollars, students might study composition and elocution in an elementary and English grammar school in the same town.[11]

The president of the newly founded state university outlined a comprehensive program of rhetorical training in his announcement of the school's opening in the fall of 1841. Among other subjects, the sophomore class were to study oratory and rhetoric; juniors, Cicero's *De Oratore*; seniors, Whately's *Rhetoric* and *Logic*. Moreover, one of the five professorships established in 1843, when the University began instruction, was a chair of rhetoric combined with logic, metaphysics, and English literature.[12]

As did many other schools offering advanced studies, the Uni-

---

[8] *History of Howard and Cooper Counties*, 160.

[9] Bowling Green *The Salt River Journal*, August 22, 1840, p. 3; Alexander Jamieson, *A Grammar of Rhetoric and Polite Literature . . . With Rules for the Study of Composition and Eloquence*, 35–36.

[10] Columbia *Missouri Intelligencer and Boon's Lick Advertiser*, March 10, 1832, p. 2.

[11] Jefferson City *Jeffersonian Republican*, July 14, 1838, p. 2, and April 24, 1841, p. 4.

[12] Bowling Green *The Salt River Journal*, September 18, 1841, p. 5; Thomas Jefferson Lowry, *A Sketch of the University of the State of Missouri*, 18. For the first two years the University was little more than a continuation of the older Columbia College.

versity admitted only young men, but private schools for girls had existed since the French and Spanish period. The early schools for young ladies stressed accomplishments considered more appropriate to their sex than rhetoric. Needlework and the arts, instruction in reading and writing French and English, and lessons in history and morality made up the usual curriculum. As early as 1824, however, and four years before an irate St. Louis editor declared that Frances Wright had abdicated her proper sphere by speaking in public, a course in rhetoric had been offered in a seminary for young ladies.[13] By 1830, although sentiment for separate education of the sexes still dominated, girls were studying much the same subjects as young men and were taking part in programs of literary societies and school exhibitions.

The interest in rhetoric and oratory was not limited to boys and girls of school age. In 1809 the St. Louis *Gazette* offered for sale *"The American Orator;* containing rules and directions, calculated to improve youth and others in the ornamental and useful ART OF ELOQUENCE." The leading men in the community showed concern for improving their ability in speaking. Frederick Bates, acting governor of the territory from 1807 to 1808 and later elected governor of the state, sent to Baltimore for a copy of Blair's *Lectures on Rhetoric and Belles Lettres,* presumably from a desire to improve his own speaking ability.[14]

Popular on the Missouri frontier was *The Columbian Orator,* first published in 1797. The author and editor, Mr. Caleb Bingham, stated in his Preface, "The art of oratory needs no encomium. To cultivate its rudiments and diffuse its spirit among the youth of America is the design of this book." Included as models for study were extracts from speeches of the Greeks and Romans, of William Pitt, and of American heroes, as well as plays, dialogues, and a forensic dispute on the question, "Are the Anglo-Americans endowed with capacity equal to the Europeans?" A poem entitled "Lines Spoken at a School Exhibition by a Little Boy Seven Years Old" and be-

---

[13] St. Louis *Missouri Republican,* May 17, 1824, p. 4.

[14] Thomas Maitland Marshall, ed., *The Life and Papers of Frederick Bates,* I, 337.

ginning "You'd scarce expect one of my age,/ To speak in public on the stage" offered something for even the younger children to recite. The thoroughly American quality of the selections was epitomized in an oration on eloquence "pronounced at Harvard College on Commencement Day, 1794." The orator on that occasion had promised:

> That refinement of taste, that laudable ambition to excel in everything which does honor to humanity, which distinguishes the Americans, and their free and popular government, are so many springs, which though not instantaneous in their operation, cannot fail to raise Columbian Eloquence "above all Greek, above all Roman fame." [15]

Such sentiments could hardly fail to evoke a favorable response from the audience.

True Columbian eloquence was cultivated in the school exhibitions and literary societies. When Missourians set up their schools, such exercises and public programs were already well-established customs in the older settlements. Missourians enthusiastically followed the practice. "Reading of compositions, oral addresses, and discussion of questions will take place each week with visitors invited to attend" was a typical part of the announcement of a new school session.[16]

Important as was the weekly program, it was minor and routine compared to the closing exhibition, the great school event of the year. The teacher knew that he would be judged by the performance of his students on closing day. Contemporaries, pleased by student recitations and orations, boasted that a favored school would not suffer in comparison with similar institutions in Kentucky and Virginia and expressed the thought that the performance of the students was a guarantee that certain teachers were amply qualified for their

[15] Caleb Bingham, *The Columbian Orator: Containing a Variety of Original and Selected Pieces; together with Rules. . . .*

[16] Such an announcement was made by the Fayette High School in the Fayette *Boon's Lick Times*, April 21, 1841, p. 3.

stations. Mark Twain's picture of the schoolmaster in *The Adventures of Tom Sawyer* is an accurate representation of many a teacher whose severity increased with his desire to have the school make a good showing on examination day. Not all were so dependent on the rod and ferrule as Tom Sawyer's master, but these instruments of teaching were widely used in the era. Twain's description of the festive scene on exhibition day is also realistic, with its picture of the schoolroom adorned with festoons of foliage and flowers, the front benches occupied by dignitaries and parents, and, on a temporary platform, rows of small boys "washed and dressed to an intolerable state of discomfort," "gawky big boys," and "snowbanks of girls and young ladies." [17]

The program was generally preceded by a demonstration of the students' proficiency in subjects studied, the length of the oral examination depending upon the extensiveness of the course of study. Listeners were disposed to be lenient. Not many had enough education to justify valid criticism. Perhaps the pride in a son's or daughter's accomplishment was greater when the parent recognized his own shortcomings. One father wrote with pride to friends in his old home:

> I am also Sending Marth to Schol. She has went 3 months and learns very fast. She Can spell in five Sylables. prety smart. She will go 3 months more if She is well and I pay 4 Dollars per Sholar for Six months.[18]

The pride in a child's learning to read and spell was minimal compared to that experienced when he performed well in the exhibitions. Audiences were generally prepared to approve the efforts of student speakers even when perfection was wanting. A member of an audience before whom a young orator had the misfortune to forget his lines reminded him that "a strong retentive memory . . . is

[17] Samuel Clemens, *The Adventures of Tom Sawyer*, 135–38.

[18] Letter of A. Wilson from Clay County, Missouri, July 6, 1835, in "The Wilson Letters, 1835–1849," Durward T. Stokes, ed., *Missouri Historical Review*, LX (July, 1966), 498.

acceptable to all men" but praised the other evidences of promise in the student speaker.[19]

Although there were occasional variations, the exhibitions followed a predictable pattern. The program at Tom Sawyer's school began with a small boy's recitation of Bingham's "You'd scarce expect one of my age . . . ," spoken with "painfully exact and spasmodic gestures." It continued with recitations and original compositions. Twain's pattern was drawn from life. At the Union Academy west of Fayette, for example, a visitor reported that the exercises began with a speech entitled "Self Conceit" delivered by a young Ciceronian, who, though scarcely three feet tall, spoke very well. The speech was the prelude to the examination in arithmetic, grammar, geography, philosophy, and Latin. Following the examination, the younger students declaimed "On the Character of Napoleon," "General Washington's Address to his Troops," and "Rullo's Address to the Peruvians." Dialogues on dancing and physiognomy were also "delivered with much success." The declamations emphasized courage, morality, and patriotism. Dialogues offered entertainment and moral advice. The dialogues each made a moral point. Dancing, for instance, was strongly disapproved, and the idea that character could be told from physiognomy was a subject for ridicule that could be counted on for a laugh. The older students presented various themes, the young ladies reading compositions and the young men orating.[20]

The exhibitions of the more advanced schools included a greater array of musical and rhetorical talent than the smaller schools could offer, but followed a similar plan. In 1842 the program at the University of Missouri began with music and continued with six orations on political, historical, literary, and philosophical subjects. Music provided an interlude between these speeches and others that followed. Listeners heard a disputation on the question "Was the confinement of Bonaparte in St. Helena justifiable?" before a third musical bridge introduced ten additional orations and a second debate, on the comparative merits of Columbus and Washington. An

[19] St. Louis *Missouri Gazette*, September 18, 1813, p. 3.
[20] Fayette *Boon's Lick Times*, March 27, 1841, p. 3.

essay by an anonymous author on "Sleep" that preceded the final musical number must have seemed fitting to the audience.[21]

Although the program seems in this day almost unbearably long, it was in accord with customs of the era. At Princeton, for example, in 1784 sixteen graduates spoke for almost five hours. Since the teachers made an effort to have every pupil take part in the program, the affairs were necessarily extended. The audience did not generally object to the length; for mothers, especially, a contemporary observed, the exhibition was the most important event in history.[22] A member of an audience at an early commencement of the University of Missouri reminisced:

> To our adolescent mind there was no more possibly impressive event than that of the senior on Commencement day, in faultless broadcloth, with deep stentorian tone and profuse wealth of gesture, delivering his oration and then amid a shower of boquets [sic] and applause retiring blushingly from the platform. Commencement day . . . never failed to draw a large and long-suffering crowd who would sit with placid patience through the protracted theses and orations, applauding promptly the bursts of florid rhetoric, and generously weeping in response to the pathetic passages of the valedictories.[23]

The pathetic passages heard by the audiences at University functions came from speeches of young men, since girls were not admitted until 1867, when they were accepted as students in the Normal College. At other schools young ladies spoke on the proper sphere of women, described a girl's experiences in school, or praised their teachers and looked to the future in such compositions as "My Boat is Launched, but Where Is the Harbor?" They so often dwelt on the solemn ordeal of death that Mark Twain justifiably spoke of the "nursed and petted melancholy" of their compositions. These young speakers recalled former classmates who were no longer with them and acknowledged a "melancholy duty to pay the tribute due

[21] Columbia *Herald*, February 25, 1892, p. 3.
[22] Reminiscences of North Todd Gentry, North Todd Gentry Papers, Folder 219.
[23] Columbia *Herald*, January 21, 1892, p. 1.

to departed worth — to drop a tear over the tomb of a departed friend and classmate." They envisioned the possibility that on this occasion they were with their classmates for the last time and that death would come prematurely to others of their number and sighed:

> Those joyous countenances, that have so often lighted our pathway, are now to part, never more to meet, until that great day when we shall all be called to the Judgment bar of God. But these familiar faces and loved friends can never be forgotten until death shall have wafted us to another state of existence.[24]

The thought of death was generally only a digression in the orations of the young men, who chose topics from history, politics, and philosophy as subjects of their orations. They spoke on internal improvements, education, the power of eloquence, literature and the West, the development of the mind, and the need for morality in public life.

Eloquently they praised eloquence, which they compared to music in yielding pleasure and refinement to social circles. It was the source of light, liberty, and knowledge, they proclaimed. Eloquence made tyranny impossible and kept the fires of patriotism burning. The most worthy eloquence was that of the pulpit, asserted the orators, for it brought transgressors to repentance.[25] All eloquence was a power mightier than the force of arms, they declared, while asking:

> Who is there that is not moved by the power of Eloquence? Who, that has not felt his eye dilate, and his breathing become deep and wrapt, and himself becoming the creature of a better and brighter order, as the spirit of eloquence, like the baptism of pure fire, continued to fall upon him, and to overwhelm him?[26]

Deploring the lack of attention given to rhetorical training in their own day, young speakers pointed to the intellectual and artistic

[24] George Everett, "Valedictory Address," *Pleasant Ridge Pearl*, published by the Union Literary and Padeusian Societies of Pleasant Ridge College, July, 1859.

[25] John R. Kelso, "Eloquence," *Pleasant Ridge Pearl*, July, 1859.

[26] Address of John H. Blue to the Chariton Polemic Society, Fayette *Boon's Lick Times*, January 9, 1841, p. 1.

heights reached in Greece and Rome and called for emulation of Cicero and Demosthenes. Though Cicero and Demosthenes were the models held up for imitation, Washington, Clay, and Webster figured almost as prominently in the speeches. Sentiments of national pride flowed like an undercurrent through orations, and the measure of the worth of a proposition was its benefit to the nation. The United States was declared to be the great center of culture, eclipsing all Europe; it was guarded by the watchful eye of the Almighty, Who had it under His special protection; it was hailed as a Christian nation, a place of freedom and moral progress where even the trees of the forests yielded to civilization by "bowing their heads" to the axe. In contrast, the heathen world — which to Protestant Missourians could mean Catholic Europe as well as Muslim Turkey — was shrouded in clouds of despotism and barbarity, lost in superstition and tyranny, and inhabited by groaning millions of suffering humanity. Student speakers boasted of the growth of the United States and its material prosperity. They told each other and heard from older speakers that their duty was to govern their country wisely. Strangely enough, the office seeker was generally pictured as a blind partisan or bigoted demagogue who mounted the political stage in self-interest. Ignoring the exigencies of politics, students saw the statesman as a patriot and philanthropist who governed without the necessity of seeking office.

Young orators saw no limit to the possibilities of the future. "Onward and upward" was a basic assumption as well as a literal motto for students, who asserted that education would promote the general progress. Young Robert Todd voiced the belief of many of his fellows when he said in a valedictory address:

> To what condition is it possible for society ultimately to be brought by a proper discipline and education of every member of it; what may be the degree of moral and intellectual force it may then attain to, what may be the capacities of the race for making still further advance, is a subject over which the imagination of the philanthropist may linger in unsatisfied delight.[27]

[27] R. L. Todd, Valedictory Address, North Todd Gentry Papers.

35

Audiences could expect to hear the advantages of education extolled. Speakers compared ignorance to a dark cloud overshadowing the earth, knowledge to a sun bursting forth in its glory. They declared that education was more to be desired than diamonds and rubies, for it developed character and benefited both the individual and the nation. Urging citizens to establish a college in the town, a young woman cried out that young men, who with education could win fame and honor, would waste their youth in toil and drudgery without it. Despite the prevailing idea that higher education was less important for women, she asserted that the future of daughters depended as much as that of the sons on education. Without such advantages, young women would be condemned to premature aging from plying needles by the midnight lamp, the speaker said, but she predicted that if girls were allowed to go to college they would probably marry wise and good men and enjoy lives of ease and influence.[28]

The vision of a girl as a future mother and homemaker was in accord with prevailing ideas, as was the belief in education as a means of influence. The speakers at the female academies emphasized the importance of the moral influence of the home. They declared that the girl, who was destined to be the companion of man and to preside over the thoughts and feelings of infancy, must be taught to reverence, regard, and read the holy word of God.

Often a teacher or one of the local dignitaries spoke at the exercises after the students had completed their speeches. These speakers almost invariably emphasized the moral worth of an education. They warned against the evils that tempted young minds from biblical authority. They pointed to the habit of novel reading as a particular danger, declaring that novels cultivated the imagination and led to the neglect and weakening of the reasoning faculties. A clergyman, in addressing a class of young ladies, denounced novels as falsehoods dressed in glowing language that undermined religious sentiments and destroyed the power of application and profound thought. Better, he said, to read Voltaire and Paine, whose infidelity

[28] Liberty *The Weekly Tribune*, January 16, 1847, pp. 1–2.

was "disgustingly manifest," than to enervate the mind, destroy its powers of application, and make of it a wilderness of thorns and rankest weeds by reading novels.[29] The denunciation of the novel was almost invariably accompanied by admonitions to read the Bible and to be faithful to religious duties.

Student orators identified the mind with the soul. "I must be measured by my soul/ For 'tis the mind that makes the man," quoted the young orator.[30] Students, in their speeches, subscribed to the belief that the purpose of education was the promotion of morality. A young man voiced the common sentiment in his support of the proposition that man is born to duty, the great work of education being nothing more than preparation of mind and heart for carrying out his moral obligations.[31] Seemingly idealists all, they vividly portrayed the lack of morality in the world about them, the charlatans in professional and public life, the natural tendency of man to grovel in vice and ignorance. They cited the downfall of Rome, the captivity of the Jews, and the long night of barbarism as lessons of history. These disasters were the consequences of moral failure, they declared, and they urged citizens to support the Constitution, honor the Sabbath, and guard that "palladium of liberty," the ballot box, from danger. Young orators praised their teachers for making plain to them the paths of morality, and speeches of teachers at closing exercises give evidence that they were unsparing in pointing out moral responsibilities.

The sentiments expressed on exhibition day suggest either that early teachers were truly remarkable or that students were effusive in their compliments at the time of farewell. One student orator eulogized his science teacher as a man to whom the forked lightning, the deep-toned thunder, the burning mountain, the fearful avalanche, and the frightful hurricane were merely themes for speculation;[32] schoolboys and girls declared they would never forget

[29] The Reverend W. H. Porter, Address delivered before the Female Department of Howard College, Fayette *Boon's Lick Times*, October 23, 1841, p. 1.
[30] D. F. Moody, "The Mind," *Pleasant Ridge Pearl*, July, 1859.
[31] R. L. Todd, Valedictory Address.
[32] George Everett, "Valedictory Address."

their teachers, that when life was drawing to a close the memory of the hours spent in the society of their schoolmasters would bring sweet repose to their dying hours. Speakers declared that the community owed a great debt to the teachers. If praise had sufficed to pay it, much of the debt would have been wiped out on exhibition day.

The value of the instruction in the schools varied, to be sure, with the ability of the instructor. The Jesuits and many of the other priests in the Catholic schools were well trained, as were some of the Protestant clergymen who came to Missouri from the eastern states. Young men who taught school while they were preparing for the bar generally had a better than average education. Other teachers had little more learning than their pupils. As did Elizabeth Ann Cooley McClure and her husband, who came from Virginia to Jackson County and held a series of subscription schools, they studied at night to be able to teach the subjects they offered in school. Elizabeth Ann wrote in her journal: "I do little besides study. I sit up nights and cipher, of days study geography and grammar and get along very well." [33]

Though Elizabeth Ann was a force for morality and prayed that the Lord would brighten her ideas and keep her from error, John Mason Peck charged that a third of the schools in southeast Missouri did more harm than good, that the schoolmasters were drunken and almost illiterate. [34] The charge can be partially discounted because of Peck's religious prejudice, but it cannot be dismissed. In 1841 a citizen, pleading for some plan of examining teachers before they were allowed to teach, observed that many were extremely ignorant persons. [35] The quality of the rhetorical training also varied. The ministers and prospective lawyers could be counted upon to be interested in speaking. Some teachers had participated in debating or literary societies, and they carried on these traditions with their stu-

[33] "The Journal of Elizabeth Ann Cooley," Edward D. Jervey and James E. Moss, eds., *The Missouri Historical Review*, LX, 2 (January, 1966), 162–66.

[34] Rufus Babcock, ed., *Forty Years of Pioneer Life, Memoirs of John Mason Peck, D.D. Edited from His Journals and Correspondence*, 109, 123.

[35] Fayette *Boon's Lick Times*, April 17, 1841, p. 2.

dents. Others were ignorant of any formal training in speaking; yet they could point to models among the many speakers of their day. Youthful speakers tended to emulate similar patterns. They generally followed Cicero's advice in demonstrating a becoming modesty as they began to speak. Typical were the introductory remarks of a young man who said:

> Like my fellow students I stand before you to discharge a duty, which, though pleasing in itself, is nevertheless embarrassing to one of my youth, inexperience, and inability — yet feeble as my powers of mind may be, I shrink not from a task which has for its object the entertainment of my friends, the satisfaction of my teachers, and the improvement of myself.[36]

The conclusion was even more predictable than the introduction. Whatever the theme might be, the speaker was relatively certain to conclude with an exhortation to students to make their lives a blessing to the country and a credit to the school. The future of the country depended upon youth, speakers proclaimed. "You are soon to guide the wheels of this great nation"; "the road to usefulness and fame is open before you," young orators cried to their classmates as they admonished them to strive to reach the glorious heights of intellectual greatness. The admonitions were clear and direct, with no attempt to disguise their nature. Speakers often prefaced the exhortations with "Let me . . . ," but the moral was not weakened by the request. Appeals were ordinarily as fervent and as direct as that of the young man who sought to enlist his schoolmates in saving the nation:

> Let me exhort you by the zeal you maintain for your institution, by the love you bear to your fellow men, by all you hold sacred, or inviolate, to bear your part in shielding our common country from national suicide.[37]

The conclusion was also the part of the speech in which the

---

[36] Isaac Campbell, Student Oration . . . at close of the last session of Monticello School, Fayette *Boon's Lick Times*, April 1, 1843, p. 1.

[37] James Dunlap, "The Charlatan," *Pleasant Ridge Pearl*, July, 1859.

speaker expressed his thanks to all who had made his education possible and bade farewell to his school associates. Occasionally, the ending of a school oration expressed all the fervor of a protracted religious meeting as a speaker lifted his voice in prayer that not one of the "scholars" would be lost but would all meet around the heavenly throne. Young orators thanked the community where they had gone to school and bade it, too, farewell. They blessed the school and took sad leave of its classic halls. They thanked the members of the literary societies and urged them to continue their pursuits toward rhetorical effectiveness. An occasional student speaker rambled around his subject, but the rambling was more likely to come from the older citizen called upon to say a few words after the students had completed their speeches.

It was not the ordered arrangement, however, but the flourishes of language that brought the most vociferous applause from hearers. Some words and phrases were so much admired that they were consistently introduced into the speeches. Metaphors came, not from daily life, but rather from literary sources, and thoughts were phrased in what doubtless seemed to the speakers to be terms of elegance. Young orators alluded to Christ as a compass and spoke of the need to have their barques well trimmed and supplied for the ocean of life. Critics laughed good naturedly that students could not make a speech without alluding to Greece, Rome, Cicero, and Demosthenes. In academies whose buildings were of hewn logs young speakers referred to the institution's classic halls, their own Olympian struggles, and the sacred temples of learning in which they had studied.

Students strove for original poetic expression, but it frequently bogged down in well-traveled ruts: The passage of time was marked by "the sun's having rolled its destined round"; to study was "to drink deep from the springs of knowledge" or "to rend the veil of ignorance"; death was "the sleep that knows no waking." Sin and ignorance were associated by being referred to in the same figures of speech. *Groveling* was a term applied equally to both. *Fetters and chains* bound a man meshed in either state; both were *blighting blasts,* places of *rank weeds, dark night, clouds overshadowing the earth.* Christianity and knowledge, in contrast, were *streams of light, stars of progress, beams of glory, priceless pearls, jewels,* or *brightest gems.*

Schoolgirls were likely to hear such phrases as *domestic circle, helper and companion, servant of God, useful and substantial knowledge* from the speakers who addressed them. Eloquence called forth the term *adornment* and, if praised, was spoken of in images of *flight* or *feasts;* if condemned, it became a *collection of set phrases* and *flowers of rhetoric.* The thought of parting was certain in those pre-Freudian times to bring a reference to *sweet intercourse enjoyed in school days,* and the smiles of schoolmates or teachers were always *genial.* The world was *cold, uncharitable,* or *unfriendly;* wine was the *fashionable glass* or the *fiery demon; greatness* was preceded by the adjective *genuine* or *true,* and *requisite* was modified by *essentially.* Although students recognized the *feebleness of their powers,* their *hearts swelled* or *thrilled* with *pride* or *grateful emotion* at *tokens of esteem tendered to them,* and they pledged *undying zeal* in *striving for the advancement of knowledge and morality.*

Student orators often quoted poems, moral in sentiment and of a quality that might be expected from admirers of Felicia Hemans and Mrs. Hannah Moore. Typical are the lines quoted by a young orator who wished to express his horror of intoxicating drink:

> More fatal than the serpent's fang
> That crawled in Eden's cradled bliss,
> It poisons peace with many a pang,
> And kills you with a flatterer's kiss.[38]

More than the phrase or figure, the formal, stylized composition characterizes the speeches. Typical is a sentence from the speech of a young man presenting a fellow student with honorary membership in a literary society: "We regret that the distance of your field of labor will preclude the possibility of your personally co-operating with us, but we are persuaded that, in the capacity of honorary

[38] Campbell, Student oration.

41

member you will strive to promote the welfare of our beloved society."[39] Auditors noted the quality of delivery and praised students for modesty and humility of bearing, for grace and elegance of gesture, and for full clear tones and voices rich in melody.

Though some students disliked the rhetorical training and harbored no desire to emulate Cicero and Demosthenes, many regarded speaking so highly that they formed literary and debating societies. Membership was voluntary, and students generally paid an initiation fee and dues for the privilege. The organizations served many of the functions of a modern sorority or fraternity, but their primary purposes were to improve speaking and writing, combined with training for citizenship.

Teachers encouraged but did not supervise the organizations. Students drew up constitutions, elected officers from among their number, levied and collected fines for infraction of rules, and served as speakers and critics at their meetings. Schools that admitted young ladies maintained separation of the sexes, but the societies of men and women were similar. The constitution of the young ladies' Philalethian Society at the University of Missouri stated its objects to be literary culture, elocutionary training, and the promotion of good fellowship.[40] The young men at the same school were somewhat more sophisticated in procedure and more serious about improving speaking skills. They carefully observed parliamentary procedure and conducted sessions with a considerable degree of formality.[41] They fined members who failed to carry out their speaking assignments, had to be prompted, were disrespectful to the critic, approached a task with unbecoming levity, or conducted themselves in an ungentlemanly manner.

Declamations, essays, and occasional addresses were included in the programs of literary societies, but the emphasis was on debate. Some debates were expressive of student opinion rather than rea-

---

[39] James Dunlap, Presentation speech, *Pleasant Ridge Pearl*, July, 1859.

[40] Philalethian Constitution, North Todd Gentry Papers, Folder 190.

[41] Records of the Youth's Debating Society, James A. Love Papers; Records of Athenaean Society of the University of Missouri 1842–1925.

soned investigations. Students debated "Is novel reading beneficial?" and decided in the negative; "Is the mind of man superior to that of woman?" and decided in the affirmative; and "Does oratory exert a greater influence over the nation than poetry?" deciding in the affirmative. Other topics were drawn from discussions current in the legislative bodies. Students debated the questions of extension of United States territory, the period of time required for naturalization of foreigners, the justification of the support of common schools by taxation, the election of the judiciary, and the protective tariff. The question of the right of a state to secede was debated in the eighteen-forties, although it was such a sensitive issue that a speaker in Fulton who attempted to discuss it was fined for disorder and the discussion postponed. Even so, the question was later discussed in the Fulton society.[42]

Students also debated moral questions. They took sides on the justifiability of war, asked whether it was right to tell a lie in any circumstances and whether conscience or law provided greater restraint. They spoke on the problem of slavery and debated whether the white man had committed the greater wrong against the Indian or the Negro at the same time their elders were still declaiming about the savage yell and the scalping knife.

Young men valued the literary and debating societies sufficiently to continue similar organizations after they had left school. Prominent men of the region enrolled as honorary members of the student organizations and upon request addressed the students. Participants and listeners repeatedly commented upon the values of the rhetorical training.

Student speakers were idealistic and sometimes naive in approaches to problems; they were guilty of circumlocutions and affectation; they were extravagant sometimes to the point of being ludicrous. Not their faults, however, but their certainties of the virtues they celebrated mark them most clearly as belonging to the pio-

[42] Fulton Lyceum Book, March 14, 1843, Love Papers.

neer period. They believed that the future was filled with promise; they believed that the government of the United States was the best in the world, that it offered the greatest freedom to the individual and provided him the widest opportunity; they honored the man who served his country on the battlefield; they praised courage; they believed that they were the chosen people of God and that He had concern for them as individuals. They accepted the Bible as the authoritative word of God and believed that success was reached by following the paths of wisdom and morality. These were the themes of the model essays and speeches in their textbooks, the lessons of their teachers, and the assumptions in their speaking.

In his rhetorical training the young speaker learned some lessons that would later be useful to him in expressing his views as a citizen. He learned how to use his voice to advantage; he gained confidence in his own ability to speak, and his practice promoted ease on the platform. In his school debates he gained experience in refuting or supporting a proposition and adapting to his opposition, but more important were the attitudes developed through hearing and repeating the themes of patriotism, courage, morality, and independence.

Higher education did not promote equality on the frontier. Rather, it tended to draw lines between the educated and uneducated. On the frontier the Jacksonian democrat tended to preach the ability of the uneducated common man to govern and to deride the classical learning stressed in the academies. In an inaugural address the president of an early college on the Missouri frontier charged that, if a man learned to speak Latin, he was decried as an aristocrat. The speaker saw the Western population as energetic and shifting, with little time or inclination to investigate the merits of any subject unrelated to immediately apparent values. He warned that this character made the Western man an easy prey for the demagogue who boasted of his lack of learning. The speaker demonstrated the rift between the educated and uneducated by denouncing the unlettered as men with no hope of arriving at respectability, without wealth or merit, and as subscribers to the creed of a "noiseless and senseless democracy who inclined toward degradation and talents desecrated."[43]

Although the speaker's comments are unpleasantly snobbish, he correctly stated the attitude of a thorough Jackson man toward a classical education. The frontiersman took an ambiguous position on rhetorical training. J. W. Ward, in *Andrew Jackson: Symbol for an Age*, points to John Quincy Adams' Harvard professorship as a factor in the New Englander's unpopularity on the frontier.[44] Adams, former Boylston Professor of Rhetoric, symbolized for the Jacksonian the corruption of real intelligence. In the campaign of 1828 the Republican General Committee of New York City issued a statement that found much support on the frontier:

> That Mr. Adams is possessed of *learning* . . . we are willing to admit. We are not ignorant that he has received a college education — that he has been a professor of rhetoric. . . . That he is *learned* we are willing to admit; but his *wisdom* we take leave to question.[45]

The man on the frontier felt little enthusiasm for the kind of education symbolized by Adams. In political campaigns he was inclined to ridicule an opponent for his skill in rhetoric and to boast that he was himself a plain, blunt man. Nevertheless, the same plain, blunt man made strenuous efforts to see that his children had the advantages of the best education he could afford, including rhetorical training. He realized that ignorance and inarticulateness emphasized the distinction between the rulers and the governed, and he acted upon the assumption that eloquence increased his sons' opportunity to move up in politics and society.

[43] J. W. Miller, Inauguration address as President of Columbia College, Columbia, Missouri, Columbia *Missouri Intelligencer and Boon's Lick Advertiser*, December 13, 1834, pp. 1, 2.

[44] John William Ward, *Andrew Jackson: Symbol for an Age*, 64.

[45] Ward, *Andrew Jackson*, 65.

III

"*What thunders are these resounding o'er earth,
Whence these shouts rapturous this sound of mirth;
A people 'tis, magnanimous and free,
Hallowing th' era of their liber[t]y . . .*"

Ode composed by an anonymous Missourian for the Fourth of July, 1820.

The Blessings of Republicanism

A man who could speak well was in great demand in frontier communities. Esteem for him rose when the townspeople wished to celebrate the Fourth of July, give a flag to departing troops, welcome a distinguished visitor, or praise a hero; for the pioneer considered that a historic event was not properly marked unless an orator had spoken.

The rhetoric on the most successful of these occasions was exuberant and florid. Speakers lauded the blessings of republicanism in terms chosen to show both their ardor and their learning. When Samuel Clemens reminisced about the speeches heard in his boyhood in Missouri, he described them as "full of gunpowder and glory, full of that adjective piling, mixed metaphor and windy declamation which were regarded as eloquence."[1] That Clemens did not exaggerate is evident in the speech of an orator who proclaimed, "If I possessed the elocution of Demosthenes, and could mount the Hippogrip or winged horse Pagassers, I would peregrinate from Spitzburgen to Table Bay . . . incite mankind to rend their chains of despotism — declare their unalienable rights, and vindicate their inherent liberties."[2]

Early French settlers had some indication of the American's interest in speechmaking when Upper Louisiana was formally transferred to the United States. A parade, soon to become a familiar part of these occasions, opened the ceremony as Captain Amos Stoddard, preceded by American troops, marched to the government house to be received by Lieutenant Governor Charles DeLassus. Citizens of

[1] Samuel Clemens, "A Campaign that Failed," *The Art, Humor and Humanity of Mark Twain*, Minnie M. Brashear and Robert Rodney, eds., 215.
[2] T. N. Cockerill, Fourth of July Address delivered at Richmond, Missouri, Fayette *The Western Monitor*, July 28, 1830, p. 2.

St. Louis heard DeLassus make the formal announcement of the transfer, saw the signing of the document, and listened to Captain Stoddard thank officials for his reception and express his good will for the people. No less impressive was Stoddard's address the next day, informing citizens of their rights under the new government and of his hope for their increasing wealth and power.[3] The publishing of popular rights and the expression of hope for increasing power of the people marked the transfer as vividly as did the lowering of the old and the raising of the new flag. Moreover, the public ceremony, including the address, was as typically American as the posting of decrees on the church door had been characteristic of French and Spanish officials. Certainly, it symbolized the differences between the regimes and their basic political assumptions.

In the years that followed, citizens commemorated the arrival of the first steamboat, the building of a new road, the erection of courthouses and schoolbuildings by addresses praising the event and predicting a glorious future for the state. Even the ladies, who rarely spoke in public, expressed sentiments of patriotism and regard for their fighting men by presenting flags to departing troops.

The flag presentations offer an interesting sidelight on frontier rhetoric. The flags themselves were remarkable. The ladies of Jefferson City imposed a blue satin field embroidered with numerous confident mottoes upon the Stars and Stripes presented to volunteers about to leave for the Mexican War. A young woman made the speech of presentation in a ceremony reminiscent of a lady's bestowing a token on her knight. Placing the flag in the hands of the captain, she expressed the hope that the spirit of patriotism that had animated the fathers of their country would go with him and his men. He, in turn, answered that the volunteers would defend the honor and glory of their country so long as their hearts beat. He promised that he and his men would never disgrace the flag. It should never fall, he said, unless it fell, tattered and torn, upon their dead bodies.[4]

[3] Louis Houck, *A History of Missouri from the Earliest Explorations and Settlements until the Admission of the State into the Union*, II, 360–72.

[4] Jefferson City *Jefferson Inquirer*, June 17, 1846, p. 2.

In the stylized language and the formality of the ceremony, citizens showed their support of the cause in which the troops were engaged, but both troops and citizens maintained an esthetic distance from the unpleasant realities of the war.

Considerable formality characterized the frontiersman's welcome to distinguished visitors. He took little public notice of the numerous European and American visitors who were attracted to Missouri through curiosity, but he welcomed a general, a statesman, or a famous orator with enthusiasm. Missourians turned out in numbers to greet Daniel Webster, Henry Clay, and Sergeant Prentiss when they came to the frontier, but the most memorable occasion was the visit of General Lafayette to St. Louis in 1825. The plan for Lafayette's welcome was imperiled by the conservative legislature's failure to appropriate state funds for the ceremony and the governor's refusal to participate in the activities. Other prominent citizens, however, showed that Missourians knew how to entertain a distinguished man. They did not wait for Lafayette's arrival in St. Louis but went down river to board his steamer and make the entrance with him into the city. The immense crowd gathered on the levee to greet him included some men who had fought under his command in Europe, and the welcome was enthusiastic. When the General came ashore, the mayor made a speech praising his sacrifices for and services to the United States, his spotless purity, and his republican principles. The General made a gracious reply before entering an open barouche drawn by four white horses and departing for a ball and reception.[5] Only the aristocrats were invited to the ball and reception, but the ceremony of welcome centering around speechmaking was a democratic affair where the republican principles of the great man had been praised.

Admiration of a great man was one of the characteristics of the frontiersman. Perhaps he saw in his hero an idea of what he or his sons might become. Timothy Flint remarked that "every circle, however small, had its prodigious great man, like Sancho's beauty,

[5] St. Louis *Missouri Republican*, May 2, 1825, p. 3.

49

the greatest within three leagues." [6] In their lifetime local and national heroes received the adulation of admirers, and in death even more fulsome eulogies were spoken at meetings arranged to honor their memory.

For yeoman frontiersmen, Andrew Jackson was the greatest of heroes. They commemorated his victory at New Orleans each January eighth with speeches of praise, and when they heard the news of his death they gathered in groups throughout the state to honor him. Nowhere was the ceremony more impressive than in Jefferson City, the state capital. Businessmen closed stores and offices to march with admirers from other walks of life in procession to the courthouse. There they heard an oration by a judge who had the special distinction of having once seen the great man. The speaker told how his father had taken him as a small boy to see the General. He described the scene in which Jackson placed his hand upon the boy's head and spoke of the need for vigilance in safeguarding the Republic. He stressed Jackson's love for the people, his courage, and his high morality. [7] These virtues were not only those generally attributed to the General by his admirers, but also the traits considered most desirable in a leader by the man on the frontier.

The speaking on these and similar ceremonial occasions followed rather general customs. Because it was difficult to light an evening gathering, groups assembled shortly before or after the noon hour or, if in the evening, at early candlelight. Few settlements had public buildings large enough to hold the crowds, but where churches, courthouses, or theatres would accommodate the audiences, the people assembled inside a suitable room. More often, citizens erected a speakers' stand in a grove, near a spring, or under a shade tree, and audiences stood or sat on the ground as they listened to words of praise or admonition.

Speeches were long, in accord with the community's expecta-

[6] Timothy Flint, *Recollections of the Last Ten Years, Passed in Occasional Residences and Journeyings in the Valley of the Mississippi . . .* , 180.

[7] J. W. Morrow, Eulogy of Andrew Jackson, Jefferson City *Jefferson Inquirer*, July 31, 1845, p. 1.

tions. Sergeant Prentiss held Missourians spellbound for three hours when he spoke in St. Louis in 1842;[8] an oration less than an hour and a half in length was considered scarcely worthy of the name. Unfortunately, not all speakers were spellbinders, and listeners sometimes chafed at a long speaking. A contemporary editor complained of the "fearful length" of many speeches.[9] Another critic vented his frustrations in a newspaper tirade against long orations, declaring them abuses of a man's leisure and an insult to his understanding. In Greece, he reminded Missourians, an orator won praise for speaking well, but in Missouri, he complained, the people bestowed their plaudits on the man who spoke a long time.[10]

Ceremonial addresses were formal and verbose as well as long. Speakers plainly preferred a polysyllabic word to a simple term. On ceremonial occasions listeners liked to hear words not commonly used in daily speech. In everyday conversation, the pioneer said admiringly that a man was a "real hoss," but he expected the orator to use such terms as "illustrious sage" or "veritable Cincinnatus" to express a compliment of similar value. One aspiring orator demonstrated the scope of his vocabulary by praising the rights of man as set forth in the Declaration of Independence as "coetaneous and coextensive with his birth and his being."[11] Beginning, as did most speakers, with apologies for his lack of ability, another young man told listeners, "I shall trust to the lenity and civility of my auditory to deal kindly with my stale and undigested observations."[12]

Following apologetic beginnings, speakers winged into wordy flights, as did the young Missourian who eulogized Lafayette at a meeting held to honor his memory. Reminding them that death was the fate of the great as well as the humble, the speaker poetically ad-

[8] John F. Darby, *Personal Recollections of Many Prominent People Whom I Have Known* . . . , 315.
[9] Columbia *Missouri Intelligencer and Boon's Lick Advertiser*, November 22, 1834, p. 3.
[10] St. Louis *Missouri Republican*, March 5, 1823, p. 1, from the *Aurora*.
[11] John B. Gordon, Fourth of July Address delivered at Columbia, Missouri, Columbia *Missouri Intelligencer and Boon's Lick Advertiser*, July 11, 1835, p. 1.
[12] Josiah Gregg, Fourth of July Address delivered at Jonesborough, Missouri, Fayette *Missouri Intelligencer and Boon's Lick Advertiser*, August 14, 1829, pp. 1–2.

monished his hearers that "though the language of inspiration shall fall from the lips of man; though the richest spoils of time be compressed beneath his brow; though the most elevated conceptions of an immortal soul should enlighten his bosom; yet man is but the creature of the dust, and should not arrogate to himself an immunity from that sentence of instability engraven upon all terrestial objects." [13]

A strong moral and religious tone permeated the orations. Missourians stood squarely upon the Constitution and the Bible and linked the two in their thoughts. In toasts, they solemnly pledged, "The Constitution of the United States — Its distruction [sic] would cause angels to weep, and in hell a jubilee would be celebrated by the ghosts of departed tyrants." [14] Allusions and quotations demonstrate the familiarity of speakers and listeners with the Bible. Typical was the digression made by a speaker who praised industry in the words, "Length of days are in her right hand, and in her left hand riches and honors." [15] Audiences approved the biblical allusions as evidences of the speaker's moral character. Despite his profanity and general neglect of religion, the pioneer expected ceremonial speeches to contain moral sentiments and agreed with the speaker who told listeners, "Religion is the foundation of all moral order in society. . . . Without it, man degenerates. . . . If we have religion, we shall have morals, and the whole train of social virtues; we shall become a happy people, and live the envy and admiration of mankind." [16]

Almost as popular as the expression of moral sentiments were compliments to womanhood. Speakers paid women extravagant tributes, such as that given by the young lawyer who digressed to say:

> Let me not forget to pay a just tribute of respect to the agency of woman. . . . It was she that bore into life, and rocked into man-

[13] James Rollins, Eulogy of Lafayette, Columbia *Missouri Intelligencer and Boon's Lick Advertiser*, July 19, 1834, pp. 1–2.

[14] Jefferson City *Jeffersonian Republican*, September 30, 1837, p. 1, from report of celebration at Cape Girardeau, Missouri.

[15] Joseph Ormond, Fourth of July Address delivered at Liberty, Missouri, Franklin *Missouri Intelligencer*, August 5, 1822, pp. 1–2.

[16] Ormond, Fourth of July Address.

hood, the patriots and sages of '76. It was she who gave life, and principles, and heroism to that immortal band of spartan warriors, who shed their blood, and whose bones whitened the plains of America, in defence of the rights of man. The great moral force of woman over man, is deeply felt and recognized.[17]

Of all women, the mother was most honored. The word *mother* was often an inspiration for a digression to allow the orator to praise her. Typical was the expression of the orator who marveled, "And oh! who can comprehend the mystery of a mother's love; it imbues the very essence of her life, tinges her heart, her soul, her deeds, her words, clothes its objects with all radiance, and then worships the glory it has made."[18]

The platform speaker frequently quoted a few lines of poetry to illustrate a thought or to provide a fitting conclusion to a speech. He rarely credited the lines to their author, but this omission was of little concern to hearers. For them, the poetic passages lent sweetness and grandeur to the addresses, thus placing them in the tradition of oratorical speeches.

The digressions served a similar purpose and may occasionally have had political ends. A speaker who eulogized Jackson appealed not only to the laborers and mechanics of Irish ancestry but also to the frontiersman's dislike of England when he ignored the Scottish part of Jackson's background and expressed his gratitude to Ireland for Jackson's being. "Ireland! What a world of thought your name awakens — the history of your wrongs, your poetry, you[r] eloquence, your love of freedom, and struggle for independence, gush through the mind and almost overwhelm us with the retrospection. Ireland! I thank you —"[19]

Andrew Jackson was often the hero of dramatic stories told to illustrate a point and to delight the audience. Typical of these stories was the description of Andrew Jackson's appearance before Federal District Judge Dominick Hall at New Orleans to be sentenced for

[17] Gordon, Fourth of July Address.
[18] Morrow, Eulogy of Andrew Jackson.
[19] Morrow, Eulogy of Andrew Jackson.

placing the city under martial rule during the War of 1812. Since the loyal Jacksonian looked upon the independent judiciary as a block to popular sovereignty, his hero's humbling a judge undoubtedly increased his zest for the story. The speaker described the excited public feeling against the Judge for threatening the man who had saved the city from the British. He spoke of the popular enthusiasm for the General. He took his hearers with him to watch Jackson enter the room where the Court was sitting; he recalled the shouts of the people when they perceived their hero. He pictured Judge Hall's consternation at the accused man's reception and told how Jackson had waved his hand to hush the multitude and restore silence to the courtroom. When Judge Hall complained that he could not hold court amid such dangerous excitement, the speaker told how Jackson rose and assured the Judge, "There is no danger here; there shall be none; the same arm that protected the city from outrage, will shield and protect this court, or perish in the effort." [20]

Scenes of battle, bravery, and triumph lived again for hearers as speakers told how opposing forces met and clashed. Always the plain farmer and mechanic, the man of the people, by superior courage and patriotism, was able to outwit the forces of tyranny, however strong. An orator, in an address marking the anniversary of the Battle of New Orleans, pictured the meeting of the Americans and British: "How fearfully sublime the spectacle—the contemplation! On the one side, a comparative handful of farmers and mechanics . . . collected suddenly from all the vocations of civil life, without military skill or experience . . . with no higher qualifications than native courage, strong intellect and genuine patriotism . . . were here marshalled . . . in a contest with practiced soldiers." But, the speaker continued, the professional soldiers were no match for patriot farmers and mechanics, who lined up facing the powerful British, played their national anthem, sounded the

[20] Morrow, Eulogy of Andrew Jackson. Contemporary accounts of the events leading to the trial in March, 1815, show that, in the differences between Governor Claiborne and District Judge Hall on one hand and Andrew Jackson on the other, Jackson had been tactless, even if he had not given actual grounds for the charges levied against him.

bugle to charge, and fought until they drove out the invaders. Soldiers who had conquered Napoleon, the speaker exulted, were forced to bow to an unschooled general from the banks of the Cumberland. God had decreed the victory for this man of the people, said the speaker, who concluded his oration by thanking God for His part in defeating the British.[21]

Frontier audiences responded to denunciations of the British with the same enthusiasm as did the settlers in the older regions. A Fourth of July oration was not complete until the orator had cried out against the perfidy of England, the unnatural mother who had spurned her children. Independence Day orators emphasized the patience of the colonists in the face of tyranny. "Reluctantly did our fathers break the chains of British bondage," they said. England was "the ancient friend and primitive home of their fathers, the land of their nativity, and the respository of their bones — they were but her children, the offspring of her loins, in whose veins ran her blood." [22] But the mother country had betrayed this kinship, they proclaimed, and made revolt just and inevitable by repeated acts of oppression.

Indian attacks upon the frontier between 1812 and 1815 caused the Western settler's hatred of the British to burn more hotly. Orators charged England with employing the "savage hell hounds of the forest" to fight her battles for her on the frontier, with subjecting the wives and daughters of pioneers to "licentious and brutal soldiery," with sacking villages, burning towns and cities, and destroying precious archives of science and art.[23] The generalizations were sweeping and often unsupported by evidence, but listeners thrilled with patriotic pride as the British lion was conquered and humbled to the dust "to crouch and cower at the feet of the American eagle." [24]

The fervor of the denunciations of England was matched by the

---

[21] James Birch, Extracts from Jackson Day Address, *Fulton Telegraph*, January 26, 1849, p. 2.

[22] Gordon, Fourth of July Address.

[23] Stephen Allen, Fourth of July Address delivered at Troy, Missouri, St. Charles *The Missourian*, July 25, 1822, pp. 2–3.

[24] Gordon, Fourth of July Address.

praise of liberty. The "genius of liberty" was a familiar personification to pioneer audiences. In America, orators said, liberty had found a dwelling place secure from the dangers of monarchy. Typical was the passage:

> For since its expulsion from Rome, the genius of Liberty had retired from the world; monarchy, anarchy, and despotic tyranny, stalk abroad in awful grandeur, and spread their chains of vassalage o'er the habitable globe; and man, oppressed man! yielded universal homage to their potent sway. Long had the genius mourned the fallen state of man — oft had the sympathetic tear fell for their sufferings; till her increasing emotions rose beyond the bounds of passive endurance, and she emerged from the place of her retreat, she threw a glance around, which embraced the whole line of animated and enlightened nature: she caught the first bold daring of those heroes of '76 . . . with rapture she exclaimed, "These are my children." [25]

The genius of liberty was responsible for the great progress made by the West, speakers declared. This genius sinks despotism, withers barbarism, and vanquishes ignorance, orators proclaimed; and well they might have felt some special favor had been bestowed upon their section of the country when they considered the progress that had been made in their own lifetime. They spoke of the changes almost with awe. "Who would have believed in '76 that in half a century, an audience so numerous, respectable and enlightened as the present, would be assembled at such a distance from the Atlantic," they asked. [26] In spacious phrases they gloried in the increasing population "rolling on from the east like a flood, prostrating forests, driving back and reclaiming barbarism and clothing the whole face of nature, with the beautiful and diversified garb of industry and civilization." [27] They rejoiced in the cities and towns, which they declared had sprung up like magic, and asserted that the

[25] Allen, Fourth of July Address.

[26] Thomas C. Burch, Fourth of July Address delivered at Richland, Missouri, Franklin *Missouri Intelligencer*, July 22, 1825, pp. 1–2.

[27] Stephen Austin, Fourth of July Address delivered at Potosi, Missouri, St. Louis *Missouri Gazette and Public Advertiser*, July 24, 1818, pp. 2–3.

growth of agriculture, industry, and culture had been proportionate with the growth of population.

They waxed eloquent on the possibilities of the future and foretold magnificent dwellings, extensive and productive farms, seminaries of learning, and cities of wealth, taste, and refinement on the western side of the Mississippi. Nearly always optimistic, frontier orators envisioned a consummate age when Missouri would shine as the brightest star of the Union, for had she not been intended by nature as the garden of America? Her "bounties were so profusely spread," she was so "enchantingly decorated with the choicest tints of nature," her soil so fine, her women so fair, her men so brave and virtuous that progress was inevitable.[28]

The Missourian who believed that such progress was possible only under a democratic government longed for all the world to share the blessings of freedom. Urging subjects of kings to cry out for liberty, glory, and immortality, he called for revolt against monarchies. The Government of the United States provided an example for all the rest of the world, speakers asserted. Never before had the rights of man been so well defined or understood. Americans had both the honor and duty of diffusing a knowledge of good government throughout the world until the "bright rays of our liberty play round an abject world like 'northern lustres over the vault of night.' "[29] Exulting in a South American revolt as an omen of the future, orators promised that European nations would soon awake from their slumbers, shake off their fetters, and be free.

Linked to the attacks upon the despotic sway of monarchs was the vision of a nation that encompassed the Oregon and Mexican territories. Missourians believed that it was the manifest destiny of the United States to extend its borders from the Atlantic to the Pacific. Citizens who had greeted the War of 1812 with delight and had demanded the invasion of Canada listened with interest to a young

[28] Such sentiments are found in the orations of Josiah Gregg (see note 12) and of John Heth, Esq., who delivered a Fourth of July address at St. Charles, Missouri, published in St. Louis *Missouri Gazette*, August 2, 1808, pp. 1 and 4.

[29] Joseph Ormond, Fourth of July Address.

speaker forecast the day when "one foot of this republic shall be placed upon the Atlantic, and the other upon the Pacific Ocean, and its head reared to high heaven."[30]

In commemorating the birth of independence, speakers reminded hearers that freedom had not been won without suffering. They alluded to the blood of their ancestors spilled at Lexington and Concord. Woven through their speeches were references to the sacrifices of their fathers, seven years of toil and uncertainty, death groans, and a ground crimsoned with the blood of sainted heroes who had bartered their felicity for the purchase of liberty. Sometimes the orator began his account with the suffering of the pilgrims who had braved the savage wilderness of New England, and then he proceeded in the two- or three-hour oration to the trials of the early settlers in Missouri.

Freedom was a personal as well as a national ideal on the frontier. A young member of Frémont's expedition to California recorded in his diary his feelings when the company paused on the Fourth of July to listen to the reading of the Declaration of Independence. "The words seemed to instill into each one of us that we were indeed freemen," he said.[31] The frontiersman's attitude toward freedom was more than a dislike of restraints upon his individual liberties; he loved freedom as an ideal, was braving the harshness of primitive living conditions in order to realize that ideal, and he saw a clear relation between the nation's past and the present.

The hero who had done most to guarantee his freedom, he believed, was George Washington. Washington was hailed in orations and pledged in toasts as a model of virtue, a Godlike champion, great and immortal. A resident of a frontier community spoke for all America when he offered, "The memory of George Washington, who stood as a pillar of fire to blast the mad efforts of men fighting against their brethren! On earth his name shall never fade, children shall talk of him, as the patriot who beheld them afar off, and with a

[30] Gustavus Earickson, Fourth of July Address delivered at Richland, Missouri, Franklin *Missouri Intelligencer*, July 22, 1825, p. 1.
[31] Thomas E. Breckenridge, Memoirs, 1845–1894.

parent ardour hastened to ward from their guiltless heads the curse of monarchy." [32] Toasts, pledged in wine or stronger drink, were ordinarily offered in holiday mood, but pledges to Washington were drunk silent and standing; and if music was played in response, it was a solemn dirge. On the Fourth of July all veterans of the Revolution were held to be noble, holy, and unimpeachable in honor. With tears in their eyes, speakers pictured them as cherubim hovering around the political ark to preserve it from the assaults of ambiion and tyranny.[33] But George Washington stood alone as the perfect national leader.

The Fourth of July was the most significant day of celebration on the frontier. The pioneers who settled the Upper Louisiana Territory believed that it was important to commemorate the deeds of their ancestors in the cause of independence and warned that when a people no longer remembered the day that gave birth to their freedom they would cease to be free. These settlers of the West brought the custom of celebrating Independence Day from their former homes. The Fourth of July had been celebrated west of the Alleghenies for the first time at Marietta, Ohio, in 1788. Upon that occasion, Ohio pioneers had applauded the invective of an orator and, repairing to convenient kegs, had drunk toasts to the overthrow of despotism, to the grandeur of Greece and Rome, and to the westward course of empire.[34] Missourians liked both the sentiments and the refreshments and throughout the pioneer period followed the example of the citizens of Marietta.

For the frontiersman, observance of such customs and traditions provided a link with the society that he had formerly known. The display of flags, the music, the toasts, processions, and speechmaking lent color and decorum to life on the raw frontier, and, as soon as he could, the Western settler introduced the accustomed ceremonies.

[32] St. Louis *Missouri Gazette*, July 13, 1816, p. 3, from report of celebration held at Herculaneum, Missouri.

[33] St. Louis *Missouri Gazette*, August 10, 1816, p. 3, from report of celebration held at Potosi, Missouri.

[34] Cedric Larson, "Patriotism in Carmine: 162 Years of July 4th Oratory," *Quarterly Journal of Speech*, XXVI, 1 (February, 1940), 12–25.

The pioneer enjoyed the social side of the celebrations, but the program on the Fourth was principally designed to provide a reminder that the nation's liberty had been won by sacrifice. Missourians indicated their purpose in such words as, "Let us not so soon forget the annual return of that epoch when our fathers resolved to die or purchase the inheritance of liberty for us." [35] Listeners expected to hear an account of the struggle for independence and thrilled with pride as they heard how their fathers under the leadership of the "immortal Washington" had saved the fledgling nation and prepared a dwelling place for the goddess of liberty. [36]

Citizens also paid homage to early settlers who had opened up the western territory and repulsed Indian attacks. Lifting their glasses to Daniel Boone, as well as to Washington and Lafayette, they toasted *The Pioneers of the West* — Brave, hardy and independent; much they contended against, more may they reap." [37]

The commemorative aspects did not make the occasion altogether solemn. Often, a ball concluded the day's festivities. Plentiful food, an abundant supply of liquor, colorful oratory, a chance to visit with neighbors and shake hands with a celebrity or two — all contributed to a holiday spirit. The presence of one or more distinguished personages increased the impressiveness of the occasion. These guests were honored by being invited to sit on the platform with speakers and officials. Typical of the men invited to grace the Fourth of July celebrations was William H. Ashley, a Virginian by birth, who had come to the territory when it was still under Spanish control. He had engaged in surveying, land speculation, lead mining, manufacture of gunpowder, and banking. His explorations of the West and his success in competing against the powerful Eastern and British companies for the fur trade enhanced his charm for Missourians. Missourians, who admired a military man, could look up to Ashley in this respect, also, for he was a brigadier general in the state

[35] St. Louis *Missouri Gazette*, July 28, 1809, p. 2.

[36] Among the orations containing such sentiments are those of Stephen Allen and Stephen Austin.

[37] Toast offered by a member of the Jefferson City Debating Society on July 4, 1841, Jefferson City *Jeffersonian Republican*, July 10, 1841, p. 2.

militia. Moreover, he was the first lieutenant governor of the state and a wealthy man.[38] A pro-Bank man, he received his primary political support from the wealthy mining, slaveholding, plantation-owning settlers rather than from the yeoman group; yet many a Jackson man, as well as the aristocrats, was glad to shake his hand on the commemorative occasions.

The distinguished guests did not bask alone in the spotlight. Sharing the glory on Independence Day with the readers of the Declaration, orators, and guests, were the presidents and vice-presidents of the day chosen from among the leading citizens. Wealth and social or political prominence were the chief qualifications for an invitation to serve as an official, but other reasons could bring about an invitation to take part in the festivities. Martin Parmer was uneducated, pugilistic, and often half drunk, but he had been one of the first settlers of Howard County and he could be relied on when Indians attacked. Frontiersmen with whom he shared a common prejudice against cowards, British, and Indians not only thought well enough of him to invite him to serve in official capacity on Independence Day but sent him to represent them in the state legislature.[39]

Despite the patriotic motives of celebrants and the sanction of officialdom, accidents brought about by predilections for strong liquor and fighting often marred the day. "The usual accidents that accompany the celebration of the day have not been wanting," an editor lamented in 1834. "Every year the victims of Bacchus are offered up upon the very altars our fathers erected to Liberty." [40] By the end of the nineteenth century, men estimated that as many lives had

[38] The best account of Ashley's life is by Harrison D. Dale, *The Ashley-Smith Explorations and the Discovery of A Central Route to the Pacific 1822–1829*, 57–173. Dale is also the author of the biographical account of Ashley in the *Dictionary of American Biography*, Allen Johnson, ed., I, 391–92.

[39] The life and exploits of Martin Parmer are described briefly in *History of Saline County*, 204; Alphonse Wetmore, *Gazetteer of the State of Missouri . . .* , 89–91. Contemporary references are found in Fayette *Missouri Intelligencer and Boon's Lick Advertiser*, March 15, 1827, p. 3, and July 4, 1828, p. 3; Franklin *Missouri Intelligencer*, July 29, 1820, p. 3, November 26, 1822, p. 3, June 3, 1823, p. 3, August 12, 1823, p. 3, December 16, 1825, p. 3; and St. Louis *Missouri Republican*, June 4, 1823, p. 2.

[40] Columbia *Missouri Intelligencer and Boon's Lick Advertiser*, August 9, 1834, p. 2.

been lost in the celebrations of the Fourth as were given up at Bunker Hill.[41]

The friends of temperance, seeing drink as the cause of the disturbances, tried to rally citizens to support their efforts to reduce its abuses. Sometimes they substituted for the usual patriotic address an oration upon the evils of intoxication. Colonel William Russell, in 1834, drawing an analogy with the struggle for independence, called for the waging of a new war upon liquor;[42] but his fellow citizens did not respond favorably in large numbers to the substitution of a lecture on alcoholism for the customary waving of the flag, and only a few of the Fourth of July toasts were pledged in lemonade.

The drinking of toasts was a traditional part of most festivities. Even when no orator provided inspiration for the occasion, celebrants offered toasts. In 1812 a young mechanic, who had recently arrived in St. Louis, wrote a glowing account of the ceremonies in that city. "We had a Noble Dinner for $1.25 each person and pd $2.50 Each for wine. We allso had 20 Toasts give us and cannon fird at each Toast with a clap of hands and 3 chears allso Elegant Songs," he wrote a friend.[43]

A clap of hands, three cheers, and elegant songs were well enough, but the boom of a cannon or the sound of musket fire was better liked. Citizens also enjoyed musical responses, and bands showed considerable ingenuity in their choice of songs to follow the expressions of sentiments. John Scott, who represented the interests of Missourians in Congress until they retired him for supporting Adams rather than Jackson in 1824, was often the object of toasts in the early part of the era; a pledge made to him was likely to bring the music of "Scots O'er the Border." "The Star Spangled Banner" frequently followed a drink to the Army and Navy, and "Hail Columbia" or "Washington's March" was struck up after the toast to

[41] Herbert W. Horwill, "The Fourth of July in America," *The Living Age*, XXXVI (August 3, 1907), 299–305.

[42] W. H. Russell, Temperance Address delivered on July 4, 1834, Columbia *Missouri Intelligencer and Boon's Lick Advertiser*, October 18, 1834, pp. 1–2.

[43] V. M. Porter, "A History of Battery 'A' of St. Louis," *Missouri Historical Society Collections*, II, 4 (March, 1905), 2–3.

Independence Day. "Yankee Doodle" was a favorite response to "The Boys of '76," and when the company drank the health of the American fair, bandsmen played "Come Haste to the Wedding."

Regular toasts were prepared in advance of the occasion. Though brief, these pledges made up no inconsiderable part of the speaking on the Fourth. In the early celebrations in the East, committees often limited the toasts to thirteen in honor of the original colonies, but in accord with Western expansiveness, limits were rarely imposed on the frontier celebrants. As many volunteers as could get the ears of the audience made pledges. Thirty or more toasts were commonplace, and at Liberty, Missouri, in 1830 forty-two were reported to the papers.[44] Even if the participants pledged in wine — an unlikely occurrence at Liberty in 1830 — they must have consumed a considerable quantity of liquor.

The number of responsive cheers indicated the listeners' approval of the sentiments offered. When the pioneer agreed with the toastmaker, he pounded one palm upon the other and roared out a hurrah! A proposition even mildly favored brought three cheers; a toast to the American fair generally elicited six or more. When the company was wrought to a high emotional pitch, they doubled the hurrahs!

Committees made efforts to unite the entire community in commemoration of the Fourth, and in many towns Whigs and Democrats, Masons and anti-Masons, yeomen and plantation owners, soft- and hard-money men celebrated together in partial and temporary truce. Not even the common patriotic motive could eliminate all acrimony, however. Henry Clay, idolized by many Missourians, was bitterly hated by others who believed that he had treacherously deprived Andrew Jackson of the Presidency. At a dinner in 1827 a toast to the exertions of Henry Clay in behalf of the political rights of Missourians was answered by a pledge to the virgin purity of elections and a promise that citizens would in the future avoid the "incestuous embraces" of a "Kentucky libertine."[45]

---

[44] Fayette *The Western Monitor*, July 28, 1830, p. 2.
[45] North Todd Gentry, *The Bench and Bar of Boone County, Missouri*, 55–56.

The regular toasts proposed more peaceable objects and followed a predictable pattern. Almost universally, celebrants began by drinking to the day, continued with pledges to Washington, the Constitution, the heroes of '76, the Army and Navy, Missouri, liberty, agriculture and industry, and finally to "the American Fair — last in our glasses, yet first in our affections."[46] Admirers drank to the health of Thomas Hart Benton, whom they regularly elected to the Senate for thirty years, to Benjamin Franklin, Thomas Jefferson, the Marquis de Lafayette, Henry Clay, and Andrew Jackson.

The special toasts gave clear indications of the sentiments of the group. The "large and respectable" number of citizens who met at the house of Horace Austin in St. Louis in 1814 to celebrate the Fourth showed their approval of the War of 1812 by toasting the war with the British, along with the United States of America, James Madison, "Commodore" Chauncey (actually Captain Isaac Chauncey), and the Army and Navy.[47]

Missourians attached considerable significance to the toasts, but the pledges were only preliminaries to the principal event — the Fourth of July oration. The orator was the central figure of the celebrations. His friends drank his health with such sentiments as, "The Orator of the day — his fellow youths are proud to acknowledge him as an ornament to their ranks — may the laurels of a life of virtue and usefulness be his reward."[48] Although lawyers were in such great demand as speakers and readers on Independence Day that the occasion was often called the Lawyer's Fourth, other promising young men who were considered good speakers were not infrequently invited to deliver the oration. Doctors and officeholders, as well as lawyers, were frequently selected as orators.

The pioneer took these orations seriously. He expected the ora-

[46] St. Louis *Missouri Gazette*, August 10, 1816, p. 3, from report of celebrations at at Potosi, Missouri.

[47] St. Louis *Missouri Gazette and Illinois Advertiser*, July 9, 1814, p. 3. In April, 1813, Captain Isaac Chauncey improvised a fleet on Lake Ontario and with General Henry Dearborn made an unsuccessful raid on York (later Toronto). Chauncey subsequently attacked Fort George successfully. It was probably the news of this later attack that inspired the toast and the title "Commodore."

[48] Jefferson City *Jeffersonian Republican*, July 10, 1841, p. 2.

tor to speak, in the words of a contemporary, "in the cause of Christianity, Patriotism, and *Literature* — in the cause of justice, humanity, virtue and *truth* — in the cause of the people, of the Union, of the whole human race, and of the unborn of every age and every clime." [49] For him, the orator spoke less as an individual than as a representative of the common beliefs of the people.

The speaker customarily adhered to traditional subject matter. He included brief references to topics of the moment, but rarely offered new information or novel interpretations of the past. Hearers resented innovations and were suspicious of the introduction of names not ordinarily listed in their catalogue of heroes. In 1825, when a newcomer to the state included the Revolutionary patriots Joseph Warren, Henry Laurens — one of the negotiators of the Peace of Paris — and Generals Richard Montgomery and Nathanael Greene as men to be praised along with George Washington and the Marquis de Lafayette, an indignant listener asked sarcastically why he did not add the name of the British General James Wolfe and the Plains of Abraham. [50] The orator on the Fourth was expected to inspire patriotism and to do it by hailing the day as sacred to the birth of independence, by praising the familiar heroes, denouncing Great Britain, and holding out hopes for a glorious future.

As on the Fourth of July, the rhetoric on other commemorative occasions was designed to unite hearers by voicing accepted beliefs rather than providing any close examination of them. The orator praised the object of the celebration and managed at the same time to praise the virtues admired by his audience. Generally admonishing his hearers to display courage and patriotism, he prophesied that their dreams of wealth and influence were destined to be realized. The extravagance of the prophecies was matched by the copiousness and ornateness of the language. To display his knowledge of the classics by reference to the Greeks and Romans, the ceremonial ora-

---

[49] Columbia *Missouri Intelligencer and Boon's Lick Advertiser*, July 11, 1835, p. 3.

[50] Franklin *Missouri Intelligencer*, July 16, 1825, p. 2. General James Wolfe was the British commander who defeated the Marquis de Montcalm at Quebec in 1756. To capture that city, he and nearly 5,000 men scaled the almost perpendicular cliffs and occupied the Plains of Abraham above the city.

tor traced the blessings of republicanism to their roots in Greek and Roman societies, extolled the oratory of Cicero and Demosthenes as the ideal form, and pointed to the downfall of Greece and Rome as a warning that citizens must be ever vigilant in safeguarding liberty. Drawing upon heroes of the ancient world for comparison, speakers likened great men of America to Cincinnatus, Scipio, Brutus, Leonidas, and Virginius.

Though hearers preferred that the speaker hold to traditional subjects, they were pleased when he was able, as they expressed it, to impart a novelty to his subject by his opulence of language and use of imagery. These qualities, critics said, "commanded the mute attention and secured the plaudits of all." [51] Sometimes the language was pretentious and the images inappropriate, as in the speech of John Heth, who reminded hearers that they had met to celebrate the birthday of independence, "a day on which the goddess of liberty waved in the air with hilarity, the glorious banner of liberty, the workmanship of the gods; a day on which the fair daughters of America rejoiced with gladdened hearts, in concert with their protecting patriotic heroes; a day in which Great Britain was seen in sackcloth and morning [mourning]; a day the name of which alone palsies the highest mirth." [52]

Often vitriolic in criticism of speeches made for political ends, audiences rarely found fault with the style of commemorative orations. The reason for the generosity was not complacency toward errors in figures or language, for among frontier listeners were graduates of European and American colleges; nor was the forbearance of Western settlers responsible, for duels growing out of speechmaking were frequent. The reason lay, rather, in the belief of citizens that fidelity to the spirit of the occasion was more important than the niceties of language. Hearers of John Heth who could respond to the complex intertwining of elation and solemnity that characterized the celebrations, to the sense of having been chosen by the gods, to

[51] J. W. Redd, Criticism of a speech, Franklin *Missouri Intelligencer*, December 30, 1823, p. 3.
[52] St. Louis *Missouri Gazette*, August 2, 1808, pp. 1 and 4.

the praise of virtuous womanhood and strong courageous manhood, and to the image of proud Britain sitting in sackcloth and mourning were not inclined to find his speech ridiculous. It was the spirit that counted. That the figure was confused did not conceal the admonition and the promise held out in the reminder that "it's also our indispensable duty to support with dignity the small branch of the great tree of liberty, which we have the honor to bear in Louisiana; and altho' we are not among its choicest flowers; let it be recollected . . . that the leaves are green about us." [53]

The speeches on ceremonial occasions had elements of a magic incantation. The subjects were traditional, the stories familiar, the language stylized. As to an incantation, the people responded not by reasoning but by absorbing the spirit of the words they heard. Speeches were not designed as arguments. The repeated encomiums of the common man's intellect and virtue, the praise of republican principles, and the invocation of the name of Andrew Jackson strengthened the belief of the man on the frontier that a plain man was equal to the aristocrat and qualified to enjoy the same privileges. As the man without a penny to his name rubbed elbows with the richest man in the settlement at the speakings, his concept of equality became more personal. And when the common man heard repeatedly that virtue resided in him, he began to feel that he and his kind should replace the old leaders. Ceremonial occasions brought many influences to bear on the participants. They reminded listeners to be vigilant in the cause of freedom, and they encouraged the frontiersman's optimism about the growth and development of the area. Ironically, although they were organized and directed by aristocrats, the most enduring influence of the rhetoric heard on such occasions was to promote class mobility.

[53] St. Louis *Missouri Gazette*, August 2, 1808, pp. 1 and 4.

IV

"*A candidate for office here, even for that of Magistrate or Justice of the Peace must canvass his districts and give his views on all those laws which come within his jurisdiction. He knows that he must talk or he is down.*"

Otis Adams, "St. Louis in 1849."

Servants of the People

The orators who spoke to audiences on the frontier — especially the political candidates — were instrumental in popularizing the concept of democracy as a patriotic ideal. Candidates for office frequently made blatant appeals to the voters' desires for sovereignty. At least one such accompanied the announcement of his candidacy for office with the statement that the wishes of a few monied men should not be allowed to trample under foot the rights of the majority; the time had come for the people to assert their rights.[1] Though the election of Andrew Jackson hastened the democratizing process, his victory was itself an outgrowth of the frontier attitude toward government.

Americans scornfully noted the absence of popular rights under French and Spanish rule. Frederick Bates, territorial secretary, said of the early settlers, "If their Commandant spurned them from his presence, deprived them of half their Estate or ordered them to the black Hole, they received the doom as the dispensation of Heaven."[2] Bates reported that he saw the "idea of representative government dawning on the bewildered imaginations of the people like the first blush of morning," but he radically underestimated the people's desire for a voice in their affairs.[3] Almost as soon as they heard that Upper Louisiana had been annexed to the United States, the French joined with American settlers to petition Congress for a separate territorial government with an elective council.[4]

[1] Jackson *Independent Patriot*, June 1, 1822, p. 3.

[2] Frederick Bates to Richard Bates, December 17, 1807, Frederick Bates, *The Life and Papers of Frederick Bates*, Thomas Maitland Marshall, ed., I, 242–43.

[3] Frederick Bates to Richard Bates, December 17, 1807, Bates, *Life and Papers*, I, 242–43.

[4] Clarence Edwin Carter, ed., *The Territory of Louisiana-Missouri, 1803–1806*, Vol. XIII, *The Territorial Papers of the United States*, 41.

Since the granting of their petition for a separate government gave them no power to elect their own officials, they remained discontented. They found that the governor and judges appointed by the President had no more regard for popular opinion than the French and Spanish rulers had shown. Officials thought the people incapable of self-government. Territorial Governor James Wilkinson considered them a poor ignorant lot who required a strong authority to hold them in check.[5] Secretary Bates also thought them incompetent to make any political decisions and without any conception of the obligations that accompanied rights. "The very name of liberty deranges their intellects," he wrote a kinsman.[6]

Though the citizens had to submit to the authority of the appointed local officers, they used every means within their power to influence such choices. Despite the difficulty and expense of correspondence, settlers bombarded officials in Washington with protests and accusations against the men and measures that governed their remote communities. They aired their grievances in the territorial newspaper, as did the writer signing himself "Old Farmer" who reminded readers that the behavior of the judges was only what might be expected from men hired and paid by the government and in whose nomination the people had no share.[7] Citizens couched their petitions to Congress and territorial officials in respectful language beginning, "We take the liberty of recommending . . . ," and ending, "respectfully, Your Ob'd t Serv'ts," but the implication of rights demanded was clear.[8]

In communications addressed to other citizens in the territory, the demand for rights was unmistakable. A notice posted on the church door in St. Louis called for citizens to rise up against John Lucas, one of the territorial judges:

[5] James Wilkinson to James Madison, September 21, 1805, *Territorial Papers*, XIII, 219.

[6] Frederick Bates to Richard Bates, December 17, 1807, Bates, *Life and Papers*, I, 242.

[7] St. Louis *Louisiana Gazette*, December 14, 1811, p. 3.

[8] *Territorial Papers*, XIII, 430.

PEOPLE OF LOUISIANA ARE YOU SLAVES
how long will you suffer the vile and infamous John Lucas to keep
you in the chains of oppression voilence [*sic*] and injustice . . . the
power of govern't has raised this enemy of your country above
you . . . and your power with a little hemp may raise him still
higher and to a station to which he is really entitled. . . .[9]

For a time, the popular pressure concentrated on persuading
Congress to raise the territory to second-class status with elective representation. The primary argument was that men elected to office
made better legislators than appointed officials, since they were more
aware of the needs of the people. Observers noted the desire of the
people to govern themselves and said that attempts at self-government in local matters had brought recognizable benefits. H. M.
Brackenridge acknowledged that the duties of the officials in the little towns were often of little consequence, but, he said, the titles of
office symbolizing leadership counted for a great deal in popular
opinion; the titles seemed to make the people of the community feel
that they amounted to something, and though he observed that the
"ancient inhabitants" retained the principal voice in these local governments, he thought the middle class had made the greatest advance in citizenship by their opportunity to feel and speak "with the
freedom of men."[10] Spokesmen for the great landholders opposed
the extension of popular control. They spoke of the inferiority of settlers collected from every quarter of the globe and warned that al-
lowing large numbers of propertyless men to vote would result in
unjust taxation upon property holders.

Congress responded, however, to the majority by raising the territory to second-class status on June 4, 1812, and by changing its
name to the Missouri Territory. Under the new classification citizens
were permitted to elect members of the Lower House and to send a
delegate to Congress, but democracy extended little further. The

[9] Clarence Edwin Carter, ed., *The Territory of Louisiana-Missouri, 1806–1814*, Vol.
XIV, *The Territorial Papers of the United States*, 336.
[10] "Sketches of the Territory of Louisiana," St. Louis *Louisiana Gazette*, April 11,
1811, p. 2.

Lower House supplied a list from which the President chose members of the upper territorial house; the President continued to appoint the governor and the judges of the highest court. An aristocracy of property was maintained by requiring each member of the Upper House to own at least two hundred acres of land and each member of the Lower House to be a freeholder. Despite these limitations, citizens were generally pleased with the extension of rights, and so many declared themselves candidates for office that voters joked about the impossibility of choosing among them.

In the early elections, voters chose men from the groups that had been accustomed to govern them. Virtually all the officials in the early territorial period belonged by interest or background to the aristocracy. Though the old familiar faces continued to be seen in the legislature, their electors reflected a change in their attitude by indicating strongly that legislators should be responsible to popular interests. When lawmakers voted themselves salaries that seemed exorbitant to the voters, critics reminded them that the "mechanics, peasants, and the rest of the multitude" that they were holding in contempt could turn them out at the next election.[11] Candidates showed awareness of the trend toward democracy and made efforts to identify themselves with the people and to accuse their opponents of subservience to the "big people" trying to run the territory.[12]

The raising of the territory to the highest rank in 1816 gave voters the privilege of electing members to the Upper as well as the Lower House, but this extension only temporarily appeased settlers, who soon began to petition for statehood. They justified their demands by speaking of the increased population, the long territorial experience, and the services of Missourians in the War of 1812; they listed as the grievance against territorial status the limitation upon self-government. Opponents of statehood repeated the arguments advanced against improved territorial status, but to no avail.

When the question of statehood had been decided in the

[11] St. Louis *Missouri Gazette*, July 29, 1815, p. 3; May 13, 1815, p. 3; August 5, 1815, p. 5.
[12] Typical are the charges made in "Dialogue Between a Farmer and Mechanic," St. Louis *Missouri Gazette*, July 27, 1816, pp. 2–3.

affirmative and the issue was Missouri's entrance as a free or slave state, both slavery and antislavery candidates for membership in the constitutional convention agreed that Missourians had the right to settle the question of restriction for themselves.[13] The 1820 constitution drawn up and adopted by popularly elected delegates — but never submitted to the people for ratification — emphasized self-government by terming Missouri a "free and independent republic." The new constitution made no property restriction for voters or officeholders and gave the General Assembly, considered most responsive to the electors, extensive power, including the right to fine or imprison those who held its authority in contempt. The higher courts were protected from political pressure in that judges were appointed by the governor and Senate and held office during good behavior, but inferior courts were placed under legislative control. The pressure for greater democracy evidenced itself most strongly in the election of the new state officials. Angered by the "high-flyers" in the constitutional convention who had voted themselves "big salaries," electors declared their intention of ousting the aristocrats and placing government in the hands of men like themselves. They elected as governor Alexander McNair, who had stumped the state appealing to the "honest farmers," over the incumbent William Clark and sent to the new capital at St. Charles legislators ignorant of the manners of urbane society.

In the years that followed, the ordinary citizen, increasingly confident in his ability to solve problems of government, somewhat belligerently increased his assertions that one man was as good as another. A leveling effect became apparent: Even when all rival candidates actually represented propertied interests, they sought to appear before the electorate as plain people. Citizens who had once signed communications to the newspapers with the names of *Cato, Aristides,* or *Philocles* now signed themselves *Plain Farmer, Mechanic,* or simply *A Voter.* Declaring that he had no pride in any title other than *Citizen,* a former member of the territorial council asked that the title *Honorable,* affixed to his name "without his consent," be

---

[13] St. Louis *Missouri Gazette and Public Advertiser,* January 3, 1821, pp. 2–3.

dropped.[14] Any hint that an office seeker thought himself superior to the voters was damning to his political ambitions. *Aristocrat* and *gentlemen* were terms of opprobrium in a political canvass. *Plain Farmer, Common Man*, and *Friend of the People* were the titles assumed by aspirants for office.

A college education and fashionable manners were active deterrents to a man's political hopes on the frontier. To the charge that his favorite's lack of learning disqualified him for the office of governor, a partisan answered that executing the law was neither so difficult nor mysterious as to be beyond the comprehension of a plain or vigorous mind and that he doubted that a knowledge of Aristotle's *Politics* or More's *Utopia* was a necessary qualification for office.[15] A majority of voters, in agreement, not only elected the man of plain and vigorous mind as governor, but sent to the legislature several other men who could barely read and write. Candidates successfully appealed to voters by stressing their lack of education, as did Isaac Martin, who boasted, "I never went to school but three days in my life; the third day I whipped the teacher and left."[16] Though native common sense was highly prized on the frontier, a formal education was considered nonessential for office.

The ideal candidate was a man of the people. Neal Gilliam prefaced his request to the citizens of Clay County that they elect him as their next sheriff with a summary of his qualifications: "I am a Jackson man up to the hub"; "I have killed more wolves and broke down more nettles than any man in Clay County."[17] Such qualifications were eminently satisfactory to a majority of his constituents. They had high regard for men who had cleared the land and freed it from wild animals, and his stated loyalty to Andrew Jackson, symbol of the sovereignty of the people, weighed even more heavily with them.

The men who lived at the edge of the wilderness admired a can-

[14] St. Charles *The Missourian*, August 5, 1820, p. 3.

[15] *St. Louis Beacon*, April 12, 1832, p. 3.

[16] W. B. Stevens, *Centennial History of Missouri (The Center State) One Hundred Years in the Union, 1820–1921*, I, 613.

[17] Stevens, *Centennial History of Missouri*, I, 68.

didate who was a good fellow, convivial, quick with an apt remark, and ready to devote his time and energy to the interests of his constituents. They liked a man who was charitable to those in need and generous in treating voters to plenty of whiskey. They respected a man who would not back down in a fight and could give a good account of himself with fists or pistols; their trust in the man who was not afraid of a scrap was expressed by the backwoodsman who announced that he was for Andrew Jackson "bekase as how he loves wimming and is chock-full of fight."[18] The frontiersman did not condemn an office seeker for getting drunk, swearing, or using bad grammar, but proof that he was unchivalrous or had misused public funds could deliver a serious blow to his chances for election. Candidates recognized the importance of a reputation for financial integrity and hotly resented any implication of dishonesty. They were also aware that birth in any of the Southern states, but especially in Kentucky, gave them an advantage over candidates of different origins. If the candidate was a plain farmer, had fought against the Indians or British, and, most important of all, had identified himself with the people and acknowledged their sovereignty, he was virtually invincible at the polls.

Parties were of little significance on the Missouri frontier before 1830. A letter writer in 1823 commented that no political distinctions existed in the state and he hoped they never would.[19] Rival groups organized around men and issues, and partisans shifted loyalties as issues shifted on the frontier. When party affiliations began to be significant, the Whig party generally attracted propertied and conservative men; the Democratic party evoked the allegiance of farmers, mechanics, and plain people. So successful were the Democrats in reaping votes by being termed *a tow-shirt party* composed of ignorant farmers, clodhoppers, and mechanics that Whigs began to try to outdo them in identifying with the common people. When the Whigs in 1840 adopted the democratic appeals and persuaded the public that William Henry Harrison was a cider-drinking, coon-

[18] St. Louis *Missouri Republican*, March 4, 1828, p. 3.
[19] St. Louis *Missouri Republican*, March 19, 1823, p. 2.

skin-wearing frontiersman, those who claimed superiority by aristocracy were left without a rallying point. With all groups asserting their desire to promote the interest of the common man, political division depended upon the ability of one man to do so better than his opponent.

Ordinary citizens took a strong interest in the campaigns. Since candidates for state office generally announced three or four months prior to the August vote and seekers of national offices campaigned for about the same length of time before the November election, the people were engaged with politics in election years from April to November 1. At camp meetings, horse races, militia musters, and Fourth of July gatherings, voters discussed the prospects of favorites and argued the issues. Crowds attending the stump speeches of the candidates and their friends were uninhibited in expressing approval or disapproval. They interrupted the speaker to ask questions, made audible comments on his integrity or lack of it, and spoke out to deny or support his assertions. They called for a favorite to take the platform and shouted down an unpopular speaker. They cheered, waved hats or handkerchiefs, and clapped their hands when they liked what they heard; they hissed, groaned, and stamped their feet when they did not like it. When friends of men involved in a disagreement took sides, arguments sometimes developed into brawls, and political discussions ended with torn coats, bloody noses, and black eyes. Frontiersmen were generally indulgent toward partisans who lost their tempers in election disputes. A party member, in requesting help for a colleague who had attacked two men with a pocketknife in an argument over a candidate, commented that his friend was "in a little difficulty." [20]

Factionalism was bitter within parties. Although Democrats in Missouri were united in support of Andrew Jackson and zealously observed the anniversary of his victory at New Orleans, they were often in violent disagreement on local men and issues. The clashes between supporters of Thomas Hart Benton and anti-Benton men were often harsher than between Whigs and Democrats. In 1844,

[20] Samuel A. Young to Abiel Leonard, August 11, 1846, Abiel Leonard Manuscripts.

when St. Louisans planned a Jackson Day celebration in their city, they attempted to forestall trouble by pledging the leaders of both factions in the Democratic party to make no allusion to Benton, either in support or opposition. Neither faction kept its agreement, and the free-for-all fight that ensued rivaled in bitterness, if not in bloodshed, the event being celebrated.[21] An observer commented that he had often heard campaign orators cry out that these were the times that tried men's souls, but his experiences on the frontier convinced him that their bodies were in more danger.[22]

The general excitement of the campaigns increased when citizens went to the polls. Viva-voce voting, instituted in 1824, added to the tumult. Under this system, the voter approached the clerk, customarily seated on a platform or behind an open window, and announced his choices for various offices. Any alert candidate and his friends could know how each man voted and could keep a tally of the progress of the voting. The kegs of whiskey provided by candidates and party leaders for the refreshment of the electors intensified the party spirit, and fights were common on election day. A mechanic living in St. Louis in 1838 described election activities in that year. Leaders of Whig and Democratic parties, in an attempt to increase interest in the election and avoid the long lines at the courthouse, chartered a boat to take voters to a polling place at Carondelet. The young mechanic, a Democrat, enjoyed the boat trip down the river, but found when he reached Carondelet that the Whigs had taken possession of the premises and would not allow him and his friends to vote. He joined with other Jacksonians who fought their way to the polls, with cries of "Hurrah for Benton!" and "Hurrah for Jackson!" mingling with the Whigs' shouts of "Drive them away!" and "Down with the damned Democrats!" For a time the Whigs barred the path, but eventually the Democrats forced their way past the Whig defenders to cast their votes. Even then, the

[21] Palmyra *The Missouri Whig*, March 23, 1844, p. 2.
[22] Thomas R. Marshall, ed., "The Journal of Henry B. Miller," *Missouri Historical Society Collections*, VI, 3 (1931), 222.

fighting did not cease, as men continued the brawl for the sheer pleasure of fighting.[23]

But men of the time and place demonstrated interest in the campaigns in other, less violent ways also. They marched in parades and torchlight processions and convened in meetings to praise favorites and denounce the opposition. They took pride in the banners carried in the parades and placed around the convention platforms. The Whig banner designed and painted by George Caleb Bingham indicated the nature of these emblems. Six by eight feet in size, it bore a picture of Henry Clay on one side and the eagle of Howard County on the other, with suitable inscriptions under the pictures.[24] Although few delegations had so distinguished an artist as designer, they generally had impressive emblems to display at conventions.

Party conventions were like the camp meeting in offering concentrated speaking and like the Fourth of July picnics in being social gatherings, but their primary function was to stimulate enthusiasm among the voters. The Whig gathering at Boonville in 1844 demonstrates the kind of activity connected with these meetings. On the day preceding the convention, Whigs of Howard County — women as well as men — assembled in Fayette for a three-hour march to New Franklin, located just across the river from Boonville. The marchers, who camped overnight at New Franklin, made the evening festive with songs, parades, and speeches. The next morning, augmented by their New Franklin friends, they came into Boonville, where they were welcomed by a congressman of their party. After his speech, they formed in procession — the company now increased by Whigs of Boonville — and, preceded by a brass band, moved to a hillside near town. Here, a committee had erected a speakers' stand and decorated it with evergreens, flags, and banners. Throughout the day the assembled crowd heard campaign orators praise Whigs and Whiggism and denounce the Democrats. At night conventioners marched in torchlight procession, sang partisan songs, and listened

[23] Marshall, ed., "Journal of Henry B. Miller," 260–65.
[24] A. J. Herndon to Abiel Leonard, September 12, 1844, Leonard Manuscripts.

to more speeches.[25] Possibly with sore feet, but presumably inspired, the merchants, lawyers, farmers, and tradesmen went home at the close of the convention to work with new enthusiasm for Whig candidates in the coming election.

The largest and most spectacular party gathering on the Missouri frontier took place in 1840, when Whigs held a three-day convention at Rocheport, a village located on the Missouri River in the center of the state. From all sections of Missouri and even from outside the state, visitors poured into the town. Candidates came to electioneer; Whig partisans came to express loyalty to William Henry Harrison and the party; even sundry Democrats came to enjoy the festivities and to keep an eye on their political rivals. Many of the visitors camped in the vicinity of the speakers' stand that had been set up in a grove near the town. The convention opened with a memorable parade led by a brass band. The log cabins in the line of march reminded Whigs that their candidate was a plain frontiersman. Troops of soldiers bearing the national colors and open carriages filled with old soldiers, some of whom had fought under Harrison, linked the party to patriotism. The antics of clowns amused citizens as the parade moved toward the speakers' stand, from which, for three days and nights partisan orators urged the election of Whigs.[26] As usual, Whigs failed to carry the state in the November election, but they derived some satisfaction from having made a creditable showing as a minority party.

Pageantry and parade did not, however, replace discussion of the issues. Citizens were well aware of at least some of the questions involved in an election and supported men who promised to promote what the people believed were their own best interests. A contemporary observed that any man who hoped to be elected must find the hobby of the people and ride it without mercy.[27] The frontiersman wanted no straddling of the issues. He demanded that the candidate declare himself forthrightly for or against a measure. In 1830,

[25] Fayette *Boon's Lick Times*, October 19, 1844, p. 2.
[26] Fayette *Boon's Lick Times*, July 4, 1840, p. 2.
[27] Franklin *Missouri Intelligencer*, June 5, 1824, p. 3.

when support of Jackson and popular election of judges were the two questions of greatest interest to Missourians, a citizen published an open letter asking candidates to tell how they stood on these measures. "These are the two great points of inquiry with the people," he explained, and he implied that the answers would determine popular support.[28]

The candidates recognized the necessity of bowing to the public will and, without waiting for a demand, clarified their position upon significant issues, as did William Rector, who told voters, "Having become a candidate . . . I deem it proper thus publicly to state to you my sentiments on the following important subjects," and proceeded to do so.[29] Candidates sometimes stated their positions in newspaper announcements, sometimes in public speeches; occasionally, the statements were ambiguous about the issues, but they made clear that the candidate recognized the sovereignty of the voters. "Public officers are the servants of the people," said Joseph Evans, when he asked the citizens of St. Charles to send him to the state legislature,[30] and he was no humbler in expression than others who sought the favor of elective office.

In the early frontier years a few leaders caucused to choose candidates for public office. The caucus was never popular with those who were not invited to share in its deliberations. In 1820 the editor of the *Missouri Gazette and Public Advertiser* announced candidates with the comment that they had been selected by a "self appointed tribunal of high-fliers and would-be great men."[31] The determination of the people to have a greater voice in the election of candidates led to the substitution of the popular convention for the caucus. The process of determining who should be supported for state and national offices by the party began at the local level with the appointment of delegates to conventions. Such notices as the following appeared in the newspapers:

[28] *St. Louis Beacon*, June 24, 1830, p. 2.
[29] St. Louis *Missouri Gazette and Public Advertiser*, April 19, 1820, p. 3.
[30] St. Charles *The Missourian*, August 19, 1820, p. 3.
[31] St. Louis *Missouri Gazette and Public Advertiser*, April 19, 1820, p. 2.

Citizens friendly to the election of General Jackson are requested to meet at the Baptist Meeting House at 3 P.M. on Tuesday next to appoint delegates to the convention at Jefferson on January 8 where an electoral ticket for the state will be formed.[32]

Despite repeated assertions that their party was the party of the people, leaders showed concern about attracting well-educated and propertied men to their cause. Describing those who attended a convention in 1828 as men conspicuous for wealth, intelligence, and respect for the Constitution, a friend of the Adams Administration said that any cause with such support was bound to be successful.[33] Jackson men, meeting at the state capital in Jefferson City a few days earlier to choose delegates also reported that speakers were lawyers and prominent men.[34] Both parties welcomed the support of men of wealth and prominence, but successful campaigners understood that it was necessary to present candidates, however distinguished they might be, as plain men moved by interest in the public good.

The contemporary voter was sometimes satiric about the candidates' image of subservience to the public. Assuming the character of a candidate's wife, such a satirist told how "her" husband acceded to the request of three or four neighbors filled with spirits of alcohol and patriotism to stand a poll and how he lost a part of his ear on election day when he denied the right of the people to instruct their representative.[35]

Although voters sometimes laughed at the exertions of campaigners, candidates understood that they must go to the people if they wished to be elected to office. The campaigns were indeed arduous business. Some three or four months before the election, an office seeker began a canvass of the voters in his district. Despite high water, muddy roads, and mosquito-infested prairies, he and his friends traveled through the country begging votes, shaking hands, treating electors to whiskey, and making speeches.

[32] St. Louis *Missouri Republican*, November 15, 1827, p. 3.
[33] St. Louis *Missouri Republican*, March 11, 1828, p. 3.
[34] St. Louis *Missouri Republican*, February 7, 1828, p. 3.
[35] Jefferson City *Jeffersonian Republican*, March 7, 1835, pp. 2–3.

Whiskey played a prominent part in the campaigns. On the campaign trail the candidate generally carried a treat for voters, and in the towns he enlisted support by visiting the grog shops and treating everyone present. Critics laughed that a "thorough-going" candidate made four expeditions a day through the bars—one before breakfast to shake hands with the "drouthy characters" who began to take their liquor early, one in the forenoon to meet the more respectable patrons, another in the afternoon to repeat the work of the morning, and a fourth at night to hold communion with all he was ashamed to be seen with at other times.[36]

Office seekers courted the voters privately with flattery and liquor, but they concentrated their public efforts on speechmaking. The warning of critics against the influence of speakers is evidence of their belief in the persuasive power of speeches. Party rivals cautioned the voters not to believe the "pharasaical politicians with sonorous voices" who were making reckless and irresponsible promises; only the ignorant, they declared, were influenced by the "eloquence crammed full of pathos."[37] Condemnation of eloquence, however, was directed toward the persuasive powers of the opposition. Leaders sought men who could speak well as standard-bearers for their own party. The voters expected the candidates to discuss the issues; they commented that they wished to see the office seekers in person and hear how they talked before they decided how to vote.[38] Contemporaries observed that debates and discussions promoted the interests of the people.[39]

Candidates made extensive tours in order to speak to the people wherever they could gather a crowd. Typical meeting places are indicated in the announcement of an office seeker that he would address the people during the following week at Hazelton's pond

---

[36] "Lectures on the Art of Electioneering," *Semi-Weekly St. Louis Enquirer*, August 9, 1821, p. 1.

[37] Jefferson City *Jefferson Inquirer*, June 6, 1845, p. 3, from the *Indiana Sentinel*; Franklin *Missouri Intelligencer*, June 24, 1823, p. 3; Columbia *Missouri Intelligencer and Boon's Lick Advertiser*, August 2, 1834, p. 3; *St. Louis Beacon*, October 20, 1830, p. 2.

[38] Jackson *Independent Patriot*, September 24, 1825, p. 2.

[39] St. Louis *Missouri Gazette and Public Advertiser*, March 29, 1820, p. 3.

spring, Perkins' Mill, the Widow Robberson's house, Nichol's house in Pleasant Prairie, and at McHaftee's place.[40] When possible, candidates tried to arrange speaking appointments to coincide with the sitting of the courts, the first day of a court session often being given over to political discussion.

Debate between rivals for an office was commonplace on the frontier. When opponents met by agreement for discussion of the issues from the same platform, they generally followed the plan of giving alternate speeches. One led off with a speech of an hour or more; the second followed with a slightly longer speech; the first speaker then offered a refutation. The debates provided an opportunity for the voters to make direct comparisons between opponents. In 1848, when Austin King met James S. Rollins in a debate to show which of them would be the better governor of Missouri, a friendly report praised King's "strongly logical" speech and disparaged Rollins not only for his arguments but also for his stories "too rare for respectable listeners" to hear.[41] The debates may have been less effective in changing votes than in strengthening party feelings, for an admirer of Rollins who heard the same debate praised his favorite as "decidedly a better speaker" than Judge King and prophesied that when the Judge met the Major once or twice more on the stump he would be so badly used up that he would be crawfishing "and taking some other shute."[42]

In debates or on other speaking occasions, candidates spoke "off hand." Campaigners believed that a written address hampered their freedom on the platform. They liked to speak as if in conversation with friends. A candidate frequently paused in his discussion of the issues to acknowledge the presence of notables who had arrived late, to greet a friend in the crowd, or to ask a member of the audience for corroboration of his statements. Neither the speaker nor his listeners were concerned with correctness of grammar and beauty of style. In 1849 a visitor from Massachusetts declared that he had lis-

[40] Springfield *Advertiser*, July 5, 1845, p. 3.
[41] Jefferson City *Jefferson Inquirer*, June 3, 1848, p. 2.
[42] Columbia *The Missouri Statesman*, May 19, 1848, p. 2.

tened to many of the campaign orators and, if any of their sentences were grammatical, it was more by "hit than any good wit."[43] Frontier audiences ridiculed a campaigner who affected the polysyllabic words they applauded on ceremonial occasions. Opponents cited an office seeker's definition of a tariff as a "cartel plenipotentiary or an agreement stipulatory between belligerents" as evidence of his utter ridiculousness.[44]

Despite the offhand manner of political aspirants, campaign speeches often show evidence of care in preparation. Rhetorical questions were used with skill. Typical are the questions asked by a critic of Thomas Hart Benton to cast doubt on the Senator's motive in opposing the Fugitive Slave bill: "Is he in favor of the bill as it now stands? Will he vote for its repeal or modification? Who can tell? He says it is injudicious. In what respects and for what reasons?"[45] Quotations from the poets, allusions to the Bible, to Heaven, and the Constitution appear in the campaign rhetoric, sometimes in astonishing juxtaposition. In a single speech at Arrow Rock, a campaigner referred to the casting out of the devils, to Cain, to the low state of the rich man who scorned Lazarus, and to Christ in the course of persuading the electorate that they should send him to the legislature.[46] Men made strenuous efforts to associate themselves, on a favored measure, with safeguards of the Constitution and with national heroes, as did the member of the Native American party who quoted Washington as saying in a dark hour of the Revolution, "Put none but native born Americans on guard tonight."[47] Historical and literary figures were introduced, as candidates alluded to Theseus in the labyrinth, Cincinnatus at the plough, the falseness of Iago, and the stratagems of Machiavelli.

Familiarity with Machiavelli and Iago was no requisite for per-

[43] Otis Adams, "St. Louis in 1849," *Bulletin of the Missouri Historical Society*, VI, 3 (April, 1950), 371.

[44] Columbia *Missouri Intelligencer and Boon's Lick Advertiser*, July 7, 1832, pp. 1–2.

[45] Columbia *The Missouri Statesman*, November 22, 1850, p. 2.

[46] Report of the speech of George Caleb Bingham, Fayette *Boon's Lick Times*, August 8, 1840, pp. 1–2.

[47] Report of the speech of Uriel Wright, Jefferson City *Jefferson Inquirer*, November 29, 1845, p. 2.

suading voters. The man without education spoke effectively by drawing his illustrations from the common experiences and speech of the people. A typical candidate declared himself for the kind of folks that spun tow, drank buttermilk, and churned their own butter.[48] John S. Robb's fictional but realistic "standing candidate," Old Sugar, won approval from his back-country neighbors by ridiculing a rival from the city as having an "*a* ristocracy stomach that couldn't go the native licker." [49] Recognizing the effectiveness of these appeals, men whose education would have permitted more elevated language employed the language of the common man. Thomas Hart Benton, who could speak learnedly in the Senate, chose illustrations from everyday life when he talked to his constituents on the frontier. Aware of their familiarity with the details of hog-killing in the fall, he told an audience that he intended to attack his opponents like a farmer on slaughter day and warned that, if the old sows and pigs fighting him did not get out the gap he had left them, he would kill them all without fattening.[50]

Invective delighted listeners. In an era when cholera was common, campaigners spoke of the infection in a rival party or faction and likened opponents to carrion rotting with the disease. They invoked the powers of Hell and the devil to castigate opponents, and they condemned what they disliked in terms of adultery, illegitimacy, and miscegenation. Pioneer Missourians, despite their reputation for godlessness, had a strict moral code. They generally believed that the Bible was the inspired word of God, that adultery and financial dishonesty were among the worst of sins, and that almost equally reprehensible were meanness, cowardice, and withholding hospitality. When Asaph Hubbard announced himself as a candidate for the state legislature, an opponent attacked him without ref-

[48] Columbia *Missouri Intelligencer and Boon's Lick Advertiser*, June 14, 1834, pp. 1–2.

[49] John S. Robb, *The Swamp Doctor's Adventures in the Southwest, Containing the Whole of the Louisiana Swamp Doctor, Streaks of Squatter Life and Far Western Scenes . . . by Madison Tensas, M. D. and "Solitaire" (John S. Robb of St. Louis, Mo.)*, I, 95.

[50] Report of a speech by Thomas Hart Benton, Jefferson City *Jefferson Inquirer*, November 24, 1849, p. 2, from *Ste. Genevieve Pioneer*.

erence to the issues he supported, but with the question, "Is this the man who refused to pay $1.50 for a shroud for a deceased brother?"[51] A contemporary observed in 1824 that his was the age of political paroxysm and expressed the thought that the virulence and rancor of party spirit was without parallel.[52] In 1850 a Missourian reporting a political speech declared that the spoken words were far stronger and more insulting than the text appearing in the paper.[53] Others testified that slanders too horrible for the eye were whispered into the ears of voters. Yet, in a newspaper column, an office seeker accused his rival of being "the accomplished minion of meanness, the drunken and contemptible cat's paw of every fellow who will descend so low as to demand and use him," and by innuendo suggested even worse things in the question, "Why did he attempt an act of violence on ———— and thereby come near being subjected to a very critical operation?"[54] If spoken slanders were more severe than this sample of the published charges, it is not surprising that duels grew out of campaigns.

Partisans increased the circulation of slanderous charges by distributing handbills among the electorate and publishing affidavits in newspapers. Such affidavits helped to defeat David Barton, one of the first senators from Missouri and a man once idolized by Missourians. Although the primary reason for the defeat of Barton was his support of Adams over Jackson in the contested election, his opponents made efforts to show that he was morally unworthy to represent the citizens in the Senate. The charges publicly used to discredit him were that he was often so drunk that he could not attend to business in the Senate, that he had behaved so disgracefully at a certain oyster house in Washington that the wife of the keeper had fled from the house in terror, and that he had cursed God in a drunken orgy.[55] Political rivals accused William Clark, territorial

[51] Franklin *Missouri Intelligencer*, July 10, 1824, p. 3.
[52] Jackson *Independent Patriot*, June 26, 1828, pp. 1–2.
[53] Columbia *The Missouri Statesman*, November 29, 1850, p. 2.
[54] St. Louis *Missouri Gazette and Illinois Advertiser*, September 24, 1814, p. 2.
[55] Franklin *Missouri Intelligencer*, January 1, 1825, p. 1; September 4, 1824, p. 2.

governor, of having an Indian wife and children;[56] they charged Thomas Hart Benton with being a thief, a murderer, and a father of Negroes.[57] Benton, in turn, accused James Birch, who opposed him in Missouri, with being a "sheep-killing cur dog" who had beaten his wife when she objected to his having a Negro mistress.[58]

The terms *rascal, villain, puppy, sneak, wretch, coward, swindler, liar, father of Negroes*, and *black cockade federalist* enlivened the exchange between partisans. Men cried out that rivals proposed to prostitute principle to policy and spoke of the opposition as debauched or as the tool of a corrupt combination. A really accomplished speaker could produce a stream of vivid and scathing images whose very sound was insulting, as did the new senator, Alexander Buckner, when he answered the charge that legislators had manufactured senators from rotten materials:

> If perchance some spider-legged, crane-necked, sheep-headed, wolf-hearted, dog-paid, editor of a newspaper, or swaggering, self-conceited, ignorant, sap-headed chief magistrate in leading strings; or some other great man in this State had been elected U. States' Senator, the materials would not have been considered so rotten.[59]

On rare occasions the object of the invective brought court action. He was much more likely to avenge his honor, if he took any notice of the charge, by challenging his detractor to a duel.

One of the notorious political duels occurred in 1831, when Spencer Pettis made some uncomplimentary remarks about Nicholas Biddle and the National Bank in his compaign for a congressional seat. Mr. Biddle's brother Thomas, who commanded troops in Missouri, was so offended by the insults offered to his family that he went to the hotel where Pettis was staying and cowhided the candidate. Anti-Jackson men magnified the insult by taunting Pettis for

[56] *Semi-Weekly St. Louis Enquirer*, August 19, 1820, p. 1.

[57] St. Louis *Missouri Gazette and Public Advertiser*, April 19, 1820, p. 2.

[58] Charles B. McAfee, "Riding the Circuits in Southwest Missouri," in *The History of the Bench and Bar of Missouri*, A. J. D. Stewart, ed., 75.

[59] Columbia *Missouri Intelligencer and Boon's Lick Advertiser*, June 18, 1831, pp. 2–3, from Jackson *Mercury*. Buckner did not sign his name, but he was publicly credited with authorship and did not deny it.

failing to issue an immediate challenge. Although Pettis refused to become involved in a duel until he had won the election (no duelist could be a candidate for public office), he knew that he must eventually defend himself against the charge of cowardice. When the duel took place, both he and Biddle were mortally wounded.[60] Newspaper editors and publishers, as well as rival candidates, had to be prepared to defend themselves against angry office seekers, but the danger did not lessen the use of incendiary language.

The same men who denounced opponents with blistering invective lavished compliments on their audiences. They spoke of the beauty and talent of the young ladies in the vicinity, the elegance of the homes, the richness of the soil, and the high quality of the corn and wheat in the neighborhood.[61] They flattered the voters with comments about their importance to the success of the campaign and credited them with outstanding intelligence. In the words of a contemporary, office seekers "fluttered around the electorate like bachelors round young female beauties";[62] they "bowed, scraped, and congeed" to win votes.[63] Although critics ridiculed these electioneering tactics, a citizen admitted that he and his friends liked the candidates who made them "feel that they were somebody" and that their opinion was worth consulting.[64]

Campaigners sought to convince the electorate that the favored party and its candidates were the possessors of all the virtues. When supporters of John Adams and Henry Clay met in Jefferson City in 1828, they heard the Adams Administration described as "pure as the angels that sit at the right hand of the throne of God." Clay, "a man of transcendent mind and towering genius," was contrasted with the "highhanded" and "dangerous" Jackson, to whom the government of the nation could not be trusted.[65] The highest praise that

[60] *St. Louis Beacon*, September 1, 1831, p. 2.

[61] Columbia *Missouri Intelligencer and Boon's Lick Advertiser*, June 14, 1834, pp. 1–2. The source is the campaign plea of George Dale.

[62] Articles signed "Simon Crabtree," Franklin *Missouri Intelligencer*, April 22, 1820, pp. 2–3.

[63] Fayette *Missouri Intelligencer and Boon's Lick Advertiser*, July 13, 1826, p. 2.

[64] "Missouri History Not Found in Textbooks," *Missouri Historical Review*, L, 1 (October, 1955), 111, from *Milan Republican*.

[65] St. Louis *Missouri Republican*, January 31, 1828, p. 3.

an advocate could give to a party — and it made no difference which group he supported — was that it belonged to the people and that the men seeking office under its banner were the bone and sinew of the country.

Candidates were no more modest about themselves. Timothy Flint was appalled at the "unblushing effrontery" of candidates who mounted the stump and declared that they alone were competent to make the laws and direct the affairs of government. It seemed to him that the more impudent a man appeared the greater were his chances of success.[66] The repeated re-election of Thomas Hart Benton seems to support Flint's theory, since Benton's egotism was legendary in Missouri; yet even the powerful Benton stated on numerous occasions his belief in the sovereignty of the people.

Office seekers based their claims to support on their services to the nation in opening up the frontier and in protecting the settlers from attack by Indians and the British. Much as others who had served on the frontier reminded voters of the debt owed to them, an old soldier of the War of 1812 asked for office on the basis of his service in the war against the British, his captivity by the Indians, and his miraculous escape from them.[67] Recognizing the effectiveness of such appeals, political rivals tried to minimize their power. When George Shannon, campaigning for the state legislature, reminded voters that he had lost a leg in the course of his explorations with Meriwether Lewis and William Clark, his opponent sneered that the expedition was a profitless excursion and Shannon only a "one-legged politician" seeking public sympathy.[68]

Public sympathy was an asset that could often be translated into votes. Office seekers tearfully recited the hardships they had endured in opening up the frontier, the fatigues of cold and hunger, the suffering from Indian attack and capture. They told how many of their family and friends had died in Indian forays, complained that they had been traduced or reviled by enemies, and stated that they

[66] Timothy Flint, *Recollections of the Last Ten Years* . . . , 214.

[67] Columbia *Missouri Intelligencer and Boon's Lick Advertiser*, June 14, 1834, pp. 1–2.

[68] Columbia *Missouri Intelligencer and Boon's Lick Advertiser*, August 17, 1833, p. 2.

were speaking despite illness, fatigue, or family sorrow. They declared their need for public office, as did Ambrose Colvin, who publicly expressed his hope that his old age and his grievous losses in the flood of 1844 would induce the voters to elect him as assessor in the coming election.[69] Cynics sneered that candidates managed to combine in the same speech love of country, devotion to the people, assertions of their own moral uprightness, and a "request for a lift." [70]

Candidates interspersed pleas for support with anecdotes ridiculing opponents. James Rollins, a Whig politician of central Missouri, was well known for his ability to tell stories. Admirers repeated with relish his discomfiture of a rival whose loyalty to Whiggism was in doubt. Rollins told his laughing hearers how the wise old woodchuck told a polecat who insisted that he was a woodchuck, "You look like a woodchuck, you speak like a woodchuck, but I'll be d——d if you smell like a woodchuck." [71]

Campaigners often ridiculed opponents by exaggerating their eagerness for public office. When William Russell, a lawyer of considerable dignity, was campaigning for the state legislature, a political rival told listeners how Russell became separated from his companions as they were traveling through the woods and wandered around in the snow until he came upon his own tracks. Believing the tracks to be the footprints of another member of the party, Russell was hurrying to overtake his friends, the storyteller said, when an old owl called out, "Who-who-who-a-e-i-u?" Russell stopped still, said his political foe, bowed low, and campaigned for the owl's vote by answering, "I am William Russell, sir, formerly of Kentucky, but now of Missouri, and a candidate for the legislature." [72] Ridicule was less troublesome than the practical jokes office seekers played upon each other. Charles Allen reportedly won the votes of all the "bar" counties of southwestern Missouri through a joke played on his rival

[69] Columbia *The Missouri Statesman*, May 12, 1848, p. 2.

[70] Jackson *Independent Patriot*, August 12, 1826, p. 2, from Franklin *Missouri Intelligencer*.

[71] Letter from Warsaw, Jefferson City *Jefferson Inquirer*, July 1, 1848, p. 2.

[72] William S. Bryan and Robert Rose, *A History of the Pioneer Families of Missouri . . .* , 523.

when both were campaigning for judicial office. Allen arranged with friends to misdirect his opponent when he asked the way to the place where he and Allen were to speak to the voters. Consequently, the misdirected man spent the night in the swamp, where he was bitten by mosquitoes; when he finally arrived late at the appointed place, his face red and swollen, Allen refused to surrender the platform, on the excuse that he could not recognize the claimant. When he at last acknowledged the identity of his rival, he attributed his altered appearance to his effort to get out the mosquito vote.[73]

Though crude humor and vituperation were an integral part of campaign oratory, the efforts of partisans to discredit the soundness of opponents' arguments and to establish their own candidates as plain argumentative speakers suggests the popular respect for clear, reasonable discussion of the issues. Critics observed that the story-telling speakers were like the bell that alarmed the fox until he learned that it was only a long-tongued thing with a hollow head.[74] Thomas Hart Benton explained that he filled his own speeches "brim-full of facts and reasons" because his constituents demanded facts.[75] Benton's respect for facts was shared by other frontier Missourians. In 1848 when Littlebury Hendricks, candidate for lieutenant governor, addressed the people in behalf of Zachary Taylor and the Whig party, he announced that he would omit vituperative attacks and confine himself to the facts;[76] in 1844, when an editor announced that Mr. George Hough, candidate for the state legislature, would speak to the voters of Osage County, he promised that Mr. Hough would speak only from facts.[77]

The phrase, "I'm from Missouri and you've got to show me," had not yet been popularized, but speakers operated on the assump-

---

[73] Robb, *Swamp Doctor's Adventures*, 70–83.

[74] Letter from Bloomington, May 22, 1848, Jefferson City *Jefferson Inquirer*, June 17, 1848, p. 1.

[75] Norman Mattis, "Thomas Hart Benton," in *A History and Criticism of American Public Address Prepared under the Auspices of the Speech Association of America*, Marie Hochmuth and W. Norwood Brigance, eds., III, 76.

[76] Report of the substance of the speech of Littlebury Hendricks, Columbia *The Missouri Statesman*, July 14, 1848, p. 1.

[77] Jefferson City *Jefferson Inquirer*, August 29, 1844, p. 2.

tion that their listeners demanded proof for their assertions. Campaign speakers offered statistics, examples, testimony of authorities, documents, and exhaustive reports upon the origin and history of a question at issue. James Rollins did not spend all his time telling stories; he supported his charge that the state's Democratic administration had squandered Missouri's money by citing the amount of money spent, the debt owed by the state, and the interest paid by the people.[78]

Campaigners made much use of examples. Sometimes the speaker drew from the experience of the past to predict the future, as did the Whig partisan who urged the voters to reject the Democratic administration, on the grounds that it violated property rights in setting up the Independent Treasury System. Reasoning that violation of the rights of property holders created despotic government, he warned that the examples of Philip of Macedon, Caesar, and Cromwell should teach frontiersmen how despots gained control.[79] Other examples were offered to show that the principles of the party supported by the speaker were in accord with the welfare of the people. The man on the frontier was forced to focus his attention on material benefits and, always short of cash, was interested in getting more money for what he sold and paying less for what he bought. A local politician attacked the tariff in 1832 as a device to make the people pay more for goods, with the assertion that a merchant had told him that if the tariff were repealed, seventeen-cent cloth could be bought for only ten cents.[80] Through a similar appeal, a speaker tried to persuade voters to reject candidates who advocated withdrawal of bank currency. He told his hearers that, since four fifths of the circulating medium was in bank currency, its withdrawal would reduce the value of goods by 80 per cent. He attempted further to clarify his point by telling his audience that the value of farm produce worth five dollars would sink to one and that laborers receiving

[78] Report from Louisiana, Missouri, of the substance of a speech by James Rollins, Columbia *The Missouri Statesman*, July 28, 1848, p. 2.

[79] George Caleb Bingham, Speech at Arrow Rock, Fayette *Boon's Lick Times*, August 8, 1840, pp. 1–2.

[80] *St. Louis Beacon*, June 7, 1832, p. 2.

wages of a dollar would get only twenty cents for the same effort, if the currency were to be withdrawn.[81]

Speakers could generally count on applause when they advocated the improvement of roads and rivers, spoke of the virtue of landholding, and contrasted the happiness of living in the United States with the misery of existence in monarchial Britain. Above all, a candidate must declare his republican principles. In 1825 a partisan indignantly refuted a charge of opposition to republican principles made against his party's candidate by saying that a charge of hog stealing would not have been more false or venomous.[82] The voter on the frontier observed with some pride that next to the pleasure of sustaining a good man who had done his duty and did not feel above the people was the delight in turning out of office a haughty, imperious man who acted as though he were "Lord of the Isles." [83] With their approbation for the national trend toward democracy, Missourians warned political aspirants that their support would go to friends of the people.

The great fur traders, merchants, landholders, and their adherents, who had heretofore influenced policies, received official appointments, and spoken for the less affluent inhabitants, painted satiric pictures of candidates who secretly despised the people even while they drank grog with them and begged their votes,[84] but they were fighting a doomed cause. Removal of the requirement that electors must pay a county or territorial tax, the provision for voice voting, the extension of elective offices, and the introduction of nominating conventions placed political power in the hands of the majority. By the mid-thirties, few campaigners questioned the vote-getting power of asserting the supremacy of the people. The well-educated and privileged man who was standing for office may have found it galling to assure a group of crude and ignorant voters that he would carry out their will if they would elevate him to a position

---

[81] Bingham, Speech at Arrow Rock.
[82] Franklin *Missouri Intelligencer*, November 25, 1825, p. 3.
[83] Jefferson City *Jeffersonian Republican*, February 14, 1835, p. 3.
[84] Supplement to the St. Louis *Missouri Gazette*, October 21, 1815, p. 1.

of public trust, but if he expected to be elected he knew he must assert the principles of popular sovereignty.

A poor or ignorant man might be rejected when he tried to borrow money; he might be omitted from the list of vice-presidents on ceremonial occasions; but during the canvass, he was as important as any other man on the frontier. He heard himself described as the fount of authority, and he accepted the fulsome compliment as truth. Believing that any man of good common sense was fit for office, he aspired to represent his fellow citizens in office and thus become a man of influence.

V

"*That man who can stand in the legislative hall, clothed with the people's powers, when the best interests of his country are at stake, without being able to do m[o]re than grunt out a simple "yes" or "no"; who, like the startled hare, knows not how to move — who like the sheep before the shearer, opens not his mouth: that man is unfit to represent the majesty of the people.*"

Franklin *Missouri Intelligencer*, June 25, 1822, p. 3, from St. [*sic*] Genevieve correspondent.

Demos Krateo

Thomas Hart Benton's rallying cry of *Demos Krateo*, roughly translatable as rule by the people, might serve appropriately as a symbol for the rhetoric of the lawmakers on the frontier. Its suitability as symbol derives first, from the circumstance that the term was coined by Benton, who, for the thirty years following his election to the United States Senate in 1820, was the foremost legislative orator, not only of Missouri, but of all the Midwestern frontier. Second, the phrase, in its corruption of the Greek term, characterized the self-taught frontiersman who gloried in the appearance of erudition without its reality. Moreover, *Demos Krateo* accurately describes the political situation in the first half of the nineteenth century, when the base of democracy broadened to place power in the hands of the common man.

In the territorial years from 1804–1820, lawmakers achieved their positions through qualifications other than their subservience to the sovereignty of the people.[1] They came generally from the aristocracy; a number of them could claim connection with families prominent in Europe or the United States.[2] In 1812, when the territory was

---

[1] Territorial judges, with the governor and secretary, served as lawmakers. They considered themselves guardians of the people and spent much time in deliberation of such questions as the right of a citizen to a divorce or the method of preventing rowdy characters from discharging firearms in St. Louis, as well as on problems of organizing the territory, creating and filling minor offices, raising revenue, promoting and regulating commerce. "Journal of Proceedings of Louisiana Territory, June 3, 1806 — December 24, 1818," collected and edited by William S. Jenkins.

[2] Otho Shrader, an early judge and lawmaker, had reputedly been a trusted member of the retinue of Archduke Charles; John Coburn, another of the group, was a cultured gentleman. John B. C. Lucas, born in Normandy in 1758, was perhaps the most aristocratic. He was accused by Missourians of trying to exercise special privileges of class in St. Louis. Frederick Bates, *The Life and Papers of Frederick Bates*, Thomas M. Marshall, ed., I, 118; Melvin J. White, "John B. C. Lucas," in *Dictionary*

raised to the second grade, voters continued to choose representatives from the wealthy French merchants and fur traders, the large landholders, and the lawyers who were the agents of these groups. Edward Hempstead, first delegate to Congress from the Missouri territory, was associated with the aristocrats both by his dependence upon them for legal practice and by his marriage into an old French family. William Carr, first popularly elected speaker of the Missouri territorial House, and John Scott in the Council were two of the leading lawyers in the region. Both had come to the territory soon after the cession; both were men of means; both were popular with the French land claimants. Auguste Chouteau, rich and influential, sat in the Council, as did Samuel Hammond, former lieutenant governor of the St. Louis district. Joseph Hunter, landholder under a Spanish grant, was there to continue his accustomed direction of the citizens' activities. Richard Caulk, who had come to New Madrid in 1796 with his wealthy father-in-law, sat in the assembly, and Reverend James Maxwell, Irish Catholic priest, who had come to Ste. Genevieve in 1796 as Vicar General of Upper Louisiana and had remained to guide the religious activities of the settlers and to promote his own landholdings, served as president of the Council. Far from typifying the backwoods frontiersman, who was ignorant of the observances of polite society, territorial legislators were generally early settlers who had prospered and become influential or later arrivals who moved into the professional and monied circles.

A few had a good formal education. John Scott had graduated from Princeton; Bernard Farrar, brother-in-law of former Territorial Judge John Coburn, had attended the University of Philadelphia; Charles Lucas, son of John B. C. Lucas, had studied for five years at Jefferson College; and some others had enjoyed educational advantages at colleges or academies. Characteristically, however, early lawmakers were educated by experience and association rather than by formal means. Still, as a body, they were superior to the typical frontiersman, who recognized the distinction and addressed

---

of American Biography, Allen Johnson, Dumas Malone, and Harris E. Starr, eds., XI, 485–86.

them as possessors of more wisdom, experience, and integrity "than falls to the lot of mankind generally."[3]

Despite the respect they accorded to their representatives, citizens thought they had a right to complain of current conditions and to ask for desired legislation. Consciousness of class differences surfaced when legislators were unresponsive to the popular mood; then they were accused of thinking themselves fashionable men of the world and of ignoring ordinary rules of morality; the voters, aware of their power at the polls, threatened to turn out the "'fine gentlemen and lawyers" sitting in the legislature.[4] When the time came to select officials again, however, the old attitudes prevailed. Citizens did, it is true, unseat some special targets of their disapproval, but they continued to vote for old settlers and soldiers, landowners, merchants, and lawyers. As heretofore, they placed their trust in men who had been successful in gaining property and prestige. Nevertheless, voters and candidates were aware of the growing power of the people, and candidates responded to the democratic trend by endeavoring to identify themselves with the people.

The constitution adopted by Missourians followed the pattern developed by the older states. It extended democracy by removing property qualifications for voters and officeholders and by adding to the number of elective offices. The first election under the new constitution was a clear victory neither for government by property and experience nor for the masses. The election of Alexander McNair as first governor of the new state was considered a triumph for the farmer and mechanic, but voters also returned a number of the old territorial lawmakers to the legislature. Among them was Benjamin Emmons, who had asked that the newspapers omit the *Honorable* from his name when he announced his candidacy. Samuel Perry, wealthy merchant from Ste. Genevieve, had been re-elected, as had Henry Geyer, lawyer from St. Louis. Frederick Bollinger, a large

[3] Open letter from a citizen, in St. Louis *Missouri Gazette*, December 4, 1813, p. 3.
[4] St. Louis *Missouri Gazette*, July 29, 1815, p. 3; May 13, 1815, p. 3; *Missouri Gazette Extra*, August 5, 1815, p. 1; supplement to the *Missouri Gazette*, October 21, 1815, p. 1.

landholder, continued to represent citizens of Cape Girardeau, as he had done almost without interruption since he had migrated to the territory. But the old leaders were now joined by newcomers who came to the temporary capital at St. Charles wearing homespun, buckskin leggings, and coonskin caps. Some of these people's representatives were as capable as former legislators, but others were as ignorant of legislative procedure as they were of the manners of society.

Their behavior aroused better-educated citizens both to mirth and consternation. The Reverend Timothy Flint told how some jokers inscribed around the speaker's chair the words, "Missouri, forgive them. They know not what they do." [5] Ever interested in observing the customs and attitudes of the people around him, Flint commented that men in the western country thought that "almost any timber could be worked into the political ship," and he proved himself a master of understatement by saying that some of the people's choices were neither Solons nor Solomons. [6]

One man came without a certificate of election because he did not know that it was necessary to have such a document. The literal interpretation of political language caused other problems. Men told how the doorkeeper, having sworn to uphold the constitution and keep the doors of the House open, swung wide the doors despite the sub-zero temperatures; he resigned rather than prove false to his oath of office when officials ordered them closed. [7] Martin Parmer, by his own testimony, a "ring-tailed painter," was said to have tested McNair's professions of belief in equality by insisting on sharing a bed with him so that he could tell the folks at home that he had slept with the Governor. [8] Upon being invited into the homes of aristocrats of St. Charles, some frontier legislators committed notable so-

[5] Timothy Flint, *Recollections of the Past Ten Years* . . . , 215.

[6] Flint, *Recollections*, 215.

[7] Thomas D. Clark, *The Rampaging Frontier: Manners and Humors of Pioneer Days in the South and Middle West*, 134. Mr. Clark cited as his source *Spirit of the Times*, XVI (December 12, 1846), 449.

[8] W. B. Stevens, *Centennial History of Missouri (The Center State) One Hundred Years in the Union, 1820–1921*, I, 115.

cial errors in their first acquaintance with carpeted floors, canopied beds, and pianos.

The democratic influence was evident in the creation of a series of new counties, the proposal for a reduction in the salaries of governor and judges — while increasing that of the members of the General Assembly — in abolishing the unpopular office of chancellor, and in the memorial addressed to Congress on the right of preemption. The power in democratic government of men of little property was evident in the passage of the act for relief of insolvent debtors and the involvement of the state in the issuance of loan office certificates designed to serve as a circulating medium. From the first, creditors, merchants, and lawyers opposed the Loan Office and Debtor bills. At Franklin, opponents of the measure arranged a dinner in honor of representatives who had voted against the bills and promised to teach supporters of the acts to honor the known wishes of their constituents by recalling them at the next election.[9] In their confidence that their own desires were the will of all the people, the opponents of the measure were wrongly assuming a unanimity of opinion, for although legislators had thwarted some electors in the passage of the bill, they had carried out the wishes of others who, distressed by the financial stagnation of the state and the falling off of immigration, warmly supported the measures. Increasingly, as the financial measures illustrate, the common man influenced legislative decisions.

The Loan Office and Debtor bills failed to solve the economic distress, however. The courts held the act for relief of debtors unconstitutional and the Loan Office bill added to, rather than subtracted from, the state's financial woes. The majority of the electors, unschooled in finance, absolved the frontier legislators from blame and held the city men — the merchants, lawyers, doctors, and judges — responsible for the condition of the economy. In the ensuing election, voters returned the backwoodsmen, who, while declaring themselves possessors of little political knowledge, asserted firm be-

[9] St. Louis *Missouri Gazette and Public Advertiser*, August 8, 1821, p. 3.

lief that the rights of the people should triumph over the will of the courts and propertied men. On these bases, they asked the voters to place them in a position of influence in the state's affairs.[10]

The increasing tendency to hold up a plain man of "just and natural reflections" as the ideal legislator was deplored by some Missourians. In their view, one or two ignorant and illiterate men in the legislature would not necessarily cause disaster, but the large number of unqualified members impeded legislation and endangered the interests of the state. Critics charged that a majority of the men elected to office were incapable of just and unselfish legislation and asserted that every measure passed by them was a gross burlesque of the law. They pleaded with the voters to send these ignorant men back to the place in society from which they had been raised and to replace them with men of competence and sagacity. The triumph of Jackson in 1828 increased the tendency among his opponents to equate support of Jacksonian principles with ignorance and belligerence. Assuming a humanitarian motive for their objections, conservatives suggested that placing an uneducated man in an office for which he was unfitted was an injustice to him. Inferring that the yeoman legislator should be sent home for his own happiness as well as for the public good, an anti-Jacksonian editor published a letter ascribed to a Jackson man who said, "This thing of legistin is not what it is crack up to be."[11]

Democratic electors, their antipathies aroused by the charges made against them, chose as their representatives such frontiersmen as Joseph Buford of Shannon County, who introduced himself in the legislature with: "I was born in a cane-brake and cradled in a sugar trough and my thirst for legislation has never been choked by the weeds and tall grass of education."[12] Buford had counterparts in Jacob Groom, a "tearing critter of the catamount school"; Billy the

[10] For such an appeal, see the announcement of E. Criddle in the Jackson *Independent Patriot*, June 1, 1822, p. 3.

[11] Fayette *Missouri Intelligencer and Boon's Lick Advertiser*, February 27, 1829, p. 2.

[12] Legislative proceedings reported in Jefferson City *Jefferson Inquirer*, January 17, 1845, p. 3. (This issue is bound with a front page dated January 16.)

Buster McDaniel, "High Bird of Liberty Compton"; and Benjamin Young, who could not read or write, but who ornamented his cabin with prints of Thomas Hart Benton's speeches.

With the exception of the act for relief of insolvent debtors, legislation passed in the frontier era did not reflect decidedly radical policy. Acts in the early legislatures brought judges under increasing control of the electorate; advocated but did not effect a system of education for all the people; made some adjustments in representation; and doubtlessly distributed some state money unwisely. Nevertheless, the generally conservative constitution adopted in 1820 remained relatively unaltered until after the Civil War. Many of the plain men elected to the legislature were men of good practical sense, although some of them lacked social graces. Moreover, the voters continued to send lawyers and aristocrats as well as the plain citizens to represent them. Country editors, rejoicing in the election of a good proportion of farmers, often praised the return of the old members to the General Assembly, men whose experience had taught them the real wants of the people. The buffoons created some merriment for the more sophisticated legislators and served anti-Jacksonians as examples to be deplored, but the regular business of legislation was carried on much as in the territorial legislature.

Though less frequently than when canvassing for votes, the legislator sometimes sounded the appeal to the sovereignty of the people as he spoke to his colleagues. Members referred to their duty to constituents, supported measures on the ground that they were carrying out the will of the people, and opposed legislation on the basis that it infringed upon popular rights. For instance, opponents of the state bank charter fought the measure by asserting that banks were designed to keep the mass of the people dependent upon a few privileged individuals.[13] The legislative speaker sometimes rose to eloquence in defense of the will of the people, as did the member who urged direct election of circuit attorneys by comparing elective sovereignty to the mountain stream and the belief that it is purest at its

[13] Legislative proceedings, Jefferson City *Jefferson Inquirer*, March 4, 1846, p. 2.

103

source: "Every remove from its fountain brings it near to the dangers of corruption."[14]

Despite his talk about subservience to the will of the electorate, the legislator did not always conduct himself as a servant of the people. He was ready to carry out the wishes of his constituents — as soon as he could decide what they ought to wish. Lawmakers generally agreed with the evaluation of Frederick Bates, who said in his gubernatorial address to the joint houses, "Surely, within the sphere of human action, there can be nothing of greater importance and dignity than the business of legislation for a virtuous people."[15] Election bestowed a kind of dignity upon a man. Martin Parmer, for all his insistence upon equality, thought of himself as superior to ordinary men. When his keelboat hit a snag and dumped him into the water on his way to the assembly, he indicated his assumption that he was deserving of extraordinary respect, even from natural forces, by declaring that the river was no respecter of persons. Further, he believed the stream's respect was due him as a representative of the people, for the river had cast him away, he said, with as little ceremony as a "stray bar-dog would be turned out of a city church . . . notwithstanding he was the people's representative."[16]

In keeping with the belief that legislating was a matter of dignity and importance, members conducted sessions with a considerable degree of formality promoted by adherence to parliamentary rules. Declaring that laxity in decorum would embarrass the infant councils, William Carr, first popularly elected speaker of the House, apologized for his lack of expertise in parliamentary matters and promised to discharge his duties in a manner conducive to the dignity and proper conduct of business.[17] Presiding officers continued to recognize the need for mastery of the intricacies of advancing and delaying tactics. Sometimes they frankly admitted their dependence upon

[14] Speech of Foster Wright, legislator from Pike County in Committee of the Whole, Legislative proceedings, Jefferson City *Jeffersonian Republican*, December 31, 1836, p. 1.

[15] St. Louis *Missouri Gazette and Public Advertiser*, October 30, 1818, p. 3.

[16] Alphonse Wetmore, *Gazetteer of the State of Missouri*, 91.

[17] St. Louis *Missouri Gazette*, December 19, 1812, p. 2.

more knowledgeable members, as did Lieutenant Governor Daniel Dunklin when he told senators that he needed their help, since he had little experience in conducting parliamentary sessions.[18]

Despite their respect for parliamentary rules, members recognized no need for training in order to speak. They declared that a man should say what he had to say in as few words as necessary and then take his seat. Critics inside and outside the legislative halls ridiculed legislators who made speeches and presented "foolish" amendments in order to get their names in print. They denounced such speechmakers as wasters of time, asserting that the least qualified were the most troublesome in imposing speeches upon the assembly. A voter who used the pen name *Philocles* advocated reducing the number of representatives to get rid of some of the "windy minded speech-making men" who consumed "time and the public treasure in soporific prosings and caballistic compromises."[19] Legislators, recognizing the popular demand for deeds rather than words, apologized for making a speech in the assembly. Even as they rose to speak, they protested that they did not wish to inflict a speech upon colleagues, but were impelled to raise their voices in defense or attack of a measure important to their constituents and the welfare of the country.

Following the custom of his Missouri predecessors in the House of Representatives, Spencer Pettis began a speech — which required nearly 11,000 words to report — by saying that were he to consult his individual interests, he would not trouble the House with another word, but when all the powers of eloquence and argument had pressed a measure so injurious to his own state, he must speak or be recreant to the interests of those whom he served.[20] A speaker frequently disclaimed powers of eloquence, presenting himself as a plain blunt man. "I am not a speaker by profession," Mr. Barkhurst, an early Missouri assemblyman, said in typical fashion. "I do not ex-

[18] Fayette *Missouri Intelligencer and Boon's Lick Advertiser*, November 23, 1828, p. 3.

[19] St. Louis *Missouri Republican*, July 26, 1824, p. 3.

[20] *Register of Debates*, 21st Cong., 1st Sess., January 14, 1830, p. 523.

pect to deal in fanciful sketches, or in an oratorical display of words; but simply to present the truth, in a plain unvarnished style." [21]

At the same time that critics condemned speaking as a waste of time and equated *rhetoric* with false reasoning, they praised the eloquence of speakers whose sentiments they approved. They termed attractive speechmaking of the opposition *rhetoric*; speaking done by their favorites was *eloquence*. In 1844 a writer illustrated the distinction in the popular mind when he warned citizens against the "blandishments of Whig oratory," but implored Democrats to select able speakers who could "tear off the mask" from the Whigs. [22] Voters showed concern that their representatives should be capable of contending against an impolitic measure with the fire of eloquence and indicated that men who could not speak well were not qualified to represent the people. Particularly, in the early frontier period when Missouri had only one delegate in Congress, men thought it imperative that their delegate should be an able debater who could refute attacks upon measures that advanced the interests of the state. [23] The belief that a delegate should be an able communicator was affirmed by the ardor with which partisans defended their public men against a charge of ineffectiveness in speech.

The limited access to news on the frontier increased the significance of speeches by prominent men. In 1820 Missouri had only five newspapers, located in four towns; though the number increased in later years, settlements outside the county seats rarely had a newspaper, even by the mid-nineteenth century. Further, these newspapers depended heavily on reports of speeches for interpretation of the issues. They often followed a favorite in editorializing about a question. Political speeches supplied themes for debating societies, specimens for declamations, and suggestions for orations. Crowds traveled hundreds of miles, often by tedious and tiresome

[21] Legislative proceedings, Jefferson City *Jeffersonian Republican*, January 14, 1843, p. 1.
[22] Jefferson City *Jefferson Inquirer*, February 8, 1844, p. 3.
[23] A typical statement is made in the speech of Robert Wells, reported in the *St. Louis Beacon*, October 6, 1831, p. 2.

methods of transportation, to hear the great men speak;[24] even the
ordinary legislator frequently drew an audience of interested citizens, who sat in the gallery and applauded a telling phrase or a popular sentiment.

Speeches were designed for the voters at home as well as for listeners within the sound of the speaker's voice. Newspapers at the
state capital generally printed the legislative proceedings, frequently
including all or parts of speeches. Senators and representatives in
Washington took care that the speeches they considered significant
should be disseminated among the voters back home, who, rather
than their colleagues, were often the audience that they hoped to
persuade.

The lawmakers recognized the importance of establishing themselves as men whose advice should be followed. In taking a stand
upon a measure, they declared their freedom from personal or partisan considerations and stated that their sole motivation was the promotion of the best interests of their constituents. In a time of distress
they recalled the words of advice that they had earlier offered and
implied or boldly declared that, if their earlier advice had been
taken, the present crisis would not have occurred. The prudent lawmaker, however, established his wisdom with a becoming modesty.
W. V. N. Bay, a frontier legislator and an astute critic of speechmaking, voiced the opinion that the self-complacency of James S. Green
had kept him from oratorical eminence. Green's frequent laugh at
his own cleverness irritated Bay, who asserted that any indication by
a speaker that he thought himself superior always detracted from his
effectiveness.[25] Ordinarily, the people's representatives sought to
demonstrate a becoming humility by minimizing their own talents.
Thomas Hart Benton, believed by many of his contemporaries to be
the epitome of egotism, prefaced a speech in the United States Senate with the declaration that he was no advocate of unprofitable de-

---

[24] Charles P. Johnson, "Personal Recollections of Some of Missouri's Eminent
Statesmen and Lawyers," *Proceedings of the State Historical Society of Missouri at
Its Second Annual Meeting Held January 22, 1903*, 54–60.
[25] W. V. N. Bay, *Reminiscences of the Bench and Bar of Missouri*, 523.

bate, but "in some cases speaking did good" and "even moderate abilities produced great results." [26] Usually, members elected to positions of authority by their fellows mentioned their diffidence in accepting the honor, declared that their own feelings urged them to decline it, but they bowed to the will of their colleagues. They spoke of their limited abilities and promised that effort would make up for lack of capacity.

Legislators for a frontier constituency not only understood the need to demonstrate becoming modesty; they also well understood the power of associating themselves or their ideas with a respected leader. They linked their stands with those of Jefferson, Franklin, and Washington in discussion of measures. They assumed knowledge of the approval or disapproval of national heroes long dead when they wished to discredit a measure, as did David Barton when he made his attack in the Senate upon his colleague from Missouri. Upon that occasion Barton praised Washington's "Farewell Address" and, pointing to Benton, declared that the Father of his country had penned a solemn warning against such Catilines, demagogues, and aspirants to personal power.[27]

Friendship or even acquaintance with a great man lent a halo effect to a speaker, as did nativity in certain parts of the country. "I was born in old Kaintuck" or "I first saw the light of day by the Roanoake River" was almost as persuasive in Missouri as a quotation from Washington or Jefferson. Relationship to a prominent man added to the prestige of a less well known individual. That William Clark profited from being the brother of George Rogers Clark, that Nathaniel Watkins' kinship to Henry Clay aided his legislative career, or that James Winston's being a grandson of Patrick Henry contributed to his authority with the people can hardly be doubted. Despite his boasted acceptance of a man for *what* he was rather than *who* he was, the frontiersman showed a marked preference for selecting his leaders from men with approved family connections.

The lawmaker who, as a candidate, had appealed to the voters

[26] *Register of Debates*, 21st Cong., 1st Sess., May 11, 1830, p. 428.
[27] *Register of Debates*, 21st Cong., 1st Sess., February 9, 1830, p. 146.

to reward him for services in the Revolutionary War or protection of the frontier, asked his legislative colleagues to follow him in voting upon a measure for the same reasons. A reminder that a man had suffered the fatigues of war and had heard the roar of cannon and the ring of savage yells was strongly persuasive at a time when many of his listeners had shared such experiences or had listened to their fathers tell of them. Benton played upon this appeal in the Senate when he opposed Foote's resolution of inquiry into the sale of public lands. He recalled his twelve years of suffering in Tennessee and sixteen years of carnage in Kentucky as he asked his fellow senators to reject a bill that he believed would jeopardize the future of an area settled by men who had risked the horrors of Indian warfare; he spoke of the sleeping family awakened in the night in the midst of flames and slaughter, virgins led off captive by savage monsters, and mothers compelled to witness the smashing of infants' heads against trees.[28]

The legislator who could not claim kinship with a famous man or recite his exploits in opening up the frontier was not without resources, for he could take his stand with his colleagues upon the Bible and the Constitution. Voters judged men and measures by standards of morality and patriotism, and morality and patriotism were measured by their conformity to the Constitution and the Bible. The frontiersman revered his state constitution almost equally with the federal document. He acted upon the premises that the rules had been set down in the state constitution and that legislation must conform to those rules. The differences of opinion in the legislature arose from interpretation of their constitution, not from attitudes toward its authority. When the lawmakers in the Lower House debated a bill to prevent dueling, Mr. Byrd declared himself friendly to the concept of the bill but opposed to the third section, which, in his opinion, was contrary to the Constitution and the Bill of Rights. He asked his colleagues to apply the maxim *expressio unius est exclusio alterius* and not to exercise a right denied in the

---

[28] *Register of Debates*, 21st Cong., 1st Sess., February 2, 1830, pp. 99–100.

Constitution.[29] The man on the frontier as well as dwellers in older settled communities jealously resented any constitutional interpretations that ran counter to his own beliefs. When Jackson vetoed the National Bank bill in 1832, an angry editor denounced the President as an ignorant and illiterate man who had no right to "undertake to expound the constitution to such a body of men as composed the Senate and House of Representatives." [30]

Legislators claimed the Bible for their guide. Few speakers were as direct as the Missouri lawmaker who announced his support of a bill with the declaration that he had been raised by Old Ironside Baptists who taught him to read the Bible and believe what it said.[31] Even if less explicit, legislative speakers customarily asked for divine guidance and committed the outcome to the God of justice when they were about to vote upon a measure. In the day when the Bible was not only the best read but often the only book read in the frontier areas, a speaker frequently identified himself with revered biblical characters and denounced his opponents as Judas Iscariots, Herods, or devils of discord. David Barton took advantage of his being named David as he spoke in the Senate of arming himself with his slingshot and pebbles to ward off the attack of some opposing Goliath. His colleague Benton also borrowed biblical phrases to praise a fellow senator by saying of him, "This is Peter, and this Peter is the rock on which the church of New England's Democracy shall be built," adding in a lower tone not intended for his colleagues, "and the gates of hell shall not prevail against him." [32] The belief in the Bible as the foundation of good government was so strong that Missourians, delegated to draw up a new constitution in 1845, declared ineligible to office any candidate who denied the being of God or the belief in rewards and punishments after death.[33]

Just as the legislative speaker sought to enhance his own reputa-

[29] St. Louis *Missouri Republican*, November 27, 1822, p. 2.
[30] Columbia *Missouri Intelligencer and Boon's Lick Advertiser*, July 28, 1832, p. 3.
[31] Mr. Compton in the legislature, Jefferson City *Jeffersonian Republican*, December 17, 1842, p. 3.
[32] *Register of Debates*, 21st Cong., 1st Sess., March 4, 1830, p. 231.
[33] Jefferson City *Jefferson Inquirer*, December 23, 1845, p. 3.

tion for wisdom and morality, he tried to discredit that of his opponents. Attack upon the judgment or character of an opponent was an effective weapon in debate. The language of a bill, the delivery of a speaker, his motives, the place where he lived, and his character were all ammunition for the cannonades fired in the General Assembly. The forms of courtesy were carefully maintained, but meticulous reference to a colleague as a gentleman in no way inhibited the speaker's implied or direct charges of ungentlemanly conduct. Three epithets were anathema to the frontiersman, and Martin Parmer managed to combine them all in his retort to a detractor when he said, "the Jentle man . . . is a dam lier a torey and a dam coward."[34] Some terms such as *lawyer* became epithets because of the frontiersman's attitude toward them. Few men since Cicero have been greater masters of invective than David Barton of Missouri. Angered at the attack upon the supporters of Adams in the House of Representatives, he denounced opponents as Catilines tearing out the vitals of the Union and scattering them to the dogs of civil war, warned ladies not to risk their jewels of virtue to the protection of such ruffians, and personified the alliance of the South and West as a union whose heir would be poised across the backbone of the continent, his eastern half squalling "No West, no West," and his western half vociferating "The West, my own Imperial West."[35]

At no time in the Missouri assembly did a legislator draw a pistol on a colleague as did Senator Henry S. Foote on Thomas Hart Benton in the United States Senate, but Missouri lawmakers supported their political conflicts with physical violence. Men recounted with relish the story of the brawl that began in the legislature at St. Charles when Andrew McGirk threw a pewter inkstand at Duff Green and other members took sides in the quarrel. Challenges were offered and duels fought over differences, but the encounters proceeded according to the code and outside the legislative assembly. Tempers often flared in debates, forcing the chairman to call for order, but legislators usually maintained a degree of decorum.

[34] Franklin *Missouri Intelligencer*, August 12, 1834, p. 3.
[35] *Register of Debates*, 21st Cong., 1st Sess., February 11, 1830, p. 159.

The frontiersman's sense of humor turned some of the potentially threatening incidents into laughter. When a legislative committee made up of city men was appointed to visit the tobacco warehouses in St. Louis, Mr. Hough of the frontier county of Scott sneered that the lawyers on the committee knew nothing about tobacco except how to snuff, smoke, and chew, and only wanted to go to the city at legislative expense to drink wine and see the ladies. A member of the committee answered by inviting Mr. Hough to accompany them, assuring him that if wine did not please him, he knew where to get some "ball face rot gut whiskey." Having refuted the implication of being an effete wine drinker, the city man further boasted that he could take an axe and beat Mr. Hough chopping wood any day. Restored to good humor, Mr. Hough told colleagues that he had no idea the St. Louisan was so thoroughly educated, and he publicly begged his pardon.[36]

Obviously, the humor tended to be rough and earthy. In 1835, when agitated Whigs deplored the "hatred, malevolence, and discordant feelings" engendered by the resolutions praising Benton and predicted that their passage would turn the legislature into a "residence of the furies," a Benton supporter gravely proposed that the doorkeeper should bring in a couple of buckets of water to dash upon the maddened members as men did upon afflicted dogs.[37] Using a similar kind of humor, Mr. William Compton of Carroll fielded the argument of a member who was asking for the establishment of a branch bank in his town on the basis of its commercial importance. Mr. Compton asserted that, by the standards of production and population, the honors belonged to his own county, where one woman had produced five boys at one time and "all Democrats, too."[38]

Any bill proposing additional rights for women inspired humorous speechmaking, some of it more suitable for the barroom

[36] Legislative proceedings, Jefferson City *Jefferson Inquirer*, December 26, 1844, p. 2.

[37] Legislative proceedings, Jefferson City *Jefferson Inquirer*, December 26, 1844, p. 2.

[38] Legislative proceedings, Jefferson City *Jeffersonian Republican*, December 24, 1842, p. 2.

than the legislative assembly of a sovereign state. Some divorce petitions were treated with levity; when one lady's petition was presented, a member proposed that it should be considered by the tobacco committee rather than by the customary Judiciary Committee.
The proposal of an amendment exempting from paying school taxes
persons over fifty who were without children incited a discussion of
bachelorhood, the relation of poverty to the number of progeny, and
other peripheral topics until the mover of the amendment withdrew
his motion with the statement that his "purpose in stimulating wit"
had already been served.[39]

Though lawmakers enjoyed the recesses, they customarily carried on business with reasoned argument supported by figures, examples, and authority. Benton's encyclopedic speeches in the United
States Senate were filled with facts and figures, and, in this respect,
he had counterparts on the frontier. A visitor to the state capital in
1831, when anti-Jackson men were loudly deploring the ignorance of
lawmakers, reported that he was favorably impressed by the legislators' respectable appearance and their orderly conduct of business.
Noting that members "elucidated very perspicuously," he remarked
that he found more talent in debate than he had expected.[40] Since
the *St. Louis Beacon*, in which the visitor's account appeared, was
strongly Jacksonian, prejudice might be assumed, but the record of
legislative proceedings shows that speakers analyzed issues, produced
quantities of relevant statistical evidence, cited legal precedents, and
read supporting facts from documents. A state senator began his
speech in opposition to a bill for limiting the terms of judges by re-
stating the arguments of the advocates and alleging fallacies in their
reasoning, continued by showing the effect of similar legislation on
county judges and justices of the peace, and, citing specific examples
of the harmful effects of limitation, concluded with an appeal to his
colleagues to reject the measure.[41] Even Joseph Buford, considered

[39] Legislative proceedings, Jefferson City *Jefferson Inquirer*, February 2, 1847, p. 1.
[40] *St. Louis Beacon*, January 29, 1831, p. 2.
[41] Charles Jones in the Missouri Senate, Jefferson City *Jefferson Inquirer*, December 23, 1844, p. 3.

by many Missourians one of the most ignorant men in the assembly, cited the cost of traps used by hunters and the value of domestic animals killed by wolves in support of his appeal for defeat of the bill abolishing bounties on wolf scalps.[42]

No doubt more persuasive with frontiersmen in the legislature than his facts was Mr. Buford's reminder that a city man had originated the motion for repeal. City men looked down on the men who represented the frontier counties, he said. He characterized legislators from St. Louis as "nice silk stocking, kid-gloves, fine-linen collars, mahogany coffins, silver plate, brass tack'd St. Louis fellows," who thought it a great degradation to be a hunter or wolf catcher. To them, he said, nice hands and feet and small ears were the only qualifications for being a gentleman or a representative. He was not ashamed of being a frontiersman, Mr. Buford boasted: "I feel proud of my broad, rough hands, and big mud slachers, and big broad shoulders, for they have been made so by honest industry." Having appealed to frontier solidarity, he showed awareness of the strong affection of many of his listeners for Kentucky by reminding them that it was the wolf hunters of Kentucky who had humbled the British lion and caught some of the British wolves. He appealed to the sympathy of his hearers as he described the wanton killing of innocent lambs by predators and pictured the plight of frontiersmen whose necessities of life had been destroyed by wolves. He made his colleagues laugh by reminding them that the repeal of the bounty would arouse the anger of his constituents against him and cause his defeat. "If I was to go for repeal my constituents would hop upon me . . . like a duck upon a June bug," he told his fellow legislators, and he successfully urged other members from new counties to join him in voting against repeal lest they lose the sight of his "pretty little face" in the legislature.[43]

Spokesmen played classes and groups against one another in their efforts to win votes for a measure. For example, Mr. Neal Gilliam sought passage of a measure to help debtors, with the assertion

---

[42] Legislative proceedings, Jefferson City *Jefferson Inquirer*, January 16, 1845, p. 3.
[43] Legislative proceedings, Jefferson City *Jefferson Inquirer*, January 16, 1845, p. 3.

that merchants and lawyers opposing the bill "lay in the shade in the summer and toasted their heels by the fire in the winter as they studied how to defraud and check the laboring class." [44]

The language of legislators, especially in what appears to have been prepared speeches, reflected the admiration of the nineteenth century for ornate style and literary allusions. When James Rollins, considered a fine orator by many of his contemporaries, appealed for legislation to provide care for the insane, he asked members to follow the leadership of the Savior who had descended from heaven to help those who could not help themselves, quoted from *Macbeth* on ministering to a mind diseased, illustrated his arguments with examples from Greek and Roman history, and recited poetic passages. A typical sentence shows the style:

> Spring, and summer, and autumn, and winter, return again and again bringing along in their trains a thousand delightful associations, but to him without that lofty attribute, which distinguishes man above the lower orders of creation, the whole world is one deep solitude, a trackless barren waste.[45]

Occasionally, speakers who attempted figurative flights floundered in a mixture of metaphors, as did the legislator who pleaded with opponents of the Hannibal-St. Joseph Railroad bill not to "raise the parricidal arm against the mother that sustains them" Judas-like, with a kiss.[46]

Often figures of speech represented familiar experiences. A speaker could accuse a man who attempted to push a measure past the opposition of trying to ride the community booted and spurred, or he might comment that a controlling faction was in the saddle and be fully understood by his audience. Borrowing terms from the domestic side of life, speechmakers personified the state as a mother, counties as members of a family, the West as an infant. Representa-

[44] Legislative proceedings, Jefferson City *Jeffersonian Republican*, March 4, 1843, p. 2.

[45] Liberty *The Weekly Tribune*, March 20, 1847, p. 1.

[46] Mr. Kirk, Legislative proceedings, Jefferson City *Jefferson Inquirer*, February 24, 1849, p. 1.

tives from frontier counties accused leaders in the assembly of treating their districts like stepchildren and making a pet of St. Louis. When men refused to sanction a bill, they termed it a bastard bill or declared they would not stand godfather for the measure. The contempt for racial mixture was evident in likening the alliance of disparate factions in the legislature to a calico child with a patch of European white, the deep red of the Sioux, the jet black of the African, and a touch of the Asiatic. Legislators opposed the operations of banks by contrasting them to agriculture, declaring that their favorite bank was one of rich alluvial soil, or by likening them to Indian atrocities, shouting that banks scalped the people. Recollections of wars against the Indians or the British inspired allusions to opponents as barbarians who desired only to imbrue their hands in the blood of their victims, admonitions to a colleague to keep his eye on the fugleman, and by comparing a man who had changed his vote to an unworthy sentinel or a deserter of his post.

Speakers frequently illustrated a point with a long-drawn-out story that usually centered upon the action of some stupid person. Joseph Buford made a typical digression in the debate on the annexation of Texas with his story of a patriot farmer who lived near a British camp in the "Old Revolution": The Hessian soldiers, who had heard about hummingbirds but had never seen one, ordered the farmer to bring one to camp. The patriot obtained instead a hornet's nest, stopped up the hole, and took it to the soldiers with the warning that they must not unstop the hole before he left camp lest the birds follow him home. Describing how the hornets later swarmed out of the hole and routed the Hessians, Mr. Buford promised to turn loose just such a hornet's nest on the "jackleg lawyers" from St. Louis.[47]

Purposeful even in their digressions, frontier legislators made speeches, not for display, but for their influence on others. The speeches of frontier legislators are so closely involved with the situations out of which they grew that some familiarity with the problem being discussed is generally necessary in order to follow the argument of the

[47] Legislative proceedings, Jefferson City *Jefferson Inquirer*, December 12, 1844, p. 2.

speech. Without preliminaries, other than an apology for taking the time of the assembly, speakers plunged into discussion of the issue under debate, said what they had to say — often at considerable length — and closed as abruptly as they began.

The rhetoric in the legislative halls reflected the conflicts between groups on the frontier. Factionalism flourished, with yeoman farmers from the back country lined up against the lawyers and merchants. Debtor and creditor groups naturally viewed an issue from opposite sides, as did Benton and anti-Benton Democrats, pro- and anti-Bank forces, Democrats and Whigs. Obviously, the solidarity of the West was a myth without foundation so far as the politics of the Missouri frontier were concerned.

Despite the sometimes heated exchanges between members and the occasional lapses into conscious burlesque, legislative sessions were carried on with a degree of dignity. Government on the Missouri frontier tended to bear out the Jacksonian belief that a plain man of good sense was able to legislate for his fellows, especially if he had the advantage of working with men of experience. Legislators were liberal in extending the suffrage and increasing the number of elective offices, but they were far from radical. Their conservatism slowed the progress of the state university and caused the state to lag behind its neighbors in the building of railroads and other internal improvements; but with the exception of the early Loan Office bill, legislators did not embarrass the state. They offered little or no original legislation; they followed the examples set by Illinois, Kentucky, and the older states and thus contributed little to experiments in legislation or new forms of government.

Legislators not only repeated the slogans of popular sovereignty but also tended to respond to the will of electors in the choice of a United States senator. Although they usually supported measures favored by the electors and explained to the public their votes upon controversial questions, they scarcely considered themselves servants of the people. They thought of themselves, rather, as custodians of the people's rights and believed that election to public office gave them a measure of superiority.

VI

"Legal arguments were worth listening to in those days."

Charles B. McAfee, "Pioneer Lawyers in Southwest Missouri," in *The History of the Bench and Bar of Missouri*, A. J. D. Stewart, ed.

At the Bar of Justice

The early settlers of Upper Louisiana had extended — at best — a cool welcome to the lawyers who arrived in their communities. They viewed those who hastened to the area after the transfer of government with suspicion and "prayed for deliverance from the children of Belial."[1] Their distrust came from fear of the unknown rather than from unpleasant experience, since they knew little of lawyers and their profession's *raison d'être*. French and Spanish officials, reserving judicial power for themselves, had excluded attorneys from the territory.[2] Under French and Spanish rule the people had the right, theoretically, to appeal the lieutenant governor's decisions, but the expense and difficulty of carrying a suit to higher authorities, as well as the inexpediency of questioning official decrees, made any request for redress of grievances all but impossible.

The severity with which officers dealt with any questioning of their power is illustrated by the ten-year banishment of a citizen for the remark that "if all young men were like him, they would not work for forty sous a day in peltries."[3] French and Spanish settlers seemed content; they had always been subject to autocratic control and they raised few problems for their officials. The Americans who had come more or less surreptitiously into the territory or had been admitted by officials on the promise that they would be loyal were also quiet for obvious reasons.[4]

[1] St. Louis *Missouri Gazette*, November 2, 1809, p. 2, from Baltimore *Evening Post*.

[2] Amos Stoddard, *Sketches, Historical and Descriptive, of Louisiana*, 285.

[3] J. Thomas Scharf, *History of St. Louis City and County from the Earliest Periods to the Present Day: Including Biographical Sketches of Representative Men*, I, 170.

[4] Major Amos Stoddard, who took command of the territory for the United States, estimated that ten thousand Americans were scattered throughout the territory in 1804. Stoddard, *Sketches*, 226.

After the establishment of the United States territorial courts, the contentment of the people was shown to be more apparent than real. A jury of citizens avenged themselves against Louis Lorimier, last Spanish commandant at Cape Girardeau, by indicting him for horse stealing, and plaintiffs named Lieutenant Governor Charles DeLassus defendant in land suits. Much of the litigation came as a result of the land hunger of newcomers who hurried into the territory. Even the old inhabitants were infected by land fever and vied with new arrivals for ownership of tracts of land. More trouble arose because the Missouri frontier, as other frontiers, attracted adventurers and lawless men, and the lack of restraints encouraged violations of the law.[5]

Judicial authority was not universally respected by men living at the edge of civilization. Even those citizens determined to punish wrongdoers occasionally resorted to extralegal methods. Distrusting the judiciary, irritated by the absence of a law covering an offense, or annoyed by the slowness of legal procedure, impatient frontiersmen organized into bands of regulators and dealt with offenders as they saw fit.[6] Some men despaired of law on the frontier and charged that the courts themselves were a "rendezvous of tumult, confusion, and iniquity."[7] The criticism was not fully justified. Most judges in the territorial period, whether they had been trained in the law or drawn from the people as lay magistrates, seem to have been competent. That tumult and disorder existed cannot be denied; the unfamiliarity of the American judicial officers with the French and Spanish law, the lack of written statutes, the confusion over land and mineral rights, and the avid desire for land produced emotional tensions in the courts. Too, the judges were uncertain which code of law they were to enforce. John Coburn, an early territorial judge, in a letter to Secretary of State James Madison, described the problems arising from the "few indigested Laws . . . extremely inadequate to the proper administration of Justice" and the difficulty of

[5] Charles P. Johnson, "Recollections of Criminal Practice," in *The History of the Bench and Bar of Missouri*, A. J. D. Stewart, ed., 94.

[6] *St. Louis Enquirer*, February 3, 1824, p. 2.

[7] *St. Louis Missouri Gazette and Illinois Advertiser*, November 12, 1814, p. 1.

ascertaining the usages and customs of the Spanish government. He questioned whether the Spanish law or the common law should prevail in the territory.[8]

The confusion over laws increased the need for lawyers. At the same time, the introduction of the jury system with its opportunities for the forensic pleader, the litigation over land claims, and the possibility of rapid political advancement made practice in the territory attractive. By the spring of 1805 at least twelve professional lawyers were practicing in the area;[9] by 1815 over thirty applicants had been admitted to the territorial bar; by 1820 almost one hundred attorneys either were practicing on the Missouri frontier or had previously practiced there.[10]

Early requirements for admission to the bar were relatively strict. Law was the only profession to be regulated by the statutes of 1804. Under these regulations a lawyer seeking initial admission to the bar was required to submit a certificate to the judges of the general court attesting that he had studied for at least two years with a legally qualified person. The judges then examined a candidate as to his qualifications for practice. If he passed the examination, was twenty-one years of age, and was able to furnish satisfactory testimonials of character, he was admitted after taking an oath that he would uphold the Constitution and conduct himself honestly in practice. Only after he satisfied all these requirements did he receive a license. An attorney already admitted to the bar in another state found the process somewhat simpler, but was required to furnish testimonials of character.[11] This careful scrutiny resulted in a generally

[8] Coburn to Madison from Maysville, Kentucky, August 15, 1807, in James Alexander Robertson, *Louisiana Under the Rule of Spain, France and the United States 1785-1807*, I, 355-61, cited in William Francis English, *The Pioneer Lawyer and Jurist in Missouri*, 56. For a comparison of Spanish law with American court system, see English, 36-40.

[9] "Records of the Superior Court of the Territory of Louisiana," I, 15, cited in English, *Pioneer Lawyer*, 24-25.

[10] Frederic L. Billon, *Annals of St. Louis in Its Territorial Days from 1804 to 1821*, 162; Louis Houck, *A History of Missouri from the Earliest Explorations and Settlements until the Admission of the State into the Union*, III, 12-23.

[11] English, *Pioneer Lawyer*, 49-50.

superior bar. Observers testified that the territory was noted for its able and profound lawyers.

Later, qualifications were relaxed in response to the need for lawyers and the frontiersman's belief that disputes should be settled on the bases of common sense and justice rather than by application of abstruse legal principles. Even the minimum age requirement was disregarded when John S. Brickey, who was only nineteen, was admitted to the bar.[12] In 1832 legislators eliminated the clause requiring a definite period of study and further lowered qualifications by placing admission of attorneys in the hands of circuit judges, who often made only a perfunctory examination of the applicant.[13] An attorney of the time, while reminiscing about frontier conditions, explained that an applicant who had read the statutes and Kenney's questions and answers was admitted to the bar if he could present good credentials.[14]

Some young attorneys received a license although they commanded almost no knowledge of the law. John B. Clark, a popular lawyer in central Missouri, was admitted to the bar after merely serving as clerk of the court. Even less learned was a cabinetmaker, who confessed that he had read neither Blackstone or Kent. He was, nevertheless, licensed by a judge who facetiously remarked that the aspirant could do as little harm as anyone he knew.[15]

Although the educational requirements declined, professional training continued to be important for lawyers who practiced in the cities or conducted cases where the stakes were high. Such men were generally knowledgeable in the law and frequently well educated for their day. More than any other profession on the frontier, the

[12] W. V. N. Bay, *Reminiscences of the Bench and Bar of Missouri, with an Appendix, Containing Biographical Sketches of Nearly All of the Judges and Lawyers Who Have Passed Away . . .* , 101.

[13] *Laws of a Public and General Nature of the State of Missouri Passed Between the Years 1824 and 1836 not Published in the Digest of 1835*, II, 206, and *Laws of the State of Missouri Passed by the First Session of the Eleventh General Assembly*, 16, cited in English, *Pioneer Lawyer*, 96.

[14] Charles B. McAfee, "Pioneer Lawyers in Southwest Missouri," in *The History of the Bench and Bar of Missouri*, A. J. D. Stewart, ed., 73.

[15] Bay, *Reminiscences*, 48.

practice of law attracted men who had attended college. A small fraternity could have been formed of Missouri lawyers who had attended Transylvania College in Kentucky; nevertheless, the frontier bar also included men with little education. A contemporary estimated that a fourth of the pioneer lawyers were "destitute of the rudiments of an English education."[16] A number of men with little formal education became highly successful lawyers on the frontier, where shrewdness in argument and ability to manipulate others were more important than knowledge of legal principles.

Preparation for the bar followed a common pattern. A young man studied for a period in the office of a practicing attorney, reading law, drawing up briefs, and listening to debates in court. Pioneer lawyers who approved such a practical education were critical of legal training gained in schools as being too full of theory and too lacking in practice. The professors of law, on the other hand, pointed out that simply reading books on the law in a lawyer's office for a short time without capable clarification of their contents was inadequate preparation for professional practice. They cited Chief Justice Butler's dictum that a student should not even try to read Coke unless he could devote at least three years to the study.[17] Some young lawyers dealt with legal questions of the frontier against a background of both kinds of training. They attended law school and also spent some time as an apprentice in a lawyer's office.

Thomas Anderson's experiences were typical of the preparation and practice of the frontier lawyer. Anderson attended the common schools of his native Kentucky, learned a little Latin, and when he was about nineteen borrowed some law books from an attorney and read at night after the day's plowing was done. When he had read for some time, he apprenticed himself to a lawyer until he received his license. Anderson practiced in Kentucky for about a year, then decided to go to St. Louis. Just twenty-two, poor and friendless, he walked most of the way, camping out at night. In 1830 he arrived in

---

[16] Bay, *Reminiscences*, 383.
[17] Daniel Mayes, *An Address to the Students of Law in Transylvania University*.

St. Louis, but soon went on to St. Charles, where he learned to adapt to the ways of its French citizens, began to be employed by them, and established a reputation for competence. With his marriage to the daughter of the politically and socially prominent Rufus Easton, he might have been expected to remain in St. Charles, but once more a newer area attracted him and he moved on to Palmyra where other Southerners were living. For nearly fifty years he practiced successfully in that area.[18]

Often a young man supported himself by teaching school until he was admitted to the bar, as did George Tompkins, who in many ways exemplified the frontier lawyer. Born in Virginia about 1780, Tompkins added to his scanty education by reading as broadly as he could until he qualified himself to teach school. About 1806 he went to Kentucky, where he remained some three years, teaching school and reading law books borrowed from friends. The lure of the new frontier in Upper Louisiana then called him, and he moved on to St. Louis, where he continued to teach and to read law. In 1816 he moved to the Boon's Lick country in central Missouri and advertised his willingness to practice in the courts.[19] His rise in his profession culminated in appointment to the bench of the state supreme court.

Both Anderson and Tompkins are examples of the lawyer with little formal education. The preparation of H. M. Brackenridge, who practiced in Missouri around 1810, typifies that of the better-trained lawyers. After his graduation from Jefferson College in Philadelphia, Brackenridge studied law in the office of a prominent attorney in Pittsburgh. He became familiar with authorities on general law, on the law of shipping, bills of exchange and promissory notes, chancery, and equity. Like most lawyers he was a student of effective speaking. He joined a debating society in college and participated in a similar group after graduation. He studied Blair's *Rhetoric*, Abbe Maury *On Eloquence*, Curran's speeches, and Demosthenes' orations. He read the works of Quintilian and Cicero to find what the

[18] Thomas L. Anderson, "Autobiography."
[19] Bay, *Reminiscences*, 30–36; English, *Pioneer Lawyer*, 31.

ancients had said about speaking, and he attended courts to listen to the pleading of lawyers whom he admired.

Brackenridge might have begun the practice of law in Pennsylvania, but the frontier seemed to him to offer greater opportunities for beginning his legal career. In the new West he would have no older, well-established lawyers as competitors; he could begin on an equal footing with others practicing at the bar. Too, he had lived as a child in Upper Louisiana, where his father had sent him to learn the French language. His ability to understand and to speak French, German, Spanish, and English was an invaluable asset in the Missouri territory, with its mixed population. Furthermore, stories of the rewards to be gained from suits over land and mineral rights had drifted back to Pennsylvania and stimulated the ambition of a young man.

Although he was no stranger to frontier conditions, Brackenridge found practice in Missouri more rugged than he had expected, and he left the Western bar after a year or two. He had won his share of cases and had made some money, but he opposed the widespread practice of dueling over differences of opinion or over real or imagined slights. He determined to quit the bar before he took some one else's life or lost his own in an affair of honor.[20] Clearly, frontier lawyers did not generally share his opposition to dueling.

By adopting the dueling code and adding *esquire* to his name the lawyer assumed status as a gentleman. Even though he might lack much in education, his being better informed than most of his neighbors placed him in a position of leadership in politics and civic affairs. Though attorneys generally came from middle-class families and denied claims to aristocracy, their conservatism and their association with men of property made them suspect by the laboring and debtor groups. Charles Drake, who practiced law in St. Louis, defended himself against the accusation that he had predicted a time when mechanics would not be allowed to attend balls with the better classes. Drake declared his loathing of pretensions to aristocracy, but, like other lawyers, his association with men of wealth gave

[20] H. M. Brackenridge, *Recollections of Persons and Places in the West.*

some credence to the charge that he thought himself better than men who worked with their hands.[21]

Lawyers who came to the frontier with few assets often amassed considerable property. Edward Bates arrived in Missouri with only $3.50 in cash to his name;[22] but four years after his admission to the bar he was listed among the one hundred largest taxpayers in the state. Association with propertied men and advance information on forced sales gave attorneys financial advantages over other citizens. A young New York lawyer who visited St. Louis in 1836 wrote a friend that "all the gentlemen of the legal profession, who have means, engage in speculation in the west," and he observed that men who had a little capital could make fortunes in a few years on the frontier.[23]

Though fees were generally small, a lawyer who handled a large number of cases could make a comfortable living by his legal practice alone. Thomas Anderson, who rarely handled cases involving large amounts, made three to five thousand dollars a year in a day when butter was five cents a pound and chickens fifty cents a dozen.[24] Not all attorneys were financially successful, but a lawyer who was popular with judges and juries and willing to follow the hard rough circuit practice had a good chance of making a comfortable living.

Riding the circuit was a necessity on the frontier. Not even the St. Louis lawyers had enough practice in the city to keep them busy and, like lawyers in other areas, traveled the circuit.[25] Some popular lawyers practiced in neighboring states as well as throughout the settlements in Upper Louisiana. The circuits were a way of bringing the courts to the people. The difficulty and expense of travel, together with the frontiersman's tendency to settle disputes by direct

[21] Charles D. Drake, "Autobiography."

[22] Trial of Nathaniel Childs, St. Louis *The Missouri Republican*, January 6, 1850, p. 1.

[23] Ferris Foreman to Clark Hyatt, Ferris Forman Letters.

[24] Anderson, "Autobiography."

[25] The territory was originally divided into five districts: St. Louis, Ste. Genevieve, St. Charles, Cape Girardeau, and New Madrid. Later, the county was the unit of division.

methods, discouraged the people from seeking out the courts. It was also easier to get witnesses when cases were tried near the place where the disputes arose. Hence, the lawyers and judge rode the circuit as long as settlements were scattered and population sparse. Until 1843 even the supreme court went on circuit twice a year, a practice common in the West.

The circuits were huge. In 1815 the St. Charles district comprised all the territory north of the Missouri River and west as far as the jurisdiction of the United States extended. The New Madrid district stretched from the southern boundary of the district of Cape Girardeau to the Territory of New Orleans.[26] A quarter of a century after statehood, Thomas Anderson traveled a circuit reaching from Pike County to the Iowa line.

When the state constitution of Missouri was drawn up, it provided for terms of court to be held three times a year in each county. The dates for the opening of each term varied. Later, longer sessions were held twice a year, but whether two or three terms were held, officials arranged dates to permit lawyers and judges to attend a series of courts. They would set a term of court at one end of the circuit on the third or fourth Monday of January, May, or September, to be followed, usually at weekly intervals, by sessions in the other counties on the circuit.[27] Since completing the circuit took six to eight weeks, attendance at two or three terms meant that lawyers and judges were away from home for long periods.

Travel was hazardous. Every traveler faced difficulty in finding his way through unmarked forests and prairies and danger from robbers. Attorneys had more to fear than most, since many of them acted as agents for creditors and often carried large sums of money in their saddlebags. Angry litigants seeking revenge were active threats to safety. Judges and lawyers usually journeyed together in groups of four or five and commonly carried weapons as safeguards. Numbers and firearms were no protection, however, against the forces of nature: the snows and icy cold of winter, the flies and heat

[26] English, *Pioneer Lawyer*, 47.
[27] English, *Pioneer Lawyer*, 81–83.

of summer, and the storms of wind and rain that might come at any season. Travelers had no means to cross the deep streams except to swim their horses across or "coon it" over on a log. At night they slept on the open prairie when they were too far from the house of a settler. In the towns they stayed at the crowded inns, where they considered themselves lucky to have a bed, even if it had to be shared with one or more other guests. The hardships are typified in the letters of a young lawyer that tell of "being out of sorts" after sitting up all night and of a cold contracted from the wind and rain blowing in his face all day.[28]

Though riding the circuit required fortitude and resourcefulness, reminiscences of lawyers indicate that they enjoyed their experiences — at least in retrospect. James Broadhead, president of the American Bar Association in 1898, spoke of his experiences fifty-five years earlier when he was a young attorney practicing on the frontier. Young men began a career in the law with nothing more than a few books, a horse, bridle, and saddlebags, he recalled; but he asserted that they did not feel deprived, as their ambitions and hopes stimulated their energies and they dreamed of a bright future.[29]

Lawyers rarely took with them on the circuit any of the few books they owned, but despite the lack of books they learned much as they proceeded from court to court. Sometimes the lawyers and judges traveling together discussed principles of law; sometimes they argued philosophical questions; sometimes they played practical jokes on each other.[30] One who traveled the circuit said later that the "continual communion with nature" and the contact with the people strengthened the bench and bar and made its members leaders in questions of law and politics.[31]

Courtrooms were generally makeshift arrangements. Court was held in a private house, a church, a tavern, or even on a grassy place

[28] Charles Yancy to Mary Bedford, Yancy Letters and Papers, 1839–1865.

[29] James Broadhead, "Reminiscences of Fifty-Five Years of Practice," in *History of Bench and Bar*, Stewart, ed., 55.

[30] Thomas Shackelford, "Reminiscences of the Bench and Bar of Central Missouri," in *The History of the Bench and Bar of Missouri*, Stewart, ed., 406.

[31] Shackelford, "Reminiscences."

under a tree. In some instances, a townsite served as the court's lo-
cale; after the court had been established, the town developed. In
Gasconade County, court met in one small log room, and litigants,
witnesses, jurors, judges, and attorneys shared the accommodations
provided by the single three-room house nearby.[32] In Montgomery
County the log structure used as the courtroom served as shelter for
sheep between sessions.[33] As a community's resources grew, the people built better courthouses, in many places the most attractive structure in town and a source of civic pride to the inhabitants.

Early courtrooms, already filled with witnesses, jurors, and attorneys, were still more crowded by citizens who came to listen to
the examination of witnesses and the pleadings of the lawyers. No
other event, except possibly the camp meeting, election day, or
Fourth of July, excited so much interest as the convening of court.
Not all the excitement was generated in the courtroom. A Methodist
circuit rider spoke with disgust of the "great fuss" in the little cabin
where court was being held, but deplored still more the "fiddle playing," dancing, and swearing that went on in the doggeries where at-
tendants at the sessions relaxed from the contests in the courtroom.[34]

Court sessions generally provided ample entertainment for the
people of the locality, some of whom walked miles to hear an outstanding lawyer plead and to marvel at his "matchless" oratory.[35]
Cases of wide interest increased the attendance to the extent that
numbers of spectators, unable to find seats, remained standing to
hear the four- or five-hour speeches that were common. On occasion
chivalrous judges surrendered their own seats to ladies and sat with
the jury.[36] Since many of the spectators had come to be entertained,
they participated in the proceedings. They cheered, applauded, and

---

[32] Bay, *Reminiscences*, 312–13.

[33] W. S. Bryan and Robert Rose, *A History of the Pioneer Families of Missouri*,
230.

[34] Jacob Lanius, "Diary," December 12, 1838.

[35] James Williams, *Seventy-Five Years on the Border*, 130–31. Mr. Williams told
how he admired Alexander Doniphan, an early lawyer, and how he "marveled at
his brilliant pathos."

[36] John D. Lawson, ed., *American State Trials*, XVI, 126.

stamped their feet when they considered that a lawyer had made a telling point, laughed at his satire, and wept as he played upon their pity. The litigating lawyers, on their part, tried to keep jurors from being influenced by popular reaction adverse to their clients. They spoke scornfully of the exhibitions as being out of place in the courtroom and warned jurors not to allow the cheering of friends "so extraordinarily exhibited" or the tears shed upon occasion to turn them from consideration of the facts.[37] When the reaction of spectators was favorable, however, an attorney exploited the mood of the audience to his client's advantage.

The reaction of spectators undoubtedly influenced juries, who ordinarily decided the outcome of a case. The jury system and common law were basic features of United States court procedure. The laws of 1804 regulating procedure in Upper Louisiana required jury trials if the amount in dispute was a hundred dollars or more and if either party demanded a hearing before a jury.[38] After statehood any litigant who chose to advance twenty-five cents for jurors was entitled to a jury, even in the magistrate courts. Jury trials were as much favored by lawyers as by litigants. Charles Drake thought that more than anything else the jury trials in the magistrate courts gave young lawyers a chance to exhibit their ability and eloquence, and he declared that a single trial could make a young lawyer favorably known in the community.[39]

Jurors had to meet few qualifications other than acceptability to the attorneys involved in a case. In territorial days they were required to own property valued at a hundred dollars or more, but the property restriction was removed after statehood. The villagers and farmers who made up the juries would not have impressed a visitor accustomed to more formal courtroom atmosphere any more than would the behavior and appearance of frontier judges and lawyers.

A contemporary belittled the Western courtrooms as scenes to

[37] Lawson, ed., *American State Trials*, XVI, 312; St. Louis *The Missouri Republican*, December 23, 1849, pp. 1–2.

[38] *Laws of a Public and General Nature of Missouri up to 1824*, I, 5, cited in English, *Pioneer Lawyer*, 49.

[39] Charles D. Drake, "Autobiography."

"make Dame Justice smile."[40] Young lawyers rolling quids of tobacco in their mouths, unkempt after riding the circuit for weeks;
judges no better dressed, occasionally half intoxicated, and often less
learned in law than the attorneys practicing before them; impudent
witnesses; noisy auditors — such a cast of actors did not make for
dignity in the courtroom. But despite the careless dress and seeming
disrespect for officials, trials were customarily carried on according
to the forms and in the language of accepted legal usage.

The intricacies of pleading and the formalities of legal language
annoyed those frontiersmen who wished to do away with elaborate
forms. With the increasing strength of Jacksonian democracy came a
demand that judges be elected rather than appointed by the governor. The agitation for an elective judiciary was accompanied by
efforts to sweep away the technicalities of common law. Proponents
of the bills to simplify legal language and eliminate special pleading
argued that deliberate misrepresentation, known to the court as
such, had been practiced through demurrers, nonsuits, and the
"muddy mass of barbarous Latin and Norman French" used by
lawyers.[41] These advocates for less intricate procedures declared that
a lawyer could never say a thing simply but must cloud his meaning
with legal jargon.

Lawyers tried to make their opposition to the changes appear to
be motivated by concern for the welfare of the people. They argued
that an elective judiciary would invalidate the governmental system
of checks and balances and destroy protection of the weak and
obscure.[42] Frontiersmen were somewhat skeptical of these arguments. Though they praised the gentlemen of the bar for their wit
and eloquence, they observed that the most successful lawyers had
the greatest abilities to pervert justice, screen the guilty, implicate the
innocent, and increase their own fame by shrewd and dishonest

[40] Columbia *Missouri Intelligencer and Boon's Lick Advertiser*, August 16, 1834,
p. 1.

[41] Jefferson City *Jefferson Inquirer*, February 28, 1845, p. 3.

[42] Typical is the speech of Mr. Pitt in the state constitutional convention of 1845,
found in Jefferson City *Jefferson Inquirer*, February 4, 1846, p. 1.

tactics.[43] Critics charged lawyers with oppressing rather than protecting the poor and with trying to monopolize political office, promote fraud, and encourage perjury.[44]

Aware of the suspicion directed against them, lawyers achieved success in the courtroom by adapting their methods to the attitudes of jurors who would bring in the verdicts in the cases being tried before them. Attorneys made strenuous efforts to identify themselves and their clients with the common people. Thus, Henry Geyer, considered head of the St. Louis bar in his day, declared his own and his client's democratic principles in his defense of William Darnes, a mechanic on trial for murder. The case was one of wide interest. Following a series of insulting newspaper articles, Darnes had waylaid Andrew Davis, publisher of the *St. Louis Argus*, and beat him about the head with a cane. Davis was carried to a doctor's office, where he underwent an operation. He survived the operation but died soon after, and Darnes was indicted for his murder. Geyer, in defense, presented his client as a man of the people defending himself against a licentious press. Davis, in contrast, was pictured as having assumed aristocratic airs and scorning Darnes as a plebeian and low fellow. Geyer expressed his horror of such class distinctions. For himself, he told the jury, he never spoke of men by classes but judged individuals by their actions; he considered a mechanic as honorable as a newspaper publisher.[45] The verdict of murder in the fourth degree in the trial of a crime for which the accused might well have been sentenced to hang demonstrates the effectiveness of Geyer's appeal.

Lawyers frequently used the device of picturing a client as a poor and humble man against whom the rich and powerful were arrayed in all their might. When Uriel Wright, famous throughout the territory for his eloquence, defended Nathaniel Childs, minister and bank teller, against the charge of embezzling funds from the Bank of Missouri, he characterized the bank as a soulless corporation, brought into being by the legislature, "Who endowed it with

[43] St. Louis *Missouri Gazette and Illinois Advertiser*, March 19, 1814, p. 3.
[44] St. Louis *Missouri Gazette*, September 5, 1812, p. 3.
[45] Lawson, ed., *American State Trials*, XVI, 252.

passions, but breathed into it no soul." [46] Paralleling biblical condemnation, he denounced the bank with: "Eyes it hath, and there is 'speculation' in them; hands it hath, and enough of them to touch at once every interest of society; but there is no heart in its anatomy." [47]

The defense lawyers in that trial consistently pictured the bank and its officers as haughty, imperious men who hid behind a great, monied power; they presented Childs as a common man, moral and energetic, but defenseless against a ruthless, faceless corporation. They ranged themselves on the side of the rights of the individual against tyranny and castigated the prosecution for searching the home of a young widow who was alleged to have secreted papers and money for Childs. Edward Bates, senior counsel for defense, quoted from a speech of Chatham, "A man's house is his castle, no matter how poor the man or mean the house," but when he reached the line, "The king of England dare not enter there," he digressed to praise the higher liberty in America and the consequent obligation for greater protection of the weak and defenseless. [48]

Prosecution lawyers tried to counter these appeals by showing Childs as a cunning and immoral man who had indulged himself in extravagance at public expense and by presenting bank officials and directors as simple, honest citizens who were guarding the interests of the people; [49] but Bates and his colleagues had done their work too well for the prosecution, and Childs went free despite the evidence.

[46] Wright was born in 1805 in Virginia. He attended West Point for a time, but left before graduation and began the study of law with Judge Philip Pendleton Barbour, a distinguished justice. In 1833 he moved to Marion County, Missouri. He represented the citizens of that county in the state legislature before moving to St. Louis, where he became active in the practice of criminal law. He was generally praised in such terms as, "his words flowed from his lips like a placid stream." His voice was described as clear and musical, and the beauty of his diction was noted along with the keenness of his logic. Scharf, *History of St. Louis*, II, 1485; Charles P. Johnson, "Personal Recollections of Some of Missouri's Eminent Statesmen and Lawyers," *Proceedings of the State Historical Society of Missouri*, 84; Daniel Grissom, "Personal Recollections of Distinguished Missourians — Uriel Wright," *The Missouri Historical Review*, XIX (October, 1924), 94–97.

[47] St. Louis *The Missouri Republican*, December 9, 1849, p. 2.

[48] St. Louis *The Missouri Republican*, January 6, 1850, p. 1.

[49] Plea of Henry Geyer, St. Louis *The Missouri Republican*, January 6, 1850, pp. 1–2; plea of Willis Williams, *ibid.*, December 10, 1849, p. 2.

Perhaps the most blatant appeal to class distinctions between the propertied and the propertyless — the only real distinction on the frontier — was used to prejudice the jury in a trial over the ownership of a horse. John S. Brickey, a country lawyer with no great pretensions to learning, represented a client who sought to retain possession of a horse that he had bought in full awareness that it was stolen. Brickey's client was a poor man with eight children; the rightful owner was a doctor in better financial circumstances than most other citizens in the community. Brickey made no effort to deny the evidence, but he closed his defense with the tearful plea:

> Gentlemen of the Jury! Will you take from poor Coatjohn his only horse, and his only means of making bread for his poor starving children, and hand it over to this rich Shylock, who has not a child in this world, though able to support a hundred? No gentlemen, you cannot do it, God forbid![50]

As Brickey sat down, sobbing as if his heart would break, the doctor's lawyer glanced at the jurors, who were wiping away their tears, and whispered to his client that the horse and the case were lost.

Lawyers made equally strenuous efforts to characterize themselves and their clients as true Americans and sons of the West. Appeals to prejudice against foreigners were common on the western frontier, where men were belligerently American. A more than usually interesting example of an attempt to sway jurors by playing on this prejudice occurred in a trial in which the prosecution defended against the implication of dishonesty a witness who had come from Germany. An attorney for the prosecution declared that it made him indignant to see this honest German, scarce knowing the English language, imposed upon by opposing counsel. The defense lawyer dared not be too open in his ridicule, since at least one of the jurors was also German; hence, his response must suggest the superiority of birth in the United States without offending the juror or other Germans in the audience. He gently satirized the witness by asking and answering the question, "And why so 'honest'? Because

[50] Bay, *Reminiscences*, 102–3.

'he was born in Germany and breathed the pure air of her mountains.'" Observing that German air apparently "beat the baptism of Achilles in the fabled Styx," he pretended to regret that his own client was not so happy as to first see the light in Germany. "It was his misfortune," he said, "to be cradled in the land of Washington and Madison, of Franklin and Jefferson." His "native hills — the hills of freedom," in contrast with Germany's mountains, brought him no exemption from suspicion of guilt.[51]

Appealing to the easily aroused prejudice against England, lawyers capitalized on the English origin of common law to denounce it as un-American when it was unfavorable to their side of a case. Basing his defense of a client against a charge of murder on the right of an individual to resist tyranny, Henry Geyer attacked the prosecution for using English law. In England, he said, people were but subjects who must petition for rights from a king; but in America, each man held his rights and privileges to be original and inherent, not granted by any superior human power. Americans acknowledged no such power; here all men were sovereigns, not subjects. It was absurd, he declared, to apply English law in America where God had made special rules for men. He argued that these rules were higher than man-made law; God's plan could not be questioned. He had with His own finger inscribed resistance to oppression upon the human heart.[52] The law was not only God's law. "It was the law of the West," the attorney pointed out, "to resent indignities on the spot."[53]

Attorneys declared that English law was not adaptable to the legal problems of the frontier. Blackstone's dictum that man must retreat to the wall before he could defend himself was repugnant to a frontiersman, Geyer said on his client's behalf, and, playing upon the Westerner's contempt for cowardice, he turned to the spectators in the courtroom and asked:

[51] St. Louis *Missouri Republican*, December 16, 1849, p. 1.
[52] Lawson, ed., *American State Trials*, XVI, 177.
[53] Speech of Joseph Crockett, in Lawson, ed., *American State Trials*, 131.

Is there a man in this vast crowd, who if he were attacked, would flee to the wall, or hesitate to strike down his assailant in his tracks? If there be one, he is a craven and a caitiff, unfit to breathe the pure atmosphere of Missouri, and ought to leave it immediately.[54]

Deriding any man that would run from his assailant, Geyer identified himself with the jurors as a fellow Westerner and the opposing counsel as outsiders. Prosecution lawyers had not been long in the West, he said, or they would know the people better. He turned to the prosecution and advised:

Go to the frontier, among our hardy pioneers, the moccasin boys, as they are called, tell one of them in the presence of his sons, that there is a law in Missouri imported from England, by which, if a man is assailed, he must run to the wall . . . before he resists; he will exclaim, "boys, do you hear that?" and his hand will be instantly on the cock of his rifle.[55]

The jurors responded to these appeals with a mild verdict, despite the evidence.

Jurors were inclined to listen sympathetically to Geyer's defense arguments, not only because he appealed to well-established attitudes, but also because he was acceptable to them. He was an old settler, and long residence in the West enhanced his prestige. The Westerner honored those who had come early to the rough frontier and helped to develop and tame it. Aware of this prejudice and that stories of the old days reinforced it, some lawyers customarily digressed to talk of days past. Jurors and spectators especially liked to hear Edward Bates, who had arrived in St. Louis in 1815, tell about the early times. The nature of his digressions is indicated by the reprimand of a judge who said to him:

Mr. Bates . . . you have given us a very interesting history of the early settlements of the country and of the privations and difficulties encountered by the early inhabitants; you have given us a glowing description of the velvet forests with their creeping vines and

[54] Lawson, ed., *American State Trials*, XVI, 177.
[55] Lawson, ed., *American State Trials*, XVI, 179.

honeysuckles, and of the beautiful prairies carpeted with lovely flowers; you have talked of the red men and their scalping-knives and tomahawks — *now Mr. Bates, please tell us something about the case we are trying.*[56]

Lawyers recognized that ability to handle juries was as important a factor in success as knowledge of the law. Perhaps the greatest resource of the pioneer lawyer was his knowledge of men. The man who could stir jurors to laughter, anger, and tears had a good chance of winning a favorable verdict. Armed with the history of each man on the jury and with knowledge of his likes and dislikes, peculiarities, and desires, successful pleaders placed themselves close to jury boxes and spoke to individuals, often calling them by name and speaking to them as if relying on their judgment alone for justice to be served in this case.[57]

Appeals to the jury were direct. Edward Bates closed a defense by telling jurors that his client's fate was in their hands and pleading: "Restore him, gentlemen, restore him . . . to the position in society which he has so worthily won."[58] Uriel Wright frequently used this technique. After a long and emotional plea for compassion for a client charged with murder he closed with:

And now, jurors, the defense is ended. . . . The lawful power of death is in your hands, the life of my client is like that of the sparrow which the Greek boy held in his closed hand before the Oracle, with the words "alive or dead?" . . . The life of the bird hung upon the caprice of a mischievous youth; that of the prisoner hangs upon the judgment of his peers, sitting to administer the humane and merciful spirit of our law.[59]

Attorneys, when asking a jury to return a verdict of guilty, recognized the reluctance of men to take away another's freedom or life and reminded them of their obligation to do what might be difficult in order to bring about the greater good of society. Declaring that

---

[56] Bay, *Reminiscences*, 130–31.
[57] Bay, *Reminiscences*, 497; Shackelford, "Reminiscences," 396–98.
[58] St. Louis *The Missouri Republican*, January 6, 1850, p. 2.
[59] Lawson, ed., *American State Trials*, X, 106.

human and divine law had imposed the duty upon them, one attorney pleaded with a jury to return a verdict of murder in the first degree. God had commanded that the guilty be punished, he said, and he reinforced his statement with a biblical quotation, "the land cannot be cleansed of the blood that is shed therein but by the blood of him that shed it." He closed his plea with a prayer that the Almighty would direct their minds to the right verdict, which was, presumably, that the man was guilty.[60]

Lawyers, interested in winning verdicts, showed deference to jurors and complimented them upon their intelligence, patience, and attentiveness. Frequently they apologized for taking the time of jurors with speechmaking; the jurors' superior abilities made arguments really unnecessary, and they stated or implied their own willingness to omit the arguments and leave the decision in the jurors' capable hands without further persuasion. When the law was unfavorable to his client, an attorney advised jurors to determine cases by their own good judgment and the law of nature, declaring that it was an invasion of the jurors' function to ask them to render a verdict according to an arbitrary technical point of law.

The examples and comparisons in lawyers' speeches seem to have been selected to appeal to jurors as well as to illustrate a point of law. Often, attorneys spoke of parallel incidents in Kentucky, not to cite a precedent but to appeal to the general idealization of Kentucky. Missourians in general thought of Kentucky as the garden spot of the world, and the frontiersmen among them delighted in the legends of Kentuckians' rough eloquence and courage. A story that circulated on the frontier quoted what was purported to be the speech of a lawyer in defense of his client:

> Gentlemen of the jury, do you think that my client, who lives in the pleasant valley of Old Kentuck . . . would be guilty of stealing? . . . I guess gentlemen of the jury, that you had better bring my client in not guilty, for if you convict him, he and his son John will lick the whole of you.[61]

[60] Speech of W. V. N. Bay, in Lawson, ed., *American State Trials*, X, 150–53.
[61] Jefferson City *Jeffersonian Republican*, July 29, 1837, p. 4.

That the story is probably fictitious does not detract from it as evidence of the admiration of Missourians for the land and people of Kentucky. Uriel Wright, in an effort to destroy circumstantial evidence against his client, chose Kentucky as the setting for a story of another case based on circumstantial evidence. He told how a man charged that his neighbor had bitten off his nose in a fight and how the plaintiff, apparently suffering, appeared in court with his face bandaged and proved by three witnesses that the defendant had committed the outrage. But when the defendant demanded that the bandage be removed, lo, the nose was whole and unscathed, Wright said.[62] The frontiersman delighted in this kind of common-sense argument in which legal maneuvers were defeated by wit and strategy; placing the scene in Kentucky enhanced the story's appeal.

Contemporaries noted the exceeding fondness of the lawyer for special pleading and the readiness of the public to praise the attorney who nonsuited his opponent, quashed a writ, or succeeded on a demurrer over the advocate who conducted a case on its own merits.[63] Despite these instances of adroitness in court, the special pleading of the country lawyer might lack subtlety. Typical was the defense against the argument of plaintiff's lawyer that the defendant had repeatedly "inched" the bottom rail of a fence over a boundary line until he had stolen an acre of his neighbor's land. The defense lawyer made no denial of the fact, but asserted that an act of God had made his client cross-eyed and any encroachment on his neighbor's land was an honest mistake. Further, he pointed out, his client would never have thought of such a scheme; only a smart lawyer like opposing counsel would have conceived of such a crooked way to acquire land.[64] An equally ingenious plea influenced the jury to find for the defendant in a case brought to recover money paid for a horse, guaranteed to be sound, that had "sickened and died on plaintiff's hands." Defense argued that there was no evidence to show that the horse "died on plaintiff's *hands*." The evidence showed

[62] St. Louis *The Missouri Republican*, December 16, 1849, p. 1.
[63] William B. Napton, "Notebooks," cited in English, *Pioneer Lawyer*, 97–98.
[64] Henry Lamm, "The Pettis Bar," in *History of the Bench and Bar*, Stewart, ed., 368–69.

"that the horse died lying on the ground . . . while the plaintiff was gathering corn in the field" and presumably had his hands with him.[65]

The attorney who practiced in the city was more subtle in his use of strategy, but he, too, relied upon it, particularly in the selection of issues he chose to emphasize. The trial of Nathaniel Childs, previously referred to, brought together the most distinguished lawyers in Missouri. The prosecution had on its side John Ryland, member of the supreme court; Henry Geyer, famous for his knowledge of law and his ability in handling witnesses; Charles Lackland, considered a power in pleading; Willis Williams, against whose "electrical eloquence" defense lawyers warned jurors; and two other able but less well known lawyers. Defense had gathered three lawyers who were to become governors of Missouri: Hamilton Gamble, Willard Hall, and Trusten Polk; Edward Bates, one of the most sought-after lawyers in the state and the future attorney general in Lincoln's Cabinet; Uriel Wright, whose oratory was said to have allowed many a criminal to go free; Richard Blennerhassett, also famed for eloquence; and Roswell Fields, who had won a reputation in land suits. The strategy of the defense on this occasion was to attack the management of the bank. They ridiculed the bank for being unable to tell what it had lost, scoffed at its method of arriving at balances and counting its assets, jeered at its "nominal cashier" who was paid by the state but did no work, and charged that if the bank had been managed correctly it would have been impossible to embezzle any money from it.[66]

Strategy was of primary importance in the examination of witnesses and introduction of evidence in the frontier period, even as it is today. Counsel argued hotly over the legality of introducing a document or a piece of testimony. They devised schemes to confuse a witness until he contradicted himself or became uncertain in his statements. They sometimes staged theatrical scenes or brought in

[65] Lamm, "Pettis Bar," 370.

[66] Lawson, ed., *American State Trials*, II; St. Louis *The Missouri Republican*, November 8, 1849, pp. 1–2; January 6, 1850, pp. 1–2.

objects purportedly for illustration, but with full awareness of their emotional impact. They argued points of law and, by raised eyebrows, derisive grins, and yawns, belittled testimony and arguments of opposing witnesses and counsel.

It was, of course, necessary that the lawyer present himself to the jury as a bulwark of society, safeguarding morality, chivalry, and order. He sought also to establish his own clients and witnesses as men and women of good reputation. By praising honor, an advocate implied his own honorable behavior. When an attorney told hearers that frontiersmen held reputation dearer than life itself, he was trying to persuade them that he and his client shared this regard for reputation. Lawyers, describing clients as saints, even as Christlike, grew tearful over the damage being wrought on hitherto impeccable reputations. Typical was Edward Bates's eulogy of a client whose Christian conduct, according to Bates, proved his innocence; his injured client, he said, had suffered great wrongs, but "accused, he did not recriminate, reviled, he reviled not again." [67]

An advocate tried to reduce the force of unfavorable testimony or argument by discrediting opposing witnesses or counsel. He tried to show that opponents were insincere and motivated by large fees or desire for personal glory. He charged them with prostituting themselves at the bidding of men of wealth. Some lawyers became famous for their skill in discrediting witnesses. Among the foremost in this regard was Henry Geyer. His method is exemplified in his attack upon Dr. William Beaumont, the physician who had performed the operation on Davis, victim of Darnes. Beaumont had earned an international reputation by his publication on digestion, a process that he had been able to observe when a patient's stomach wound had not healed properly. Dr. Beaumont had testified that, when Davis was brought into his office, he had found the skull so badly fractured that he had performed the operation known as trephining. The prosecution exhibited the skull in court with "electrical effect" and pointed to its splintered condition. To counteract the effect of this grisly exhibit, Geyer introduced other medical witnesses

[67] St. Louis *The Missouri Republican*, January 6, 1850, p. 1.

to cast doubt on the doctor's ability, but he relied primarily on ridicule of the operation of trephining as a more probable cause of the victim's death than the blows of the cane. He described the instrument used to perform the operation as a large punch with teeth like a saw that cut out a round piece of skull. Any man, he said, subjected to such an operation, could expect to be saved only if his skull was so empty that a few more holes could not harm it. He likened the trephine to a divining rod used to bore for treasure and punned, when he was reprimanded for smiling in the early part of the case, that only a trephine could have bored him into gravity. He ridiculed Beaumont as not very learned and sneered at his publication on digestion as merely the diary of a patient's stomach kept open to satisfy the doctor's curiosity.[68] Prosecuting lawyers were indignant at Geyer's tactics, but the public generally applauded him, and his conduct of the case earned him a national reputation.

References to moral courage, the still small voice of conscience, and the great judgment when all the secrets of the heart would be made known before God permeated the legal arguments. Attorneys were generally regarded as men of good morals and good standing in the community. They customarily led in support of education and religion, but not all of them lived by the moral code they preached. Uriel Wright, who denounced gambling so fiercely and pathetically that men trembled and wept, was himself an inveterate gambler. Others advocated temperance in thrilling tones but drank freely. The free thinkers, who were numerous among lawyers, quoted biblical authority and invoked divine law to serve their own purposes, but rejected organized religion.

Though their sincerity in some things might be questioned, attorneys tried to persuade the judge and jury that they sincerely believed justice to be on their side. Frontiersmen repeated with some relish the story, reportedly true, of the lawyer who pleaded two similar cases in one day, one for a plaintiff, the other for a defendant. When the jury had retired to consider the verdict in the first case and the lawyer began to speak to the second jury, the judge re-

[68] Lawson, ed., *American State Trials*, XVI, 196–277.

minded him that he was contradicting his earlier interpretation of the law. Unabashed, the attorney gazed earnestly at the judge and declared that he might have been mistaken in his first argument but that he now knew he was right.[69]

Knowing that his fellows cherished an ideal of womankind and scorned a man who disregarded the weakness of woman or refused to give her "all that civilization had established as her due," the frontier advocate was characteristically chivalrous in his expressed attitude toward women. The anguish of the mother, sisters, and children of a man on trial was invoked to melt the hearts of jurors. Opposing counsel often reminded jurors that his client had a mother, as did every member of the jury, and, one may assume, the lawyer, too. Mention of a client's aged or widowed mother was especially effective for swaying a jury. All the female relatives of a client were, according to his lawyers, noble, lofty, Christian women, who, if the lawyer's accounts were to be accepted, spent much time in prayer.

Though lawyers may have questioned privately the worthiness of some of the females whose virtues they extolled in such glowing terms, the sincerity of their respect for law can hardly be questioned. Through bar associations they tried to maintain professional ethics among their members and to exert an influence for the selection of capable judges. In the courtroom, accusing an opponent of ignorance or naivete in the law was a primary method of attack, and such was the respect for the law, that an attack of this nature was usually effective. Advocates could argue a case successfully on the premise that a decision in their favor would preserve the sanctity of law and promote order. Attorneys spoke of the majesty of the law and of themselves as its guardians. Law, they asserted, guaranteed life, liberty, and the pursuit of happiness; it was the shield to protect the rights of the humblest citizens. Obliteration of the great landmarks of law founded on wisdom and experience would deliver the land over to anarchy and chaos. Lack of respect for law would bring a time when man could not travel upon the highway or repose upon his couch at night with any security against the bloodthirsty

---

[69] Jefferson City *Jeffersonian Republican*, April 14, 1838, p. 3.

assassin.[70] Not only did prestige for the law accrue through these statements but prestige for the lawyer.

Precedents were infrequently cited in frontier courts, both because the attorneys were unfamiliar with them and because they chose to interpret the law to fit each case. Individual rights rather than precedents served as guiding principles in the interpretation of the law. In America, jurors were repeatedly told, a man was innocent until proved guilty. All had the right of a fair trial.

A fair trial did not preclude an attorney's using all the means in his power to win a verdict. His language was chosen to move the jurors. A contemporary historian asserted that all lawyers, whether from Kentucky, southern Ohio, Indiana, or Missouri, developed the same rough and ready wit, terse epigrammatic speech, and Western eloquence.[71] Timothy Flint referred to the tendency of frontier lawyers to use colloquial expressions and to substitute noise and flourish for concise statement and classical reference.[72]

Colloquial expressions and rough wit were certainly part of the resources of lawyers, but eloquent pleas, made in polished language with allusions to and quotations from the plays of Shakespeare, the works of great poets, and the orations of classical Greece, Rome, and contemporary England are also in the legal records of the time. Some attorneys had little knowledge of literature, geography, law, or grammar; but rough or polished, successful lawyers knew how to use an apt illustration and to choose language for its effect on hearers.

Typical of the manipulation of language are the terms used to describe the young widow, the alleged accomplice of Nathaniel Childs, and the visit paid to her by bank attorneys and officials. Defense lawyers spoke of her as unfortunate and unprotected, the child of an aged mother, defenseless, gentle, handsome, womanly, modest. Her visitors were described as insulting, base, revealed inquisitors. Their statement to her that officers would search the house unless

[70] This typical warning was used by an attorney in a trial reported in Lawson, ed., *American State Trials*, X, 116.

[71] Scharf, *History of St. Louis*, II, 1450.

[72] Timothy Flint, *Recollections of the Last Ten Years*, 51, 85.

she surrendered the property she had secreted for Childs became, in court, a threat to "expose her body to the vulgar embrace of police inspectors." Defense ignored the lady's admission of other gifts from Childs and ridiculed the prosecution's furor over a little gold pencil. Prosecution reminded jurors that rumors of intimacy between the lady and Childs were in common circulation, spoke of her frequent denials and sudden recollections when she was questioned, and described her visitors as kind, chivalrous men who desired to save her unnecessary embarrassment. Prosecution tried to show that defense had been unchivalrous in its examination of the modest, respectable wife of the bank cashier, but they were less skillful than defense in their charges and countercharges.

The choice of language that lent dignity and solemnity to the frontier courtrooms and the practical demonstrations used as arguments are exemplified in an excerpt from a plea by a defense attorney:

> All murders are not alike in turpitude, tried by any moral test. If you, sir [speaking to a juror], are lying on a bed of sickness and prompted by an old grudge, masked in the disguise of sympathy, I approach you, proffer my assistance, gain your confidence, tender you medicine, five grains of arsenic (which I have substituted for twenty grains of calomel, the prescription of your physician); am I not, in the sight of heaven and earth, a different criminal from the man, who, in the flush and transport of passion kills for bitter, burning words of contumely, spoken against the honor of his wife and daughter?[73]

The rhetoric of the frontier lawyer was designed to present his clients' cases in the most favorable light. He viewed the conduct of a case as a contest in which stakes were admittedly high. Nevertheless, for the attorneys and spectators a trial had many elements of a game that must be played by fixed rules. The lawyer, like a debater who argues both sides of a question, was not bound to express his own convictions, though he must seem to do so. He was not held morally responsible for his statements, since he was the agent for his client and spoke in his behalf. Knowledge of the law was important, but

---

[73] Lawson, ed., *American State Trials*, X, 29.

the abilities to bend it to his purpose, to try the case on issues that would accord with the frontiersman's cherished beliefs were even more important. Spectators delighted in the battles of wit in the courts and derived keenest enjoyment when an attorney was able to win against what seemed to be overwhelming odds.

The law undeniably offered protection for the weak and obscure, as attorneys claimed, but it was, also undeniably, more often employed in the service of the propertied classes. Perhaps because of these associations, lawyers tended to be conservative and to cling to tradition even on the frontier. Though they proclaimed the merits of democracy in courtroom pleas, they fought against popular control of judicial processes. By 1850 they had lost the battle against the introduction of a simplified code and popular election of judges, but the gentlemen of the bar never quite succumbed to Jacksonian democracy. Their rhetoric conformed to the democratic ideal, but their own image of themselves and their position in politics and social affairs was one of leadership rather than subservience to the popular will.

VII

"*Would to God I could paint for you a picture of those pioneer preachers. . . . I heard them when their appeals fell like fire from above — red hot! — from a heart anxious for the glory of the Lord.*"

R. S. Duncan, *A Memorial Sermon.*

Onward, Christian Soldiers

The comparative merits of the ministry and the law as professions emerge in the contemporary saying that fathers encouraged their brightest sons to take up the study of law and directed their less gifted toward the ministry. Despite this indication that the people did not generally credit the preacher with the highest intellectual powers, they respected him as a man who could point the way to Heaven. Clergymen of the time, however, indicated the path upward by talking more of eternal punishment than of eternal bliss.

By drawing vivid word pictures of a flaming and personal hell, pioneer clergymen sought to turn frontiersmen from their godless ways. From 1673, when Father Marquette first published the gospel to the Indian nations in the Missouri Valley, missionaries made visits to the region. After the nineteenth century the revival spirit that swept through Cane Ridge in Kentucky and overflowed in the meetings of Lyman Beecher in Connecticut poured westward into the Missouri settlements. The revival spirit was an element of that force called by Alice Tyler "freedom's ferment," another evidence of Jacksonian philosophy, which, combined with the idea of man's perfectibility, dominated Western thought in the first half of the nineteenth century.[1]

The ardor was aimed at saving souls, but its associated effects went much further. Though Protestant ministers had but scanty education, they, with the Catholic clergy, were from the first the friends, promoters, and patrons of education. Ministers opened schools almost as soon as they established churches, and throughout the pioneer era education remained primarily the concern of the churches.

[1] Alice Felt Tyler, *Freedom's Ferment: Phases of American Social History From the Colonial Period to the Outbreak of the Civil War.*

Further, the ability of a man of the people to be set apart as a religious leader demonstrated the power of the common man to gain distinction. Catholic priests stationed on the frontier were, in some numbers, the sons of aristocratic families,[2] but Protestant preachers were men of the people in birth, taste, habits, and manner of speaking. They promoted republican principles through their lives as well as their teaching.

Church and state were closely connected during the French and Spanish regimes. With the approval of the kings, priests established missions among the Indian tribes of Upper Louisiana and ministered to the French and Spanish settlers who later came to the region. The governing council at New Orleans supported the priests and contributed funds for building and maintaining churches.[3] Officials stopped short of requiring church attendance, but encouraged it by prohibiting horse racing and gaming on Sunday until Mass was over.[4]

For Catholics the church was the center of the community. Before the church door officials read government decrees, held sales of property, and required penitents to make public atonement. Religious ceremonies, processions, and festivals were social as well as religious occasions. The priests shared the popular entertainments, dancing and gambling, with their parishioners.[5] The French answered American newcomers of Calvinistic descent who questioned the frivolity of the priest and the gaiety on Sunday that men were made

[2] Henri Pratte, a native Missourian, belonged to one of the richest and best-known families in the state; the family of Pierre De Smet, who began his clerical work in Missouri in 1823, enjoyed high esteem in his native Belgium; and William DuBourg was an aristocrat who fled to America from the terrors of the French Revolution. Louis Houck, *A History of Missouri from the Earliest Explorations and Settlements until the Admission of the State into the Union*, II, 313; William J. Dalton, *Address on the Pioneer Missionary Work of Father De Smet of the Jesuit Society*, delivered before the Missouri Valley Historical Society in Kansas City, February 7, 1914; John E. Rothensteiner, "The Missouri Priest One Hundred Years Ago," *The Missouri Historical Review*, XXI, 4 (July, 1927), 566.

[3] Amos Stoddard, *Sketches, Historical and Descriptive, of Louisiana*, 316.

[4] Frederic L. Billon, *Annals of St. Louis in Its Early Days under the French and Spanish Dominations*, 276–77.

[5] Letter of Frederick Bates to Richard Bates, December 17, 1807, Frederick Bates, *The Life and Papers of Frederick Bates*, Thomas Maitland Marshall, ed., I, 243–44.

for happiness and the more they were able to enjoy themselves the more acceptable they were to their Creator.[6] They looked upon the priest as their adviser, director, and companion, their oracle in worldly as well as religious matters.[7] Some Protestant Americans, imbued with Puritan values, found the relation of the priest and his parishioners difficult to understand. The men appointed to govern the territory often resented the power of the priest and his influence upon the people. Puzzled by French customs, Americans, schooled in the Protestant ethic that hard work is a virtue, disapproved of what seemed to them the lack of ambition among the French settlers. An American territorial officer blamed the priests for the attitudes of the French:

> Surrounded by wretchedness they dance and sing; and if they have their relations and friends within the sound of their violin, they have nothing more to ask of the Virgin, provided her viceregent, the Priest, will design [sic] to forgive those sins which perhaps they have never committed.[8]

The French and Spanish officials were equally suspicious of the Protestants who came to the territory. Before the cession, a government decree had banned Protestant farmers and artisans and limited liberty of conscience for other American settlers to the first generation, but commandants never strictly enforced the order. They permitted Americans to enter the territory after answering such simple questions as: Do you believe in Almighty God? In the Holy Trinity? In the true Apostolic Church? In Jesus Christ our Savior?[9] If Protestants made no attempt to hold public services they were not molested.

---

[6] Stoddard, *Sketches*, 316.

[7] J. Thomas Scharf, *History of St. Louis City and County from the Earliest Periods to the Present Day: Including Biographical Sketches of Representative Men*, I, 286–87, citing "Governor Ford's *History of Illinois*."

[8] Letter of Frederick to Richard Bates, December 17, 1807, Bates, *Life and Papers*, I, 243–44.

[9] R. S. Duncan, *A History of the Baptists in Missouri Embracing an Account of the Organization and Growth of Baptist Churches and Associations; Biographical Sketches of Ministers of the Gospel and Other Prominent Members of the Denomination: The Founding of Baptist Institutions, Periodicals, etc.*, 45.

The laxity in enforcing religious restrictions upon the laity did not extend to clergymen.[10] In the early years of the American infiltration, the Spanish threat to imprison any Protestant preacher who dared to enter the province kept out all except such intrepid souls as John Clark, who rowed across the river from Illinois and, standing on a rock in the river, preached to Americans gathered in the darkness on the Missouri shore.[11] Later, officials showed increasing leniency. When Trudeau became lieutenant governor a few years before the cession, he relaxed the restrictions against Protestant preaching. Pretending to be unaware that a minister was in the territory, Trudeau waited until the clergyman had almost completed his circuit, then sent him a message ordering him to be gone within three days.[12] Through this device, the minister completed his circuit, and Trudeau could claim to have observed the law.

After 1804, when the United States assumed control of the area, separation of church and state left the people free to follow the faith of their choice. For a time they had less opportunity to hear the gospel than under the earlier regimes.[13] Many of the Catholic priests left the territory when they lost government support. From 1804 to 1813 St. Louis was without a resident priest, and though a visiting clergyman occasionally spoke to the people and administered the sacraments, the district was so much neglected that Bishop Benedict Joseph Flaget observed, on his visit to the territory in 1814, that children were unbaptized, marriages contracted without the blessing of the Church, Catholics buried without the sacraments, and Christian doctrines rarely taught.[14] After 1818 when Bishop William DuBourg

[10] Stoddard, *Sketches*, 314.

[11] David R. McAnally, *History of Methodism in Missouri; from the Date of Its Introduction in 1806, down to the Present Day; with an Appendix, Containing Full and Accurate Statistical Information, etc.*, I, 82–91.

[12] Scharf, *History of St. Louis*, II, 1670.

[13] Lucy Simmons, "The Rise and Growth of Protestant Bodies in the Missouri Territory," *The Missouri Historical Review*, XXII (April, 1928), 303.

[14] John Rothensteiner, *History of the Archdiocese of St. Louis in Its Various Stages of Development from A.D. 1673 to A.D. 1928*, I, 240; Francis J. Yealey, *Sainte Genevieve, the Story of Missouri's Oldest Settlement*, 99–100; R. L. Kirkpatrick, "Professional, Religious, and Social Aspects of St. Louis Life, 1804–1816," *Missouri Historical Review*, XLIV (July, 1950), 376–77.

established a residence in St. Louis, Catholic parishes were generally supplied with priests. Protestant ministers also came in increasing numbers after 1810. Eastern Presbyterian societies sent missionaries Timothy Flint, Salmon Giddings, and Nicholas Patterson to Christianize Missourians; John Mason Peck and James Welch came to convert settlers to Baptist doctrine; Methodists and other groups also soon became active. By 1820 Presbyterians, Lutherans, and Episcopalians had established organizations, and fourteen Methodist preachers rode the circuit in Missouri.[15]

Outside St. Louis and the more highly developed communities, the old puritanical religions did not flourish. To the Westerner who loudly asserted equality with his earthly betters, a heaven reserved for the elect did not make sense. The aristocrats who might consider themselves set apart from the masses in other ways could sign the Westminster Confession with good grace, but the man who was not of the elect on earth was indifferent to a religion that promised an aristocracy in Heaven. The Cumberland Presbyterians, the followers of Alexander Campbell, the Baptists, and, above all, the Methodists offered philosophies pleasing to the frontiersman.

Despite their differences — and these were often bitter — all these religions held in common the belief that man had some choice in being saved. The theology of the Universalists, which held that all men would be saved, since eternal punishment was inconsistent with the nature of God, left as little to choice as the old Puritan belief in predestination. Further, by eliminating the need for an emotional conversion, it lacked the power to exorcise the backwoodsman's fear of the devil. Methodists, Baptists, Campbellites, and Cumberlands agreed that man by nature was sinful, that Christ by His crucifixion had atoned for the sins of mankind, and that faith in Jesus was requisite to salvation. They shared a trust in the importance of a recognizable experience in conversion (they called it experimental religion) and by their belief in salvation through repentance endorsed

[15] Floyd C. Shoemaker, *Missouri and Missourians: Land of Contrasts and People of Achievements*, I, 258–59.

the idea that a man could be cleansed of sin in a lightning flash. Methodism, which held that a sinner once saved could revert to his old sinful ways and die unredeemed, was ideally suited to religious attitudes on the frontier, since its teachings made man subject to re-peated conversions. The democratic faiths had another appeal. The old puritanical groups had extended church membership only to those sanctified by a slow process of preparation; the new theology promised speedy redemption and elimination of tedious disciplines.

These religions were further suited to the frontiersman in that they took the gospel to him. In the more settled communities the people gathered in courthouses or schoolrooms to hear preaching and built churches as soon as congregations were strong enough; but much of the state was sparsely settled in the first half of the nine-teenth century, and if the souls of the frontiersmen were to be saved, the clergymen must seek out dwellers along the edges of civilization.

Their journeys were often dangerous. Roads were mere bridle paths; streams became swollen torrents in wet weather; and in the cold months a man could freeze to death on the prairie. Hardy cir-cuit riders had little tolerance for clergymen who required physical comforts. John Mason Peck spoke with disdain of a Methodist col-league who nearly lost his life in the barrens below Herculaneum. Peck believed that any man should know how to camp out, make a fire, and keep warm. Food, he thought, was not important, since a frontiersman "who could not go without food for twenty-four hours, and more especially a preacher of the gospel, ought to be sent back where he came from." [16] Physical vigor and the skills necessary for survival in the wilderness were not always enough. The Methodist circuits covered several hundred miles, and other itinerants traveled as widely as they. The rain poured down on them; they and their mounts swam rivers and spent nights in the morasses with no human company; the howl of the wolf and the scream of the panther kept ever in mind the presence of wild, predatory animals

[16] Rufus Babcock, ed., *Forty Years of Pioneer Life, Memoirs of John Mason Peck, D. D.*, 103–4.

in their solitude. Not the least of their fears was the threat of attack by savage Indians or robbers.[17]

Imagined as well as real dangers caused much suffering. One young minister, in an attempt to shorten the distance between appointments, took a new and strange path and lost his way. He had gone without food or fire since early dawn and was wet, weary, hungry, and cold when night came; yet every step took him farther into the wilderness. He was young; he was making his first circuit; and as he rode through the dense woods, he imagined bears, panthers, and midnight assassins lurking behind every bush. He went courageously on until in the silence of the night he heard a hideous howl that rose and died and rose again. Giving away to terror, he spurred his frightened horse through the undergrowth, which tore away his leggings and the skirt of his overcoat. He lost his whip, his hat, and his saddlebags, but at last was rescued by the slave of a settler, who took him to his master's house. The settler told him that he had probably heard only a wolf as badly frightened as he, but the clergyman remembered his fright for long years.[18]

The settler on the frontier welcomed the preachers as well as other passers-by, shared his corn cakes and bear beef or hog meat with them, fed their horses, and invited them to make their beds on his cabin floor. Nicholas Patterson, who traveled into the interior with John Mason Peck, found the people kind, hospitable, and, though ignorant of the outside world, not stupid.[19] Though most of the women and many of the men were unable to read, they prized the hymn books and Bibles brought by the itinerants. They often bought the books with which the Methodists filled their capacious saddlebags and almost universally expressed their appreciation of the clergyman's visit.

[17] Enoch Mather Marvin, *The Life of Reverend William Goff Caples*, 22–23; McAnally, *History of Methodism*, 156–58.

[18] J. V. Watson, "Tales and Takings, etc." from the Itinerant and Editorial Budget of Reverend J. V. Watson, D. D., in McAnally, *History of Methodism*, 338–95.

[19] Letter of Nicholas Patterson from Howard County, Dec. 21, 1818, quoted in "The Boon's Lick Country," *Bulletin of the Missouri Historical Society*, VI, 4 (July, 1950), 447.

When it was possible, the itinerant sent a notice of his planned arrival ahead, so that settlers could congregate for services at some central location. More often, he visited the families in the lonely log cabins, read the Scripture, talked with them of sin, exhorted them to repentance, and prayed with them.

He received gratitude and affection from the people he served, but little money. He had the satisfaction of seeing the improvement of living conditions of the people on the frontier, for he was a civilizing as well as a moral influence. An early preacher commented that increased attention to personal and household neatness was not the least of the blessings brought by the evangelist's visit. "Wherever the missionary goes, domestic cleanliness whitens on his pathway," he observed.[20] Noting that the use of soap and sand increased when a squalid people received the Bible, he spoke of religion as a great face washer.

Even when the itinerant was the stalwart, brawny-fisted frontier type who could eat the food and brave the discomforts of the frontier, he could not look forward to a comfortable old age. The hardships and privations of circuit riding brought about the early retirement of some ministers and the death of others. Salmon Giddings, the pioneer Presbyterian missionary in Missouri, died at the age of forty-six;[21] Felix Andreis, a missionary priest, lived to be only forty-three;[22] the Reverend Charles Robinson, worn out by his labors, died in St. Charles at the age of thirty-six.[23] Wounded by a vicious horse as he rode the circuit, Lewis Williams suffered amputation of his leg;[24] and Archibald Hite lost his life at the hands of robbers as he rode to an appointment in Adair County.[25]

The clergyman did not shrink from the exertion of visiting scattered settlers, but he recognized the advantage of gathering them together, and he rejoiced when the practice of holding camp services,

[20] Watson, "Tales," 412–13.
[21] Billon, *Annals of St. Louis*, 295.
[22] St. Louis *Missouri Gazette and Public Advertiser*, October 18, 1820, p. 3.
[23] St. Louis *Missouri Republican*, September 30, 1828, p. 3.
[24] Duncan, *History of the Baptists*, 83.
[25] Duncan, *History of the Baptists*, 513.

which originated elsewhere, was adopted by Missourians. Many ministers felt that the camp meetings were singularly blessed by God. The advantages could be demonstrated. Congregations that camped on the spot lost no time in coming and going to services; the women near the meeting were relieved of the burden of preparing food for families that came from a distance, and people received the benefits of concentrated attacks upon sin, since three services were ordinarily held during the day and another at night.

The people made careful preparation for the camp services. The men selected a grove where they could get fresh water and shelter for their families and their horses and oxen, cleared a square, and built platforms from which preachers addressed the people. They fashioned seats for the congregation from slabs of wood or trunks of trees and set up shelters around the square for families, who camped out.

Clemens' account of the camp meeting in *The Adventures of Huckleberry Finn* may well have been written from memory of services attended in the Missouri of his boyhood. The sunbonneted women in calico or linsey-woolsey, the barefooted young men, the children in towshirts, and young folks courting on the sly were familiar sights at the camp meetings.[26] The services roused the religious enthusiasm of the people as with Huck Finn's congregation who sang the hymns lined out by the preacher. The frontier audiences, like the fictional one, "woke up more and more," and as the services progressed, they groaned and shouted in religious fervor.

The worship at night was especially productive of emotional excitement. Blazing fires accented the shadows cast by the dense foliage of the trees. The light falling in yellow and uncertain beams on faces and figures of the people made the scene "singularly indistinct and awfully impressive."[27] The preacher's loud imprecations, his entreaties and calls of admonishment, the penitents' shrieks of despair and groans of agony, mingling in one mighty swell, stirred the emo-

[26] Samuel Clemens, *The Adventures of Huckleberry Finn*, 181–82.
[27] St. Louis *Missouri Gazette and Public Advertiser*, November 3, 1819, p. 1, from *Augusta Chronicle*.

tions of listeners to godly hysteria.[28] The saved moved about among the sinners, adding their own pleas to the preacher's exhortations, and as the prayers and singing increased in fervor, sobbing mourners moved forward to join the circles of prayer. In the growing excitement, sinners cried aloud in awful conviction of guilt and fell prostrate upon the ground.

Some critics punned that more sin was "conceived" than repented at the camp meetings and deplored the "indecent conduct" that sometimes passed for the influence of the Holy Spirit.[29] After the camp meeting at Cane Ridge, a conservative Presbyterian minister recorded in his diary, "Becca Bell — who often fell — is big with child to a wicked trifling school master of the name of Brown," and he noted that other young females had been "regrettably careless." [30] Such events were not unknown in Missouri. Epidemics of pregnancies followed the camp meetings. Jacob Lanius, a Methodist circuit rider, commented that the Cumberlands had given camp meetings a bad name in upper Missouri because they had tolerated almost every form of vice, but he pronounced the Methodist meeting productive of great good.[31]

Contemporary accounts testify to the power of the meetings. "Hardened wretches" were brought to the love of God and "some who had cursed, gambled, and wallowed in drunkenness" sang and praised the Lord.[32] A young man declared that he had gone to the services to scoff, but had come under such awful conviction of guilt that he had kneeled and cried for mercy until he had been filled with glory and unspeakable peace.[33]

Other accounts support the young man's testimony that the meetings were fruitful sources of religious conviction. "Fifteen

[28] St. Louis *Missouri Gazette and Public Advertiser*, November 3, 1819, p. 1.
[29] *St. Louis Beacon*, October 20, 1831, p. 1, from New York *Courier and Enquirer*.
[30] William Warren Sweet, *Religion on the American Frontier: The Presbyterians, 1783–1840, A Collection of Source Materials*, II, 89.
[31] Jacob Lanius, "Diary," April 20, 1835, and June 28, 1836. The diary, in two volumes of handwritten manuscript, covers the years 1833–1842.
[32] Letter from Otis Tiffany, St. Louis *Missouri Republican*, January 19, 1822, p. 3.
[33] Tiffany, St. Louis *Missouri Republican*, January 19, 1822, p. 3.

mourners came on Sat. and Sun. night. Their cries & screams for mercy were hideous and awful beyond the description of my pen."[34] "These meetings have been attended by the outpourings of the Holy Spirit";[35] and "no other place was so signally owned of God . . . as the camp ground" are samples of the testimonies of men who attended the meetings.[36] Both clergy and laity measured the success of a meeting by the number and fervor of conversions, and by these standards the camp meeting led all other religious services in effectiveness.

Men of the time believed in hard conversions. They thought that if a man had been regenerated and his soul cleansed from evil he should know that something extraordinary had happened to him. Moreover, they rationalized that, if revival conversions were to be substituted for a long period of preparation, the experience must be sufficiently memorable to be convincing. The pioneer who came under conviction expected to suffer intense misery until he was assured of forgiveness. Jacob Lanius testified that he could neither eat nor sleep and "was fit for nothing" after his realization that he was a sinful man, until he made a complete surrender to the Lord.[37] Converts witnessed to the joy that came with the assurance of forgiveness. Ministers often told the story of their own conversions. An old Baptist minister recalled his repentance from the wickedness of dancing, drinking, and card playing:

> I retired to the lonely grove between sunset and dark, and while prostrate on my guilty breast, pleading with the Lord for the salvation of my soul, I saw that my condemnation was just, and thought surely hell was my doom. I resolved to resign myself to the will of God without reserve. This done, 'ere I was aware, I felt something with the speed of lightning . . . flash over me; my feelings were strange indeed — all was peace — and while I mused the fire of God's

[34] Lanius, "Diary," June 28, 1836.

[35] Columbia *Missouri Intelligencer and Boon's Lick Advertiser*, August 6, 1831, p. 1, from *Pioneer and Western Baptist.*

[36] W. S. Woodard, *A Centennial Sermon or One Hundred Years of Methodism in Missouri.*

[37] Lanius, "Diary," *c.* August, 1831.

eternal love kindled within me, and I leaped from the earth, joyful and happy.[38]

Shouts and cries of rejoicing were characteristic of the sinner who had won a victory over Satan. The Methodists and Cumberlands strongly encouraged the "feeling times" as evidence of spiritual outpourings; Baptists and Campbellites accepted them rather apologetically, but accepted them, nonetheless.

Frontier congregations believed that religions should be stirring. When a priest rebuked a feminine parishioner for not only attending the Presbyterian services held by Gideon Blackburn, but weeping freely as she listened to the "heretic," the lady retorted that if the priest could only preach like Mr. Blackburn she would cry all the time at his sermons.[39] Blackburn was not representative of the Presbyterians, who were ordinarily, like the Catholics, more restrained in their manner of preaching. Congregations of the democratic religions, however, surrendered unashamedly to their emotions. As the preacher exhorted and prayed, tears running down his cheeks, repentant sinners wept aloud, called for mercy, and fell prostrate on the floor. As vigorously as they repented, churchgoers expressed their happiness in religion. When they "felt happy," they sang, shouted, and sometimes strode over the benches to shake hands with and embrace their brothers—and occasionally their sisters—in evidence of affection and Christian love.[40]

Missourians from the Southern states remembered the excitement of the hen-egg revival in Kentucky.[41] As the spasms and convulsions that marked the Great Revival spread to Missouri, mourners often became subject to attacks of writhings and contortions

[38] D. R. Murphy, "Autobiography," in Duncan, *History of the Baptists*, 602–3.
[39] Houck, *History of Missouri*, III, 224–25.
[40] Lanius, "Diary," July 18, 1835.
[41] An egg, inscribed with the words, "The day of judgment is close at hand," was reported to have been found in Kentucky. The report set off a revival of religion as ministers predicted the imminent end of the world. William S. Bryan and Robert Rose, *A History of the Pioneer Families of Missouri, with Numerous Sketches, Anecdotes, Adventures, etc., Relating to Early Days in Missouri; Also the Lives of Daniel Boone and the Celebrated Indian Chief Black Hawk, with Numerous Biographies and Histories of Primitive Institutions*, 526.

frightful to see. As their bodies jerked forward and backward with a violence that seemed sufficient to dislocate their joints, some converts gave short, sharp, unnatural cries like yelps or barks. Many of the afflicted lay unconscious upon the ground when their convulsions had ceased.[42] Clergymen could not agree about the origin of these incidents. Some thought them divinely inspired; others were as certain that the devil had a hand in them. James Welch, a Baptist missionary, was so disconcerted by his first experience with the phenomenon that he was unable to continue his sermon.[43] Timothy Flint was temperamentally opposed to such undignified behavior, but tolerated the manifestations as characteristic of the crudity of the frontier. The people, he said, were trying to get a lot of religion at once so that they could be exempt from its rules and duties until the next occasion for replenishing their exhausted stock.[44] The Southern-born Jacob Lanius rejoiced when converts shouted and "jumped about in a tremendous manner." He praised the torrents of blessing that caused sinners to cry out and fall as if dead.[45] Advocates of divine origin "proved" the correctness of their belief by pointing out that scoffers were as subject to the seizures as believers. They cited the example of a young man who, starting angrily forward to take his sister from the altar where she had joined the mourners, fell to the floor and flounced helplessly until he submitted to the divine power.[46]

That the attacks could not be explained logically was of little concern to the uneducated settler. Faith rather than logic was his guide. He generally had less confidence in the missionaries trained at Harvard and Princeton than in the plain men who prayed much and interpreted the Bible in the language that he himself spoke. The Princeton-educated Nicholas Patterson recognized the necessity of adapting to the religious climate of the frontier and acknowledged the superior effectiveness of some of the plain, uneducated preachers.

[42] McAnally, *History of Methodism*, I, 265–70.
[43] Bryan and Rose, *History*, 86–87.
[44] Timothy Flint, *Recollections of the Last Ten Years* . . . , 238.
[45] Lanius, "Diary," May 19, 1835.
[46] Bryan and Rose, *History*, 84.

He thought the Methodists knew how to address the people to the best effect, as they used words and phrases that the people understood and spoke with the eloquence of nature. The phrases and figures that would sound barbarous and uncouth to an educated ear, he said, had point and meaning to the bear- and bee-hunters who formed the congregations.[47] Young men who had gone to school to study for the ministry were warned by older preachers to take care lest they make "too smooth an edge to their sword" and lose their influence with the people.[48]

Catholics, Presbyterians, and Congregationalists required educational qualifications for their clergy, but the democratic religious groups licensed applicants upon acceptable presentation of a trial sermon and satisfactory evidence of morality and sincerity. John Mason Peck's comment that a classical and scientific education had never been regarded as an "indispensable requisite" for the ministry in the Baptist Church was a masterpiece of understatement.[49] The truth was that for several years the only ordained Baptist minister west of St. Louis was almost completely illiterate. The Cumberland Presbyterian preachers were not much better educated. At the time the Kentucky Presbytery expelled Finis Ewing, one of the founders of the Cumberland Church, they charged that he was destitute of classical learning and showed no remarkable talents.[50] As for the Methodists, one of their bishops confidently asserted that formal education for the clergy was unnecessary; if a man was called of God, he need not waste his time going to school.[51] The people were inclined to think that pulpit eloquence expressed more of the divine when it flowed from the lips of an uneducated man. Clergymen boasted that they were poor unlearned men who, like Peter and Paul, spoke only by the grace of God. A brilliant mind and a high degree of education were of little value for the preacher to frontier groups.

[47] Letter from Nicholas Patterson, December 21, 1818, quoted in "The Boon's Lick Country," *Bulletin of the Missouri Historical Society*, VI, 4 (July, 1950), 448.
[48] Letter of T. Kidd to P. G. Rea, May 23, 1840, Peter Goodman Rea Papers, 1838–1869.
[49] Babcock, ed., *Memoirs of John Mason Peck*, 151–52.
[50] Sweet, *Religion on the Frontier*, II, 91, 187–89, 341.
[51] Thomas M. Finney, *The Life and Labors of Enoch Mather Marvin*, 159.

Typical of the popular local preachers—frontiersmen who supported themselves by various means while they preached to their neighbors—was Luke Williams. He had come to Missouri from Kentucky after being dispossessed of a little clearing upon which he had failed to file the necessary legal papers. He was of a poor Virginia family of the kind known in the South as white trash. His mother's brothers were notorious throughout the West as horse thieves, but his own greatest sins were dancing and fiddling. These sins seemed grievous to him after he was brought under conviction of sin, and he determined to preach to try to save others. Although almost illiterate, he was "set apart" by a Baptist church and allowed to preach to his neighbors. When he lost his land in Kentucky, he loaded his goods in a wagon and came to Missouri where, for several years, he was the only ordained Baptist preacher west of St. Louis County.[52]

Settlers who had little cash and less inclination to give it to the preacher approved his providing his own necessities. Local preachers, who took no money, argued that accepting pay for spreading the gospel was nonscriptural. They pointed out that Christ and His disciples had preached without pay, and they charged that the missionary preachers who tried to raise some funds for their own support were carrying the gospel on silver wheels. None of the clergy, to be sure, received enough money to warrant jealousy. Timothy Flint said that, as far as he knew, no Protestant minister of any denomination ever received support sufficient to provide his living for two years in succession.[53] As a contemporary observed, "the clergy worked hard on short feed."[54] They rarely made enough to support a family. Protestant ministers took no vows of celibacy, but usually postponed marriage. Older clergymen warned young men against the smiles of "sweet little creatures" that might turn them from their fields of labor, and they admonished young preachers

[52] J. C. Maple and R. P. Rider, *Missouri Baptist Biography*, II, 291–99; Duncan, *History of the Baptists*, 246–50.

[53] Flint, *Recollections*, 115.

[54] Robert C. Ewing, *Historical Memoirs: Containing a Brief History of the Cumberland Church in Missouri*, 99.

that they belonged to God.[55] These warnings were highly practical, for when a minister married, he usually had to retire from circuit preaching and turn to other employment to provide for his family's needs.

Despite their unwillingness to contribute money for his support, church members had a high regard for the spiritual authority of the minister and meekly submitted to discipline for misconduct or infraction of church rules. Since clergymen condemned absence from church, drunkenness, swearing, card playing, theatre- and circusgoing, novel reading, Sabbath breaking, and scandalmongering as sins, members frequently faced disciplinary action.[56] If a member was churched, he could appeal to a higher authority, but accused persons generally accepted the verdict of the hearing conducted by their minister and did whatever he required to be restored to good fellowship.[57] A rare individual pleaded justification or denied the authority of the church. "Sister Sarah Fisher" gave full satisfaction to the church at Arrow Rock, which had called upon her to defend herself against the charge of playing thimble.[58] John Saling was less amenable to discipline. When a committee from Mount Prairie Presbyterian Church warned him that he would be expelled from their fellowship unless he could show that he had not been making sugar on the Sabbath, he defiantly admitted the charge and said he expected to continue to attend to the operation of his sugar camp on Sunday.[59]

Popular acceptance of the clergyman's spiritual guidance did not extend to political or economic matters. The people expected the minister to concern himself with heavenly matters and to leave worldly things alone. A minister who insisted upon preaching doctrines repugnant to his congregations or on participating in political

---

[55] Letters from the Reverend Barnett Miller to P. G. Rea, July 6, 1839, and December 11, 1840, letter of John Foster, December 25, 1840, and others of similar sentiments, all in Rea Papers.

[56] Finney, *Enoch Mather Marvin*, 146–51.

[57] Leslie G. Hill, "The Pioneer Preacher in Missouri," 34–80.

[58] Duncan, *History of the Baptists*, 481.

[59] Minutes of the Presbytery of Missouri, 1832–1851, pp. 116–25, cited by Hill, "Pioneer Preacher," 51–52.

activity lost his influence and his pastorate. Few congregations went so far as the Methodist group who tarred and feathered their preacher for using the pulpit as a point of vantage from which to advocate abolition, but the local clergy early learned that exertions against slavery were unacceptable to Missourians.[60] Congregations did not accept political speaking from the pulpit. Jacob Lanius observed that "there are many kinds of ticks, but none of them so injurious to Methodist Preachers as Polly Ticks."[61]

The question of slavery aroused surprisingly little controversy in the church, perhaps because nearly 90 per cent of the preachers of democratic faiths were from the Southern states and they shared the popular views of slavery. Few Missouri settlers owned large numbers of slaves, even though the number tripled in the last decade of the territorial period and the value of slaveholdings quadrupled.[62] Non-slaveholders identified their economic interests with the institution of slavery and defended it as hotly as slaveowners. Churchgoers deplored involuntary slavery as a great moral evil that ought to be removed as soon as the interest of all concerned would permit, but they believed that immediate freeing of slaves would be exceedingly injurious to the country as well as to the slaves.[63] The Baptists went further. Delegates from the Mount Pleasant Association, meeting in Howard County in 1819 when the controversy over restricting slavery as the price of admission to statehood was raging, entered a solemn protest against restriction, which stated that it was neither constitutional nor humane to confine the slave in one small district.[64] Methodists also supported slavery by refusing to oppose it. Declaring that he had been intimately acquainted with most of the Methodist preachers in the territory, had heard them preach, and had con-

[60] Howard L. Conard, ed., *Encyclopedia of the History of Missouri, a Compendium of History and Biography for Ready Reference*, I, 50.

[61] Lanius, "Diary," January 17, 1834.

[62] David D. March, *The History of Missouri*, I, 400.

[63] This was the position of the Synod of the Presbyterian Church in session at Marion College in 1835, as reported in the Columbia *Missouri Intelligencer and Boon's Lick Advertiser*, October 31, 1835, p. 2.

[64] Franklin *Missouri Intelligencer and Boon's Lick Advertiser*, October 1, 1819, p. 2.

versed with them in private on the subject of slavery, a spokes-man for that sect asserted that he had never heard one of them at any time or place advocate that the slaves should rise up and claim their freedom. On the contrary, he said, Methodist preachers ex-horted the slaves to honesty and fidelity. He assured the citizens that the Methodist Church would no sooner countenance sentiment for abolition than any other gross immorality.[65] The union of the Mis-souri churches with Southern Methodists in the 1840's attests to the correctness of his observation. A contemporary reminisced that the burden of the preacher's argument was that slavery must be accepted as a divine institution.[66]

Not all clergy supported slavery, despite the theory that it had approval from on high. A Methodist historian asserted that, even during the controversy over restriction, some preachers used their influence against the institution to the extent of circulating petitions against it.[67] The Methodists were generally considered proslavery, however, and John Clark withdrew his membership in the church for that reason and joined a group known as the Baptized Church of Christ, Friends of Humanity. Clark's unpopular views did not turn the people against him, but John Mason Peck found that his own opposition to slavery and his efforts to help the Negro aroused re-sentment. When he first settled at St. Louis, Peck began a Sabbath school for "Africans." He required certificates from their masters and owners before admitting them to the school, but he was consid-ered a Yankee and therefore suspect by the slave-trading interests.[68] After a time, he found it expedient to publish a refutation of "malig-nant slanders" circulated against him. He declared that, whatever his own sentiments, he had too much regard for the cause of religion and his own reputation to preach on slavery or any other subject of party politics. Further, he denied that he had ever in the course of his public or ministerial labors uttered a syllable that had the least

[65] Alexander McAlister, in the St. Louis *Missouri Gazette and Public Advertiser*, May 24, 1820, p. 3.

[66] Wiley Britton, *Pioneer Life in Southwest Missouri*, 146.

[67] McAnally, *History of Methodism*, 223–24.

[68] March, *History of Missouri*, I, 337.

bearing upon slavery.[69] He continued to teach Negro adults and children who came to his Sabbath school, instructing them in reading and in the Scriptures. They worshipped in his church with the white congregation — a practice not unusual on the frontier — until they formed a separate branch with a minister of their own race,[70] but he was careful not to offend slaveowners.

Slaves were not restricted by law in religious matters until 1847, when a statute forbade religious meetings conducted by Negro officiants or preachers unless a white peace officer was present.[71] Several denominations licensed Negro preachers; other Negroes spoke without benefit of license. Masters generally encouraged slaves to attend religious services, but one frontier preacher who baptized a slave without his master's consent was threatened with a whipping. Later, however, the owner told him that the Negro was so improved as a servant that he "wished to God" the preacher would baptize all his Negroes.[72] In general, so long as the clergy did not interfere with the institution of slavery or encourage individual slaves to seek their freedom, they were unrestricted in ministering to Negroes.

Some preachers supported colonization as a solution to the slave question. In 1827 ministers of several St. Louis congregations met with leaders in the city to consider this method of dealing with the problem. The group held several meetings and listened to orations, but the instructions to managers of the society to find out whether there were any free persons of color in Illinois or Missouri and, if so, whether they were willing to migrate to Liberia indicate the lack of reality with which members dealt with the question.[73] Despite the orations and the interest of "respectable ladies and gentlemen," the St. Louis society had a brief life. Most churches took a stand similar to that of the brethren in Lexington who declared that "the relation

[69] Franklin *Missouri Intelligencer*, June 17, 1820, p. 3; St. Louis *Missouri Gazette and Public Advertiser*, May 3, 1820, p. 3.

[70] Duncan, *History of the Baptists*, 755.

[71] Emil Oberholzer, "The Legal Aspects of Slavery in Missouri," Part 3, *Bulletin of the Missouri Historical Society*, VI, 3 (April, 1950), 333.

[72] Duncan, *History of the Baptists*, 62–63.

[73] St. Louis *Missouri Republican*, May 17, 1827, p. 3. Issues preceding and following this one carry reports and announcements of the society.

between master and slave is a critical one, with which the church ought not to meddle."[74]

If the preacher on the Missouri frontier avoided controversy on the slave question, he had no fear of engaging in disputation on doctrine. In 1832 a writer on the American pulpit charged that American sermons consisted mostly of "rhetorical phillipic upon the faith and principles of some adverse group or of an elaborate vindication of the clergyman's own religious persuasion."[75] Very much as political factionalism flourished in the atmosphere of Jacksonian democracy, rivalry grew among the democratic religions. The rivalry was partially inspired by the desire for numbers of converts, but it also stemmed from the belief that a day of judgment was coming when followers of the true doctrine would be gathered up into eternal glory and all others cast into everlasting darkness. "Come and go to Heaven with us" was the plea as each group confidently asserted that its own theology was the true doctrine. Methodists deplored the Baptists' erroneous beliefs on immersion; Baptists professed to be horrified at the idea of sprinkling babies, and thereupon they denounced Methodism; Presbyterians argued the merits of Old School, New School, and New Light doctrines; and Campbellites eagerly debated points of doctrine with anyone who would argue with them. Little Christian charity existed for a different form of baptism or communion. Downcast about the success of Baptists in "preaching up immersion" until the "illiterate people" accepted it as the apostolic method, Jacob Lanius comforted himself by the hope that the Campbellites would soon break up the Baptist Church.[76]

Lanius was no more intolerant than many of his associates. In sermons filled with vituperation, preachers labored for two or three hours to show that their doctrine was the true one. Arguments might be quite devious. An ardent young preacher exulted that he had, by the Scriptures, utterly disproved the Baptist claim that infant

[74] *Lexington Express,* July 30, 1844, p. 2.

[75] *St. Louis Beacon,* September 27, 1832, p. 2, quoting an unnamed writer in the *St. Louis Times and Free Press.*

[76] Lanius, "Diary," May 9, 1834.

baptism was unjustified. He quoted the Bible, "Faith is the substance of things hoped for" and, having shown to his own satisfaction that faith and hope were synonymous, turned to the statement, "For we are saved by hope," then triumphantly recited Psalms 22:9, "But thou art he that took me out of the womb; thou dids't make me hope when I was upon my mother's breast." [77] He was equally satisfied that he had disproved the accounts of Christ's immersion. Explaining that the Old Testament reference to passing through Jordan was in reality a crossing over on the dry ground of the river bed, he concluded that Christ came only to the brink of the river for His baptism and was never immersed.[78] A Baptist minister in the audience objected to this logic, and the two continued the argument the following day for seven hours, at the end of which time neither admitted defeat.[79]

When preachers met in public debates on the tenets of their faith, they usually began the proceedings on a high tone by quoting from Scripture but soon descended to a lower plane and ended in angry exchanges of personalities. A clergyman of another faith refuted the claims of a Universalist with, "Universalists are *imps of the Devil*, and will most assuredly *go to hell.* . . . Proof: False teachers are tellers of falsehoods, and tellers of falsehoods are imps of the Devil: Universalists are false teachers and must be . . . therefore . . . imps of the Devil, and will be eternally damned." [80] Their audiences relished such debates. They enjoyed the attack, the victim's telling response to it — or his discomfiture, and they applauded the gifted speaker who seemingly needed merely to open his mouth for the rolling phrases to flood forth.

Clergy and congregations alike considered that salvation was the most important subject for sermons. The pioneer preacher dwelt less on Heaven than on the horrors of Hell's fire and brimstone. William Caples' vivid description of the tongues of fire bursting

---

[77] Letter of Ephraim Conrad, Greenville, Missouri, to David Henkel, "Early Lutheranism in Missouri," *Theological Quarterly*, III, 3 (n. d.), 342–44.

[78] Conrad to Henkel, *Theological Quarterly*, III, 3 (n.d.), 342–44.

[79] Conrad to Henkel, *Theological Quarterly*, III, 3 (n.d.), 342–44.

[80] Fayette *Boon's Lick Times*, March 16, 1844, p. 1.

from the cracks of Hell caused terrified sinners to shriek with fear.[81] Jacob Lanius frightened the unsaved into repentance by calling on them to listen to the terrible shrieks of the doomed whose bodies were eaten by the "worm that never dies." He pictured the lost souls crying out for water as the smoke of their torment ascended to the skies and their screams echoed and re-echoed in the "awful caverns of hell." [82] Under pioneer conditions preachers could effectively emphasize the uncertainties of life. All about him the frontiersman saw sudden death; the malaria fever so prevalent in the region, the recurrent ravages of cholera, the hardships and dangers of daily life made death ever imminent and the preachers' warnings real.

A funeral provided an appropriate occasion to expatiate on the brevity of life and the inevitability of judgment. Typical was the sermon described by a member of a funeral party in St. Louis. He told how the coffin was placed over the narrow pit and how, as the people stood by with heads uncovered, the minister took his place at the head of the grave, stood silent for a moment, and then addressed the mourners. The clergyman referred to the sudden, unexpected, and hasty manner in which the deceased had been cut off from life without warning. He reminded mourners that death seized his prey in the twinkling of an eye, and he entreated them not to count on future years that might not be theirs. With tears in his eyes, he urged them to take a last farewell of their departed friend whom they must all sooner or later follow. "None can escape the relentless tyrant," he warned them; "he stalks in triumph . . . and none can stay his hand or set bounds to his power." [83] Clergymen often closed a funeral sermon with an invitation to sinners to come forward and repent. A minister, preaching the funeral of a man whose wife was not a church member, rejoiced when the widow rose from her seat and, weeping bitterly, fell down before the altar, clasping her arms around the preacher's feet and crying aloud for mercy. He exulted that he had not only been instrumental in saving her, but also that

[81] Marvin, *Life of Caples*, 82.
[82] Lanius, "Diary," December 17, 1835.
[83] *St. Louis Beacon*, January 13, 1830, p. 2.

nearly every unconverted person in the audience had come forward.[84] The preacher felt that a congregation bathed in tears was sincere in its repentance for sin.

Throughout his sermons, the preacher expressed anxiety for the glory of God and enlisted as a soldier in Christian warfare, with sin his enemy. And sin was all around him, slaying the people on every hand, "not one today and another tomorrow . . . but daily yea hourly *alas* every moment."[85] Sin was no abstraction, no mere unrighteousness. Sin was card playing, dancing, drinking, horse racing, and swearing. The clergyman decried the practice of men and women dancing together "to the strains of lascivious music" with "suggestive touch and movement." He warned that the midnight dance offered temptation and opportunity to female frailty. He condemned the wealth-seeking preoccupation of frontiersmen, as did Enoch Marvin, who not only preached a sermon against love of money, but also, observing a man who was whiling away the time of the sermon by making calculations on his boot, pointed his finger at the guilty member with the cry, "Thou art the man!"[86]

Notes left by a frontier preacher for a sermon on the sin of being wealthy show the generally used method of attack. The speaker began by conjecturing whether the story of Lazarus and the rich man was a parable or a fact. He pondered the identity of the rich man before denouncing him. He argued that the great sin of the rich man was not drinking or gambling, but in living extravagantly every day while Lazarus was in need. He digressed to congratulate Missourians on living in a day when the blessings of Christianity provided benefits for the poor and helpless, but passed rapidly over this debatable premise — the insane were incarcerated in jails or wandered about uncared for unless relatives could keep them hidden away — to describe the death of the two men. He told how Lazarus was transported by the angels to Abraham's bosom, and how the rich

[84] A. McCorkle, "Memoirs," in Ewing, *Historical Memoirs*, 164.

[85] Letter of T. Kidd from Rutherford City, Tennessee, May 23, 1840, to P. G. Rea. Rea Papers.

[86] Finney, *Enoch Mather Marvin*, 591.

man went to Hell. He pictured the agonies of Dives, his cries, his petitions, his situation.

The minister returned to discussion of the sin of the rich man. His sin was in faring sumptuously every day, wearing fine clothes, and living easily and extravagantly. Because he bore no cross on earth, he went to Hell, for man was born to suffer. The preacher noted that, when it was too late, Dives recognized that he could have avoided eternal punishment, and now he pleaded to be allowed to return to warn his brothers. For Dives, it was too late, but it was not yet too late for the congregation, as it had not been too late for Dives' brothers, to repent their sins, the speaker told them.[87] Harsh in his condemnation of sin, the pioneer clergyman saw the tides of ungodliness sweeping the western country and was in an agony of fear that man would be forever doomed in Hell. In his effort to save the souls of humanity, he eschewed gentle words; only by strong language could he convince the sinner of the Hell-deserving character of his deeds.

The real power of a preacher lay in his ability to exhort. As he progressed from interpretation of the Scripture to the ecstasy of his plea for repentance, a powerful preacher could draw men and women magnetically to the mourners' bench. Admirers told how the Methodist minister William Caples, with tears flowing down his cheeks, decried man's guilt, envisioned the day of judgment, and showed the heavenly throne and the horrors of Hell. He cried out to the unsaved, "Come! sinners, come! It is *not* too late. You are not dead yet, thank God! Come! God calls you! Fly! Death is on your track. Your steps take hold on hell. The pointed lightning shaft quivers at your breast. COME TO CHRIST! COME NOW!" As he continued his pleas against the background of the choir's singing, "Are you washed in the blood of the lamb?" penitents crowded to the altar, mingling sobs of contrition and shouts of joy with prayers for their souls.[88]

The age had its scoffers, who noted that the excitement died

---

[87] Moses Payne, Notes of Sermon, Moses Payne Papers and Account Books.
[88] Marvin, *Life of Caples*, 107.

down when the preacher relaxed his pleas or moved on to other communities. Superstitious frontiersmen speculated that the power of one preacher who wore a large silk handkerchief around his afflicted hand lay in some mysterious powders that he concealed in his handkerchief and scattered on the people until they came under his spell.[89] To some ministers the dramatic method of exhorting seemed improper and the conversions based on emotional excitement fleeting, but even the skeptics generally granted that the people's response to the revivalists' impassioned pleas was good.

Along with fear of eternal fire, the clergy used pathos as an appeal for reform. A contemporary commented that a preacher who could not bring a parent or two to the mourners' bench with a pathetic story of a deceased child resting in the bosom of the Savior was not worth his calling. Usually, with tear-stained cheeks, the preacher related the sins of his own youth and the intensity of his repentance. He told sad stories of young men called to face their Maker without having received forgiveness. He described the death of mothers whose little children were thus orphaned. He imitated the child, wailing, "My mama is dead!" Dwelling on death as the inescapable fate of all men, he told how grieving families held the transparent hands of loved ones and bent to kiss dying lips.

So vivid were the tales of some of the speakers that their transported listeners imagined themselves as participants in the events. As Gideon Blackburn visualized the scene of Moses lifting up the serpent in the wilderness, he sketched in the amazement of the people and the press of the crowd so realistically that when he called out, "Look to the woman who faints," listeners turned to aid the fainting woman.[90] A Methodist minister, well known for his dramatic presentation of Scripture, won special acclaim for his sermon urging sinners to make their way across the terrible chasm of sin and set their feet upon the rock of Christ. Acting out the struggle of the sinner, he moved forward step by step as if uncertain of his footing and

[89] Bryan and Rose, *History*, 424.
[90] J. W. Hall, "Gideon Blackburn," in *Annals of the American Pulpit*, William B. Sprague, ed., IV, 53–54.

fearful of destruction until at last he placed his foot upon the rock. Exhausted by their empathy, the crowd wept and rejoiced.[91] Perspiration mingled with tears as clergymen battled with Satan, and the chairs behind which the preachers ordinarily stood as they spoke often suffered from their violent thrusts at the devil and the archfiends. Their antics were not ridiculous to frontier audiences. Timothy Flint said that a really effective preacher left a hearer "not sufficiently cool to criticize." He believed that the ability to move "the inmost affections" was perhaps the most important qualification a clergyman could possess. He deplored Gideon Blackburn's "low words" and the bad taste of some of his images and illustrations, but he admired Blackburn's power to burst upon his hearers in a "glow of feeling and pathos." [92]

The metaphors and illustrations within the sermons were often crude, but they made the speakers' points clear. Members of Enoch Marvin's audience understood his explanation of the mystery of life when he illustrated it with a story of his father's search for good seed corn after a killing frost.[93] They had experienced the same anxiety; they and their families depended for bread upon the sprouting of the seed, and the comparison was meaningful to them. One preacher attempted to increase his audience's appreciation of Christ's sacrifice by telling of a father who scarred his hands in rescuing his daughter from burning. The figure was effective, for the frontiersman could visualize hands scarred by fire more readily than he could imagine hands pierced by nails, and he could appreciate the selfless sacrifice of the father.[94]

Men of little education often spoke with a natural eloquence, as did Wilson Thompson, a humble little preacher whose hair and clothes were both cut at home. He showed his frontier listeners the peril of their souls in an image reminiscent of Jonathan Edwards' "Sinners in the Hands of an Angry God." Thompson's geography was at fault, but his image was vivid as he visualized the river at their door:

---

[91] Marvin, *Life of Caples*, 110.
[92] Flint, *Recollections*, 183–84.
[93] Finney, *Recollections*, 46–47.
[94] Finney, *Recollections*, 46–47.

It is said that away up at the source of the mighty river that flows through your valley, there is a fountain from which two streams take their rise. One goes westward and empties into the Pacific; the other flows close beside us and pours its freight into the Gulf of Mexico. I have imagined a ledge of rocks hanging over that fountain, and from that rock a dew-drop suspended. . . . Sinner, you hang like that dewdrop. . . . A wind coming from the gates of heaven . . . may bear you to that . . . stream . . . that flows . . . by the throne of God. A wind coming from the opposite quarter shall result in the destruction of your soul for time and eternity.[95]

That the language and ideas of the preachers fitted the times and the people is not remarkable, since the preachers were for the most part frontiersmen whose only difference from their fellows was in being "set apart." Audiences did not object to mispronounced words or errors in grammar so long as the speaker supported their own ideas of theology, discomfited rival sects, and drew sinners to the mourners' bench. Undoubtedly, the frontier preacher "fed and watered the passions of his hearers" and committed a hundred stylistic faults. Dependence upon the inspiration of the moment resulted in some rambling and incoherent speeches and provided grounds for the critics' charges that some speakers went round and round a text "like a blind horse in a mill," sang their sermons, and confused logic with noise.[96]

The prejudice of the frontiersman against written sermons contributed to their inadequate preparation and lack of discipline. Audiences held a poor opinion of the preacher who had to write out his thoughts and read them off on the Sabbath. They liked to hear the words fall "red hot" from the lips of the speaker, frowned on the obvious use of notes, and considered a memorized sermon dull and

[95] W. H. Burnham, "Story of William Thompson," in Duncan, *History of the Baptists*, 808–15.
[96] Babcock, ed., *Memoirs of John Mason Peck*, 151–52. Peck, who rode in company with Elder Badgely on the circuit, commented that the old man, "like many frontier preachers," knew no rules for interpretation of the Scripture but his own fancy and thought, through which the spirit of God had taught him the meaning. Elder Badgely was a Presbyterian and Peck did not lack confidence in his own interpretations of the Scripture; hence his judgment of the old man may not have been completely impartial.

stiff. An experienced minister advised young clergymen that if they could not acquire "the gift of aptness" they had better let preaching alone.[97] Many of the preachers believed that the spirit of God would fill their mouths and inspire their messages if they prayed much and led godly lives. Consequently, they did not feel any need to study or prepare, since they believed they had only to open their mouths and let the glory pour forth. On the other hand, John Mason Peck observed that many frontier preachers would have been more effective if they possessed a good dictionary, a touch of logic, and a knowledge of rhetoric.[98] He thought preachers should train their minds to habits of thinking, systematized arrangement, and readiness of speech.

Educated and uneducated alike used the Bible as their primary text. They studied it for long hours and memorized passage after passage from its pages. Some familiarized themselves with interpretations and commentaries, read published sermons, and studied theology and church history. Whether educated or uneducated, however, the clergyman who faced a congregation on the frontier preached a practical religion.

The Missouri frontier developed no new religions, but it provided favorable climate and rich soil for those transplanted there. The frontiersman scorned metaphysical essays, preferring sermons on sound faith and human duty. Choosing such texts as "For I say unto you that except your righteousness shall exceed the righteousness of the scribes and pharisees, ye shall in no wise enter into the kingdom of heaven," preachers spoke for an hour or more on the concept of righteousness, then turned the hourglass and talked equally as long of the happiness that the righteous would enjoy in Heaven and the horrors that the doomed would suffer in Hell.

Most of the frontier clergy were good men, humble and dedicated, but, unfortunately, generally lacking in humor. The hardships

[97] Babcock, ed., *Memoirs of John Mason Peck*, 151–52.
[98] Babcock, ed., *Memoirs of John Mason Peck*, 157. By rhetoric, Peck meant logical reasoning, systematic arrangement, style of speaking, power to excite the emotions, and good use of the voice.

that they endured and their preoccupation with the salvation of sinners probably explain their solemnity. Their congregations respected them and held them in affection. Frontiersmen, despite their predilections for blasphemy, gambling, and drunkenness, showed also a hunger for the gospel, welcomed the itinerants, and formed themselves into congregations as soon as settlements warranted organization.

Faulty as their ministry may now seem, the frontier clergy earned an honest debt from the settlers. Through Sunday schools and subscription classes, the preachers promoted education, and they encouraged cleanliness, neatness, and self-respect in the people they visited. They were a force for decency and morality in every aspect of life except on the slave question, and on that issue they believed, with many of their contemporaries, that their view had divine approval. They were without political power — any suggestion of their participation in politics met with strong disapproval — and they had no economic influence. Nevertheless, the preachers of the democratic faiths were, of all frontier speakers, the most effective promoters of Jacksonian democracy. They preached that all men were equal in the sight of God, with special privilege for none, and that the soul of each man was of equal and inestimable value.

VIII

". . . they all had respect for the man who best expressed their aspirations and their ideas."

Frederick Jackson Turner, "Contributions of the West to American Democracy," in *The Turner Thesis*, George Rogers Taylor, ed.

Rhetoric: Reflection of
the Frontier

Determining whether the speaker shaped the ideas of the frontier or merely reflected them is as difficult as assessing the relative
influence of the artist and his society upon each other. To grant the
speaker no greater power than to be a reflector of ideas is to assign
him considerable significance, for the man who can identify and express the needs and aspirations of a group clarifies and strengthens
the attitudes and beliefs of his hearers. Vague feelings and undefined
values may become the bases for positive action when they are
clearly articulated.

Rhetoric has long been viewed with suspicion and has been
damned even by those who employed it in order to denounce it. The
critics of rhetoric have charged that it is concerned with appearances
rather than with reality, that it is used to mislead, that it is a "compendium of cynical protestations" applied without regard for ethical
standards.[1]

The enemies of rhetoric could have found illustrations on the
frontier for their charges, just as the friends of rhetoric could have
pointed to speeches containing clear and reasoned appeals made by
good men with ethical motivations. Frontier rhetoric was a reflection
of the frontier, with all its contradictions and ambivalences.

The frontiersman based rhetorical arguments on the myth of
the inherent virtue of the yeoman who strove to provide for the
needs of his family through cultivation of his own soil and on the
ability of the plain man of good sense to conduct the affairs of gov-

[1] Bower Aly, "Rhetoric: Its Natural Enemies," *The Speech Teacher*, XVII, 1
(January, 1968), 1–10.

STUMP, BAR, AND PULPIT

ernment. With the abundance of relatively cheap if not free land, with the preponderance of farmers in the frontier population, and with the necessary dependence of settlers in a new land on men much like themselves to make the laws and effectuate them, the myth more nearly agreed with reality on the frontier than in areas of greater industrialization and specialization. That all the elements did not always conform to observable fact is unimportant. As Georges Sorel has pointed out, myths "are not descriptions of things, but expressions of a determination to act." [2]

Frontier speakers assumed that elevating a man to the proud rank of freeholder gave him a vital interest in the country and strong motives to promote its prosperity and protect its existence. The virtue lay not simply in ownership of virgin land, however, but in fields brought under fruitful cultivation. To leave the forest in its primitive state was viewed as an actual evil. Thomas Hart Benton in the United States Senate attacked Senator Foote's resolution limiting the sales of land with the argument that such limitation would deliver up two thirds of the state to the wild beasts in violation of the divine command that man should have dominion over beasts of the forest. [3] Settlers on the frontier formed agricultural societies, and they applauded speakers who declared that whatever brought happiness and contentment to the yeomanry laid the foundations of the Republic deep and strong and gave assurance to the people's liberties. [4]

Inextricably bound up with the Jeffersonian myth of the virtuous yeoman was trust in the ability of the plain man to govern. The "will of the people" was acknowledged as a motivating power by any office seeker who hoped to be successful on the frontier, and popular sovereignty was a slogan for Whigs, the party of planters and merchants, as well as for the yeoman farmers and mechanics who made up the majority of the Democratic party. Though extension of elective office and removal of property qualifications for voting

[2] Georges Sorel, *Reflections on Violence* (London: n.d.), 132, 135–36, 137, cited in Arthur M. Schlesinger, Jr., *The Age of Jackson,* 511.
[3] *Register of Debates in Congress,* 21st Cong., 1st Sess., VI, January 18, 1830, p. 1.
[4] See, for example, the speech of Rufus Pettibone, St. Charles *The Missourian,* July 25, 1822, pp. 1–2.

preceded the Jacksonian era, in Jackson the plain man saw the symbol of his own dreams, and in Jacksonian democracy he saw the possibility of realizing his own aspirations. Candidates for office on the frontier told audiences that they relied on the good judgment of the "great body of the people," the "bone and sinew of the country," to place them in office, and they expressed their intention to carry out the will of the people faithfully and to justify the trust placed in them.

The belief in the power of the people was one facet of the objection to special privilege. Much of the opposition to banks during this period lay in the belief that banks demanded special powers, that they made money, not by honest individual productiveness, but in speculation with the people's money. Jacksonian rhetoric implied the immoral nature of banks by terming them soulless corporations. The bank, as an example of special privilege, was declared to be a threat to the liberties of the people. Speakers appealed to the fears of listeners when they prophesied that the bank, as a great monied institution, would rule the people, would raise and depress prices at its own pleasure, and would doom their children to be "born with saddles on their backs" to be "rode through life by a booted and spurred aristocracy."[5] Slowly the argument of supporters of banks that bank notes would promote material progress became increasingly effective as commerce and industry took on added importance; but even when frontiersmen accepted banks as a necessity for progress, they sought to hedge the powers they granted with safeguards for the people's protection.

The pioneer had much to say about equality, but he recognized a natural aristocracy among men. He extravagantly honored a hero who had by courage or judgment won the right to lead, but he refused to call any man his master. To accuse a frontiersman of wearing another man's collar was a deep insult. Frontier speakers loudly asserted the equality of all men. That equality never existed on the frontier did not lessen the effectiveness of these egalitarian state-

[5] See the report of a speech by R. W. Wells, *St. Louis Beacon*, October 29, 1831, pp. 2–3.

ments. Social and economic mobility was an actuality, and men could move up the scale if they acquired property. Possession of property was the true distinction between men on the frontier. To gain wealth was to gain social and political prestige; economic appeals were powerful motivating factors in the speechmaking of the time and place.

Despite the reiteration of democratic beliefs, the Negro and the Indian remained outside the pioneer's concept of equality. The Indian was a savage, and he was not welcome in the settlements. He figured largely in the current rhetoric through references to the scalping knife, ambush and massacre, savage yells and wanton bloodshed — always in unfavorable metaphor. Negroes were slaves, slaves were property, and property must be protected. Christ had not disturbed slavery, frontier speakers declared, and they saw no justification for an abolitionist to meddle where Christ had forborne to do so.

Nonslaveholding whites generally supported the slaveowners' property rights on the Missouri frontier, but the conflict between propertied and propertyless classes was strong and often bitter. In the class conflict between the "haves" and the "hope-to-haves" the yeoman farmer was linked with the laborer and mechanic against the merchant and planter. Appeals of men of little property for solidarity against the rich were made in terms of clothing and material possessions, as were those of Joseph Buford, son of the prairie, who pictured his opponents as wearing silk stockings and kid gloves in contrast to his own muddy boots and work-worn hands. He further marked the division between classes by reminding his hearers that rich men could bury their dead in fine mahogany coffins; he did not need to complete the contrast by mentioning the rough pine boxes in which many of them had laid to rest members of their own households.[6] The clergy often inveighed against riches as if wealth were sinful; yet through their striving, frontiersmen showed active willingness to risk some peril of their souls if they could only add to

[6] Report of legislative proceedings, Jefferson City *Jefferson Inquirer*, January 16, 1845, p. 3.

their material possessions on earth. It is clear that the Missouri pioneer was a materialist in his personal life. He responded most readily to appeals for support of a proposition on the basis that it would promote prosperity. Elected officials recognized the force of this appeal and made the promotion of wealth and prosperity a common theme of inaugural addresses.

Optimism in attitudes and in rhetoric demonstrated that every improvement in the conditions of their lives seemed possible. These pioneers foresaw the wilderness becoming in a few years a great commonwealth and the abode of "millions" of free men. In the very spot where the deer now browsed, cities and temples of learning would soon rise. In frontier rhetoric advance was inevitable and immanent; civilization was flowing westward and prostrating the wild forests before it. Through honest toil, speakers confidently asserted, any man could earn a competence on the frontier and be rewarded with a life of freedom and independence.

Freedom was among the most highly valued aspects of life; no word was more sacred than *liberty*. A speaker almost invariably won applause when he denounced autocratic governments and praised liberty. To be a free man meant to the frontiersman absence of government restrictions, lack of restraint in moving from one area to another, and nearly uninhibited freedom in his personal life. It also meant to him that he was a citizen of a free nation. Frontier rhetoric became more fervent when it was offered in praise of Washington and his little band of warriors who had bought freedom with courage and at risk of their lives. Only a little less honored for their contributions to freedom were Jefferson and Jackson. Citizens named counties and towns in honor of these heroes, toasted them at celebrations, and idealized them as models of patriotism and courage. Not content with his own good fortune, the frontiersman wanted all to share in the blessings of liberty and looked forward to the day when the Republic would stretch from the Atlantic to the Pacific, when peoples everywhere would throw off the yoke of tyranny and know the joys of freedom.

Frontier rhetoric reflected the belief that a man who had helped to open up the wilderness and establish a home there deserved honor. Candidates for office asked for support on the basis of having helped to clear the land and free it from Indians and wild beasts. Speakers acknowledged the debt owed to early settlers as they vividly portrayed the deprivations and dangers, the loneliness, sickness, toil, and peril to life that they had endured.

Questions in every area of life took on the guise of moral issues. The man on the frontier assumed that God had made the frontier rich and beautiful for the pioneer's benefit and that, as a freeholder, he was under the special protection of the Deity. He linked the measures he supported with morality, those he opposed with evil. Jacksonian democrats contrasted the virtuous, hard-working farmer and mechanic with the smooth-handed and corrupt capitalist, their own conscious rectitude with their opponents' shameless depravity, brave frontiersmen with effete sons of the East, and plain, unostentatious Jacksonian partisans with cunning and arrogant officeholders. It was through the speakers' ability to associate republicanism and the plain man of common sense with virtue and morality that Jacksonian democracy derived much of its power on the frontier.

Accepting the Bible as the divine word of God, speakers assured listeners that reliance on God would bring prosperity and happiness to the area, that it would attract respectable and virtuous settlers. The Bible was the final authority, not only for saving souls, but for conduct in the legislature and the courtroom. Legislators announced support of a bill with the remark that they had been taught to read the Bible and believe what they read in it.[7] Lawyers argued the guilt or innocence of a client by citing biblical passages. Speakers assumed that listeners were familiar with the Bible and filled speeches with allusions to it. Linked with the Bible in the rhetoric of the time and place was the Constitution. Frontier speechmaking contained such symbols for the Constitution as *shield* and *buckler*, *bulwark* and *defense*. Acknowledging the Bible and the Constitution as authorities did not decrease the quarrels over interpretation of both, however, so

[7] See the speech of William Compton in report of legislative proceedings, Jefferson City *Jeffersonian Republican*, December 17, 1842, p. 3.

that the same passages were often interpreted in directly opposite ways and to support opposing views.

The differences in interpretation were encouraged by the practice of rarely defining terms. Often the attitudes and feelings of a speaker so aptly matched those of his listeners that any definition was unnecessary. The Missourian who proclaimed that no man answered to the name of federalist on the frontier, that all were republicans there, had no more need to define his terms for frontier audiences than to define the term *bastard*. Listeners understood what the speaker meant and how he felt about a proposition when he used words as an expression of an attitude rather than for their denotative value.

Life at the edge of civilization created an ambivalence toward the past, since the frontier tended to cut a man off from his earlier life and his ancestors and to throw him upon his own resources. Alexis de Tocqueville observed part of this phenomenon, on which he based his statement that democracy was a force separating man from his contemporaries and his past.[8] The Missourian of the frontier period agreed, frequently asserting that in a new land every man began life anew, but his practices denied his assertions. As soon as he could, he re-established the traditions and ceremonies that he had known in his old home. He followed the familiar models in organizing his state and local governments, in drawing up a constitution, and in setting up an educational system. He also carried with him his old religious beliefs. The old traditions and beliefs underwent some changes on the frontier, to be sure, and these changes took place more rapidly than in the settled areas, but the frontiersman developed no new philosophies of government, education, or religion. The frontier was a testing ground for philosophies and dogmas originating elsewhere, but if these beliefs differed too markedly from the settler's past experience he proved hostile to them. If the pioneer was truly thrown upon his own resources as Tocqueville declared, then he just as truly moved as rapidly as he could to re-establish the old patterns.

[8] Alexis de Tocqueville, *Democracy in America*, trans. by Henry Reeve, esq., II, 99.

Even the style of his rhetoric was similar to that of speakers in his old home. In both themes and language, frontier speakers imitated models that they had admired in the older states. Speechmaking in Missouri in pioneer years often contained florid passages, but the figures were no more elaborate than many used by Daniel Webster and John Randolph. The nineteenth century enjoyed a spacious rhetoric of elaborate figures and vivid denunciation, to which the frontiersman added creative metaphor and vituperation. Colloquialism found a ready place in the persuasion of the pioneer speaker, who used homely illustrations and idiomatic speech even in the courtroom and from the pulpit. On the frontier, speakers broke the flow of more or less formal language to introduce rough wit or terse ridicule of the opposition. But similar techniques were used by men such as Mike Walsh and John O'Sullivan, who were moving laboring men in the East to action. Nor did distinction lie in love of stentorian tones and rolling periods. True, Missouri audiences were hypnotized by the music of Uriel Wright's voice, but Emerson also succumbed to the "stately rhetoric" of Daniel Webster while paying little attention to his views.

Frontier rhetoric was in the mainstream of the national rhetoric of its day. It differed, primarily, on premises accepted by the frontier. The sovereign power of the people, the mobility of classes, the glorious future of the West, and the virtue of landholding were no more questioned by the frontier speaker and his audience than was reverence due to motherhood, God, and country. That the myths did not always conform to reality mattered little; the people believed the myths, accepted the slogans as guides to conduct, and acted upon their beliefs. That free decision by people who believed in their sovereignty contributed to the success of the experiments on the frontier is a confirmation of faith in the wisdom of the plain man of good sense.

A study of speeches in their historical and social context does more than disclose the quaint customs of a bygone day. It provides a reflection of the thoughts, motives, and attitudes of the speakers and listeners. Though an examination of frontier rhetoric does not reveal all the complex factors operating in a decision to act, it shows what speakers believed would influence their contemporaries' actions. A direct cause-effect relationship between the rhetoric and the dominance of Jacksonian democracy on the frontier can no more positively be established than can the direct effect of the artist upon his society, but the speeches of the time provide evidence that the rhetoric of the political philosophy corresponded closely and interacted with the attitudes and ideas of the frontier.

Frontier rhetoric carries within itself a warning to those who come after it. Men who repeat slogans or adapt arguments to accord with the assumptions of hearers in order to win a popular verdict may find that their future actions are thereby restricted. When slogans and arguments have been accepted as facts the people may adopt them as bases for action. The need for a rhetoric founded on reason and ethics is clearly illustrated by the study of the persuasive statements of public figures in a period and their relationship to the political and social climate of their time.

Selected Bibliography

I. MANUSCRIPT COLLECTIONS

Unless otherwise designated, all manuscripts are located in the Western Historical Manuscripts Division, The State Historical Society of Missouri, Columbia.

Anderson, Thomas, "Autobiography." Typed copy.

Athenaean Society of the University of Missouri, Records, 1842–1925. 13 vols.

Breckenridge, Thomas E., Memoirs, 1845–1894.

Brown, Henry J., Papers and Account Books.

Chambers and Knapp's Missouri and Illinois Almanac For the Year of Our Lord, 1848.

Drake, Charles D., "Autobiography." Typed manuscript.

Flint, Timothy, and Salmon Giddings, Letters to the Connecticut Missionaries in the West, 1814–1822. Typed copies. The State Historical Society of Missouri.

Forman, Ferris, Ferris Forman Letters.

Gentry, North Todd, North Todd Gentry Papers.

Journal of Proceedings of Louisiana Territory, June 3, 1806–December 24, 1818. Microfilm record, collected and edited by William S. Jenkins, The Library of Congress. Photo Duplication Service, 1949. The State Historical Society of Missouri.

Lanius, Jacob, "Diary." The Diary of a Methodist circuit rider, 1833–1842. 2 vols. Photostatic copy. The State Historical Society of Missouri.

Leonard, Abiel, Manuscript Collection.

Love, James A., Papers, including Records of Youths Debating Society and Fulton Lyceum Book.

Megown, Benton, History of New London Christian Church. Typed copy.

Payne, Moses, Papers and Account Books.

Rea, Peter Goodman, Papers, 1838–1869, including letters and biography of a Cooper County Cumberland Presbyterian minister.

Shackelford, Thomas, Papers, 1820–1908.

Sheppard, Charles, Letters, 1844–1877. Typed copies.

Yancy, Charles, Letters and papers, 1839–1865.

II. ARTICLES, ESSAYS, SPEECHES

Adams, Honorable Otis, "St. Louis in 1849." *Bulletin of the Missouri Historical Society*, VI, 3 (April, 1950), 368–76.

Allen, Stephen, Fourth of July Oration. [St. Charles] *The Missourian*, July 25, 1822, pp. 2–3.

Aly, Bower, "Rhetoric: Its Natural Enemies." *The Speech Teacher*, XVII, 1 (January, 1968), 1–10.

Anderson, Hattie M., "Evolution of a Frontier Society in Missouri, 1815–1828." *The Missouri Historical Review*, XXII, 3 (April, 1938), 298–326; XXII, 4 (July, 1938), 458–83; XXIII, 1 (October, 1938), 23–44.

Austin, Stephen, Fourth of July Oration. [St. Louis] *Missouri Gazette and Public Advertiser*, July 24, 1818, pp. 2–3.

Barton, David, Speech, delivered at a public dinner given in his honor in St. Louis, July 10, 1830. [Columbia] *Missouri Intelligencer and Boon's Lick Advertiser*, August 7, 1830, p. 1; August 14, 1830, pp. 1–2; September 4, 1830, p. 2.

———, Substance of speech, delivered in the Senate February 9 to February 11, 1830, on Foote's Resolution. *Register of Debates in Congress, Comprising the Leading Debates and Incidents of the First Session of the Twenty-First Congress; Together with an Appendix, Containing Important State Documents and the Laws Enacted During the Session: with a Copious Index to the Whole*, Part 1, Vol. VI, 146–59. Washington, D. C., Gales and Seaton, 1830. 14 vols.

"A Batch of Old Letters," 1840–1854. *Missouri Historical Society Collections*, II, 7 (October, 1906), 83–93.

Benton, Thomas Hart, Report of the Speech in opposition to government factories, delivered in the Senate, February, 1822. *St. Louis Enquirer*, May 11, 1822, pp. 2–3.

———, Substance of four-day speech, delivered in the Senate, February, 1830, on Foote's Resolution. *Register of Debates in Congress, Comprising the Leading Debates and Incidents of the First Session of the Twenty-First Congress; Together with an Appendix, Containing Important State Documents, and the Laws Enacted During the Session: with a Copious Index to the Whole*, Part 1, Vol. VI, 95–119. Washington, D. C., Gales and Seaton, 1830. 14 vols.

———, Speech in opposition to renewal of the charter of the national bank, delivered in the Senate on February 2, 1831. *St. Louis Beacon*, March 17, 1831, p. 2; March 24, 1831, pp. 1–3.

———, Substance of speech, delivered in the Senate on January 2 and 3, 1834, on the removal of federal deposits. [Jefferson City] *Jeffersonian Republican*, February 8, 1834, pp. 1–2; February 15, 1834, pp. 1–2; February 22, 1834, pp. 1–2; March 15, 1834, pp. 1–2; March 22, 1834, pp. 1–2; March 29, 1834, pp. 1–2.

———, Substance of speech, delivered at St. Louis October 19, 1844, on the presidential election. [Jefferson City] *Jefferson Inquirer*, November 7, 1844, pp. 1–2.

———, Substance of two speeches, delivered to the Democratic State Convention at Boonville, July 17 and 18, 1844. [Jefferson City] *Jefferson Inquirer*, August 1, 1844, pp. 1–2.

——, "Address to Colonel Doniphan and the returned volunteers, delivered at the Courthouse in St. Louis on July 2, 1847," in J. Thomas Scharf, *History of St. Louis City and County, from the Earliest Periods to the Present Day: Including Biographical Sketches of Representative Men*, I, 382–85. Philadelphia, Louis H. Everts and Company, 1883. 2 vols.

——, Appeal to the People of Missouri, delivered in the State Capitol, May 26, 1849. [Jefferson City] *Jefferson Inquirer*, May 26, 1849, pp. 2–3; June 2, 1849, pp. 1–2. Another text of the same speech was published in the *Fulton Telegraph*, June 1, 1848, pp. 1–2; June 8, 1849, pp. 1–2.

——, Speech, delivered at Fayette, September 1, 1849, with a note that some materials from other speeches are added. [Jefferson City] *Jefferson Inquirer*, October 6, 1849, pp. 1–4.

Bingham, George Caleb, Campaign Speech, Delivered at Arrow Rock, July 23, 1840, in reply to Dr. George Penn. [Fayette] *Boon's Lick Times*, August 8, 1840, p. 1.

Birch, James, Extracts from Jackson Day Address. *Fulton Telegraph*, January 26, 1849, p. 2.

Blue, John H., Address before the Chariton Polemic Society, *circa* November 17, 1840. [Fayette] *Boon's Lick Times*, January 9, 1841, p. 1.

"The Boon's Lick Country," *Bulletin of the Missouri Historical Society*, VI, 4 (July, 1950), 442–71.

"Boon's Lick Folk Tales." *Bulletin of the Missouri Historical Society*, VI, 4 (July, 1950), 472–90.

Boone, Banton G., "A Cause Celebre — Birch vs. Benton," in A. J. D. Stewart, ed., *The History of the Bench and Bar of Missouri*, 377–83. St. Louis, Legal Publishing Company, 1898.

Bowlin, Judge James B., Charge to prisoners in a murder trial held in St. Louis in 1841. [St. Louis] *Daily Missouri Republican*, June 2, 1841, p. 2.

——, Substance of speech on occupation of Oregon, delivered in Congress on January 15, 1845. [Jefferson City] *Jefferson Inquirer*, May 15, 1845, pp. 1–2.

Breckenridge, William Clark, "Biographical Sketch of Judge Wilson Primm." *Missouri Historical Society Collections*, IV, 2 (St. Louis, 1913), 127–59.

Broadhead, James O., "Reminiscences of Fifty-Five Years of Practice," in A. J. D. Stewart, ed., *The History of the Bench and Bar of Missouri*, 7–19. St. Louis, Legal Publishing Company, 1898.

Buford, Joseph, Speech in the General Assembly of Missouri, *circa* January, 1845. [Jefferson City] *Jefferson Inquirer*, January 17, 1845, p. 3.

Burch, Thomas C., Fourth of July Oration. [Franklin] *Missouri Intelligencer*, July 22, 1825, pp. 1–2.

Campbell, Isaac, Student oration on the subject of temperance, delivered at the close of Monticello School, *circa* March, 1843. [Fayette] *Boon's Lick Times*, April 1, 1843, p. 1.

Campbell, John I., Address in commemoration of New Orleans Day before citizens and members of the Missouri House of Representatives in the House of Representatives, January 8, 1845. [Jefferson City] *Jefferson Inquirer*, March 6, 1845, p. 1.

Carondelet [Francisco Luis Hector], Baron de, "Letter of Instructions from the Governor of the Province of Louisiana to Lieutenant Colonel Don Carlos Howard." *Missouri Historical Society Collections*, III, 1 (January, 1908), 71–91.

Carr, William C., Acceptance speech upon his election as presiding officer of the Territorial Assembly in 1812. [St. Louis] *Missouri Gazette*, December 19, 1812, p. 2.

——, Address to the Agricultural Society. [St. Louis] *Missouri Republican*, June 7, 1824, p. 3.

"The Case of Pourée Against Chouteau." *Missouri Historical Society Collections*, II, 2 (July, 1906), 68–80.

"Cerré, Jean Gabriel, A Sketch." *Missouri Historical Society Collections*, II, 2 (April, 1903), 58–76.

Chambers, William N., "As the Twig Is Bent: The Family and the North Carolina Years of Thomas Hart Benton, 1752–1801." *North Carolina Historical Review*, XXVI (October, 1949), 385–416.

Chouteau, Auguste, "Journal of the Founding of St. Louis." *Missouri Historical Society Collections*, IV [III], 5 (St. Louis, 1911), 335–66.

Clark, William, Message from the Governor to the Territorial Assembly. [St. Louis] *Missouri Gazette*, July 31, 1813, p. 2.

——, Message from the Governor to the Territorial Assembly. [St. Louis] *Missouri Gazette*, December 9, 1815, p. 3.

Cockerill, T. N., Fourth of July Oration. [Fayette] *The Western Monitor*, July 28, 1830, p. 2.

Compton, William W., Speech in the Missouri House of Representatives on the bill to provide for the sale of lands forfeited for nonpayment of taxes. [Jefferson City] *Jeffersonian Republican*, January 28, 1843, p. 1.

——, Speech in the Missouri House of Representatives. *Fulton Telegraph*, February 2, 1849, p. 1.

——, Speech in caucus of Democratic members of the Missouri House of Representatives, held in the Senate Chamber, *circa* December 16, 1842. [Jefferson City] *Jeffersonian Republican*, December 17, 1842, p. 2.

Conway, Reverend J. J., S. J., "The Beginning of Ecclesiastical Jurisdiction in the Archdiocese of St. Louis, 1764–1776." *Missouri Historical Society Collections*, I, 14 (1897), 1–40.

Copes, Thomas P., Fourth of July Oration. *St. Louis Beacon*, August 1, 1829, p. 1.

Culmer, Frederic A., "Abiel Leonard." *The Missouri Historical Review*, XXVII, 2 (January, 1933), 113–31; XXVII, 3 (April, 1933), 217–39; XXVII, 4 (July, 1933), 315–36; XXVIII, 1 (October, 1933), 17–37; XXVIII, 2 (January, 1934), 103–24.

Dalton, William J., *Address on the Pioneer Missionary Work of Father De Smet of the Jesuit Society*. Delivered before the Missouri Valley Historical Society, February 7, 1914. Pamphlet [n. p., n. d.]. The State Historical Society of Missouri, Columbia.

Dameron, George W., *Early Recollections and Biographical Sketches of Log Cabin Pioneers. Prominent Citizens of Pioneer Days*, Laura V. Balthis, ed. Pamphlet. Huntsville, Missouri, Herald Print, 1898.

Darby, John F., "Address before the Missouri Historical Society April 21, 1881, at St. Louis on the occasion of the Presentation of a Portrait of Samuel Gaty. *Missouri Historical Society Collections*, I, 5 (1880–1889), 1–8.

Douglas, Walter B., "Manuel Lisa." *Missouri Historical Society Collections*, III, 3 (St. Louis, 1911), 233–68; IV [III], 4 (St. Louis, 1911), 367–406.

Drumm, Stella M., "Samuel Hammond." *Missouri Historical Society Collections*, IV, 4 (St. Louis, 1923), 402–22.

Drunert, Mrs. A. H., "Historical Spots of Montgomery County." *The Missouri Historical Review*, XIX, 1 (October, 1924), 155–57.

Duncan, R. S., *A Memorial Sermon*. Preached at the Completion of the First Fifty Years History of the Bear Creek Baptist Association at Zion Church, Montgomery County, Missouri, August 17, 1904. Pamphlet [n. p., n. d.]. The State Historical Society of Missouri, Columbia.

Dunklin, Daniel P., Address to the Missouri Senate upon assuming the office of Lieutenant-Governor. [Fayette] *Missouri Intelligencer and Boon's Lick Advertiser*, November 23, 1828, p. 3.

——, Inaugural address upon assuming the office of Governor, delivered to the joint assembly of the Missouri House and Senate. *St. Louis Beacon*, December 6, 1832, p. 2.

Dunlap, James, "The Charlatan." *Pleasant Ridge Pearl*, published by the Union Literary and Padeusian Societies of Pleasant Ridge College, July, 1859. James Cash Penney Collection, The State Historical Society of Missouri, Columbia.

——, Presentation speech. *Pleasant Ridge Pearl*, July, 1859.

Earickson, Gustavus, Fourth of July Oration. [Franklin] *Missouri Intelligencer*, July 22, 1825, p. 1.

"Early Lutheranism in Missouri." *Theological Quarterly*, III, 3 (July, 1899), 319–33, based on correspondence of Ephraim R. Conrad to the Reverend David Henkel 1824–1829 concerning the formation of a Missouri Synod. Photostatic copy. The State Historical Society of Missouri, Columbia.

Everett, George, "Valedictory." *Pleasant Ridge Pearl*, published by the Union Literary and Padeusian Societies of Pleasant Ridge College, July, 1859 James Cash Penney Collection, The State Historical Society of Missouri, Columbia.

Finkelnburg, Hon. Gustavus, "Under Three Flags or the Story of St. Louis Briefly Told." *Missouri Historical Society Collections*, III, 3 (St. Louis, 1911), 201–32.

Fisk, Josiah, May Day address at Monticello Academy. [Fayette] *Boon's Lick Times*, May 28, 1842, p. 2.

Fitzgerald, Fred, "Daniel Dunklin." *The Missouri Historical Review*, XXI (1927), 395–403.

Gentry, North Todd, "David Todd." *The Missouri Historical Review*, XXI, 4 (July, 1927), 527–38.

Gordon, John B., Fourth of July Oration. [Columbia] *Missouri Intelligencer and Boon's Lick Advertiser*, July 11, 1835, p. 1.

Green, James S., Speech in Constitutional Convention of 1845 on the bill to exclude all but native-born citizens from eligibility to become governor. [Jefferson City] *Jefferson Inquirer*, November 29, 1845, p. 3.

——, Speech in Congress, delivered on January 25, 1848. [Jefferson City] *Jefferson Inquirer*, March 4, 1848, p. 1.

Gregg, Josiah, Fourth of July Oration. [Fayette] *Missouri Intelligencer and Boon's Lick Advertiser*, August 14, 1829, pp. 1–2.

Grissom, Daniel P., "Personal Recollections of Distinguished Missourians — Thomas Hart Benton." *The Missouri Historical Review*, XVIII, 2 (January, 1924), 129–45.

——, "Personal Recollections of Distinguished Missourians — James O. Broadhead." *The Missouri Historical Review*, XIX, 2 (January, 1925), 308–12.

——, "Personal Recollections of Distinguished Missourians — Hamilton Gamble." *The Missouri Historical Review*, XIX, 4 (July, 1925), 662–63.

——, "Personal Recollections of Distinguished Missourians — Claiborne Fox Jackson." *The Missouri Historical Review*, XX (1926), 504–8.

——, "Personal Recollections of Distinguished Missourians — Abiel Leonard." *The Missouri Historical Review*, XVIII, 3 (April, 1924), 400–403.

——, "Personal Recollections of Distinguished Missourians — James S. Rollins." *The Missouri Historical Review*, XVIII, 4 (July, 1924), 526–52.

——, "Personal Recollections of Distinguished Missourians — Uriel Wright." *The Missouri Historical Review*, XIX, 1 (October, 1924), 94–98.

Hall, J. W., "Gideon Blackburn," in W. B. Sprague, ed., *Annals of the American Pulpit*, IV, 43–58. New York, Robert Carter and Brothers, 1859. 9 vols.

Harrison, A. G., Speech on bill to grant preëmption to settlers, delivered in Congress, *circa* June 12, 1838. [Jefferson City] *Jeffersonian Republican*, July 14, 1838, pp. 1–2.

Hempstead, Edward, Speech on settlement of land claims, delivered in Congress in 1814. [St. Louis] *Missouri Gazette and Illinois Advertiser*, April 30, 1814, p. 2.

Hendricks, Littlebury, Substance of speech at ratification meeting held by Whigs in Springfield, Missouri, June 22, 1848, following the nomination of Zachary Taylor. [Columbia] *The Missouri Statesman*, July 14, 1848, p. 1.

Henry, John W., "Personal Recollections," in A. J. D. Stewart, ed., *The History of the Bench and Bar of Missouri*, 384–92. St. Louis, Legal Publishing Company, 1898.

Heth [Heath], John, Fourth of July Oration. [St. Louis] *Missouri Gazette*, August 2, 1808, pp. 1–4.

"Historical Notes and Comments." *Missouri Historical Review*, XLIX, 4 (July, 1955), 376–77.

Horwill, Herbert W., "The Fourth of July in America." *The Living Age*, XXXVI (August 3, 1907), 299–305.

Hough, Miss Sarah, Address of presentation of a flag to volunteers about to leave for Fort Leavenworth, and response by Captain Eastin. [Jefferson City] *Jefferson Inquirer*, June 17, 1846, p. 2.

Jervey, Edward D., and James E. Moss, eds., "The Journal of Elizabeth Ann Cooley." *Missouri Historical Review*, LX, 2 (January, 1966), 162–206.

Jewett, W. O. L., "The Early Bar of Northeast Missouri," in A. J. D. Stewart, ed., *The History of the Bench and Bar of Missouri*, 54–71. St. Louis, Legal Publishing Company, 1898.

Johnson, Charles P., "Personal Recollections of Some of Missouri's Eminent Statesmen and Lawyers." *Proceedings of the State Historical Society of Missouri at Its Second Annual Meeting Held January 22, 1903*. Palmyra, Missouri, pp. 54–60. Pamphlet. Posey Brothers Printers, 1903. The State Historical Society, Columbia, Missouri.

———, "Recollections of Criminal Practice," in A. J. D. Stewart, ed., *The History of the Bench and Bar of Missouri*, 90–108. St. Louis, Legal Publishing Company, 1898.

Jones, Claude, Speech on Independent County Representation, delivered in the Constitutional Convention of 1845. [Jefferson City] *Jefferson Inquirer*, December 23, 1845, pp. 1–2.

Kelso, John R., "Eloquence." *Pleasant Ridge Pearl*, published by the Union Literary and Padeusian Societies of Pleasant Ridge College, July, 1859. James Cash Penney Collection, The State Historical Society of Missouri, Columbia.

Kennerly, William Clark, "Early Days in St. Louis from the Memoirs of an Old Citizen." *Missouri Historical Society Collections*, III, 4 (St. Louis, 1911), 407–22.

King, Austin, Fourth of July Oration. [Columbia] *Missouri Intelligencer and Boon's Lick Advertiser*, August 10, 1833, pp. 1–2.

———, Inaugural address upon assuming the office of Governor, delivered to the joint assembly of the Missouri House and Senate. *Fulton Telegraph*, December 29, 1848, p. 1.

Kirkpatrick, R. L., "Professional, Religious, and Social Aspects of St. Louis Life, 1804–1816." *Missouri Historical Review*, XLIV, 4 (July, 1950), 373–86.

Krauthoff, L. C., "The Supreme Court in Missouri." *The Green Bag*, III (April, 1891), 157–90.

Lamm, Henry, "The Pettis Bar," in A. J. D. Stewart, ed., *The History of the Bench and Bar of Missouri*, 366–76. St. Louis, Legal Publishing Company, 1898.

Larson, Cedric, "Patriotism in Carmine: 162 Years of July 4th Oratory." *Quarterly Journal of Speech*, XXVI, 1 (February, 1940), 12–25.

Lathrop, John H., Address on the subject of education, delivered to the joint assembly of the Missouri House and Senate. [Jefferson City] *Jeffersonian Republican*, December 31, 1842, pp. 1–2.

Lawson, L. M., "Founding and Location of William Jewell College." *Missouri Historical Society Collections*, IV, 3 (St. Louis, 1914), 275–89.

Lockridge, Miss N. F., Valedictory address at the closing of school. [Fayette] *Boon's Lick Times*, July 23, 1842, p. 1.

McAfee, Charles B., "Riding the Circuits in Southwest Missouri," in A. J. D. Stewart, ed., *The History of the Bench and Bar of Missouri*, 72–78. St. Louis, Legal Publishing Company, 1898.

McCurdy, Frances Lea, "Frontier Invective." *Quarterly Journal of Speech*, XLVI, 1 (February, 1960), 54–58.

———, "Courtroom Oratory of the Pioneer Period." *Missouri Historical Review*, LVI, 1 (October, 1961), 1–11.

———, "The Genius of Liberty." *Missouri Historical Review*, LVII, 4 (July, 1963), 331–43.

Marshall, Thomas M., ed., "The Journal of Henry B. Miller." *Missouri Historical Society Collections*, VI, 3 (1931), 213–87.

Marvin, Enoch M., *Sermons*, T. O. Summers, ed. Nashville, Tennessee, Publishing House of the Methodist Episcopal Church, South, 1877.

Mattis, Norman W., "Thomas Hart Benton," in Marie Hochmuth and W. N. Brigance, eds., *A History and Criticism of American Public Address Prepared under the Auspices of the Speech Association of America*. Vols. I, II, New York, McGraw-Hill Book Company, 1943; Vol. III, New York, Longmans, Green and Company, 1955, 52–95. 3 vols.

Mayes, Daniel, *An Address to the Students of Law in Transylvania University*. Lexington, Thomas J. Pew, 1838. Pamphlet bound in *Miscellany*, XIV, 1–32, The State Historical Society of Missouri, Columbia.

Metzger, Walter, "Generalizations About National Character: An Analytical Essay," in Louis Gottschalk, ed., *Generalization in the Writing of History*, 77–102. Chicago Press, 1963.

Miller, Henry B., "The Journal of Henry B. Miller," Thomas Maitland Marshall, ed. *Missouri Historical Society Collections*, VI, 3 (1931), 213–87.

Miller, John C., Inaugural address upon assuming the office of Governor, delivered to the joint assembly of the Missouri House and Senate. [Columbia] *Missouri Intelligencer and Boon's Lick Advertiser*, November 23, 1828, pp. 1–3.

———, Farewell message to the joint assembly of the Missouri House and Senate. *St. Louis Beacon*, December 6, 1832, p. 2.

Miller, J. W., Inauguration address as president of Columbia College at Columbia, Missouri. [Columbia] *Missouri Intelligencer and Boon's Lick Advertiser*, December 13, 1834, pp. 1–2.

Minor, James, Address at the laying of the cornerstone of the State University, July 4, 1840, in Columbia, Missouri. [Jefferson City] *Jeffersonian Republican*, September 12, 1840, pp. 1–2.

"Missouri History Not Found in Textbooks." *Missouri Historical Review*, L, 1 (October, 1955), 111.

Moody, D. F., "The Mind." *Pleasant Ridge Pearl*, published by the Union Literary and Padeusian Societies of Pleasant Ridge College, July, 1859. James Cash Penney Collection, The State Historical Society of Missouri, Columbia.

Moore, Samuel, Fourth of July Oration. [Fayette] *Missouri Intelligencer and Boon's Lick Advertiser*, August 28, 1829, pp. 1–2.

Morrow, James W., Eulogy of Andrew Jackson, delivered at a public meeting in Jefferson City, July 8, 1845. [Jefferson City] *Jefferson Inquirer*, July 31, 1845, p. 1.

Munger, George, "The Cook Family of Southeast Missouri." *The Missouri Historical Review*, XXIII, 5 (July, 1929), 568–74.

"Murder at Big Prairie." *Bulletin of the Missouri Historical Society*, VI, 2 (January, 1950), 225–33.

Norton, Elijah Hise, "The Bench and Bar of Platte Purchase," in A. J. D. Stewart, ed., *The History of the Bench and Bar of Missouri*, 358–65. St. Louis, Legal Publishing Company, 1898.

Oberholzer, Emil, "The Legal Aspects of Slavery in Missouri," *Bulletin of the Missouri Historical Society*, VI, 1, 2 (January, 1950), 139–61; VI, 3 (April, 1950), 333–51; VI, 4 (July, 1950), 540–45.

Ormond, Joseph, Fourth of July Oration. [Franklin] *Missouri Intelligencer*, August 5, 1822, pp. 1–2.

Parrish, Susan, and other ladies, Speeches to stimulate donations for establishing a college at Liberty, Missouri. [Liberty] *The Weekly Tribune*, January 16, 1847, pp. 1–2.

Peerce, Willie, Lecture on education. [Fayette] *Missouri Intelligencer and Boon's Lick Advertiser*, October 26, 1827, pp. 1–2.

Pettibone, Rufus, Address to St. Charles Agricultural and Manufacturing Society on July 17, 1822. [St. Charles] *The Missourian*, July 25, 1822, pp. 1–2; August 1, 1822, pp. 1–2.

Philips, John F., *Reminiscences of Some Deceased Lawyers of Central Missouri*. Address delivered before the Missouri State Bar Association at St. Louis, September 24, 1914. Pamphlet [n. p., n. d.].

———, "The Lawyer in Missouri One Hundred Years Ago." *The Missouri Historical Review*, XIII, 4 (July, 1919), 377–85.

Porter, V. M., "A History of Battery 'A' of St. Louis." *Missouri Historical Society Collections*, II, 4 (March, 1905), 1–48.

Porter, W. H., Address to Female Department of Howard College. [Fayette] *Boon's Lick Times*, October 23, 1841, p. 1.

Pratte, General Bernard, Jr., "The Reminiscences of General Bernard Pratte, Jr." *Bulletin of the Missouri Historical Society*, VI, 1 (October, 1949), 59–65.

Primm, Wilson, "History of St. Louis." *Missouri Historical Society Collections*, IV, 2 (St. Louis, 1913), 160–93.

———, "New Year's Day in the Olden Time of St. Louis." *Missouri Historical Society Collections*, II, 1 (January, 1900), 12–22.

Rollins, C. B., "Some Recollections of George Caleb Bingham." *The Missouri Historical Review*, XX (1926), 463–81.

Rollins, James S., Eulogy of General Lafayette, delivered at a public meeting in Columbia. [Columbia] *Missouri Intelligencer and Boon's Lick Advertiser*, July 19, 1834, pp. 1–2.

———, Speech on care of the insane, delivered to the Missouri House of Representatives. [Liberty] *The Weekly Tribune*, March 20, 1847, p. 1.

Rothensteiner, John E., "The Missouri Priest One Hundred Years Ago." *The Missouri Historical Review*, XXI, 4 (July, 1927), 562–69.

Russell, Colonel William, Farewell to troops. [St. Louis] *Missouri Gazette and Public Advertiser*, June 17, 1815, p. 3.

Russell, William H., Temperance address, delivered in Columbia, Missouri. [Columbia] *Missouri Intelligencer and Boon's Lick Advertiser*, October 18, 1834, pp. 1–2.

Schafly, The Reverend James J., "Birth of Kansas City's Pioneer Church." *Missouri Historical Review*, XLIV, 4 (July, 1950), 364–72.

Schmidt, Joseph H., "Recollections of the First Catholic Mission Work in Central Missouri." *The Missouri Historical Review*, V, 2 (January, 1911), 83–93.

Scott, John, Speech on the contested election, delivered in Congress. [St. Louis] *Missouri Gazette*, April 19, 1817, pp. 1–2.

———, Report of the Speech on the Missouri question, delivered in Congress. [St. Louis] *Missouri Gazette and Public Advertiser*, May 5, 1819, pp. 1–2; May 12, 1819, pp. 1–2.

Shackelford, Thomas, "Early Recollections of Missouri." *Missouri Historical Society Collections*, II, 2 (April, 1903), 1–19.

———, "Reminiscences of the Bench and Bar of Central Missouri," in A. J. D. Stewart, ed., *The History of the Bench and Bar of Missouri*, 393–406. St. Louis, Legal Publishing Company, 1898.

Shields, George H., "The Old Bar of St. Louis," in A. J. D. Stewart, ed., *The History of the Bench and Bar of Missouri*, 109–26. St. Louis, Legal Publishing Company, 1898.

Shoemaker, Floyd C., "Fathers of the State." *The Missouri Historical Review*, X, 1 (October, 1915), 1–32.

Simmons, Lucy, "The Rise and Growth of Protestant Bodies in the Missouri

Territory." *The Missouri Historical Review*, XXII, 3 (April, 1928), 296–306.

Squires, Monas N., "A New View of the Election of Barton and Benton to the United States Senate." *The Missouri Historical Review*, XXVII, 1 (October, 1932), 28–45.

Stokes, Durward T., ed., "The Wilson Letters." *Missouri Historical Review*, LX, 4 (July, 1966), 495–517.

Thornton, John, Acceptance speech upon his assumption of office as speaker of the Missouri House of Representatives. [Columbia] *Missouri Intelligencer and Boon's Lick Advertiser*, November 23, 1828, p. 1.

Thwaites, Reuben Gold, "William Clark: Soldier, Explorer, Statesman." *Missouri Historical Society Collections*, II, 7 (October, 1906), 1–24.

Vandiver, W. D., "Reminiscences of General John B. Clark." *The Missouri Historical Review*, XX (1926), 223–35.

Van Ravenswaay, Charles, "The Tragedy of David Barton." *Bulletin of the Missouri Historical Society*, VII, 1 (October, 1950), 35–56.

———, "Judge Mathias McGirk." *Bulletin of the Missouri Historical Society*, VIII, 3 (April, 1952), 244–48.

———, "Architecture in the Boon's Lick Country." *Bulletin of the Missouri Historical Society*, VI, 4 (July, 1950), 491–502.

Waldo, William, "Recollections of a Septuagenarian." *Missouri Historical Society Collections*, I, 2 (1880–1889), 1–18.

Waugh, Alfred S., "Desultory Wanderings in the Years 1845–46," John F. McDermott, ed. *Bulletin of the Missouri Historical Society*, VI, 3 (April, 1950), 288–322; VI, 4 (July, 1950), 503–20; VII, 1 (October, 1950), 95–123; VII, 2 (January, 1951), 216–64; VII, 3 (April, 1951), 347–65.

Weiner, Alan, "Thomas Hart Benton, David Barton and the 1824 Presidential Election. . . ." *Missouri Historical Review*, LX, 4 (July, 1966), 460–94.

Wells, Robert, Substance of campaign speech, delivered at a public meeting in St. Louis October 17, 1831. *St. Louis Beacon*, October 20, 1831, pp. 2–3.

Woodard, W. S., *A Centennial Sermon or One Hundred Years of Methodism in Missouri*. Preached for the Veteran Missouri Methodist Preachers Association before the St. Louis Conference in Poplar Bluff, Missouri, September 20, 1906. Pamphlet. Nashville, Tennessee, Publishing House of the Methodist Episcopal Church, South, 1906. Copy in the State Historical Society of Missouri, Columbia.

Yantis, J. L., An Address at the Examination of Pupils at the Columbia Female Academy, 1841. *Miscellany*, The State Historical Society of Missouri, Columbia, pp. 1–12.

III. BOOKS

Atherton, Lewis E., *The Pioneer Merchant in Mid-America*. Columbia, University of Missouri Studies, 1939.

Babcock, Rufus, ed., *Forty Years of Pioneer Life, Memoirs of John Mason Peck, D. D. Edited from His Journals and Correspondence*. Philadelphia, American Baptist Publication Society, 1864.

Barns, C. R., ed., *The Commonwealth of Missouri; a Centennial Record*. St. Louis, Bryan, Brand and Company, 1877.

Bates, Frederick, *The Life and Papers of Frederick Bates*, Thomas Maitland Marshall, ed. St. Louis, Missouri Historical Society, 1926. 2 vols.

Bay, W. V. N., *Reminiscences of the Bench and Bar of Missouri with an Appendix, Containing Biographical Sketches of Nearly all of the Judges and Lawyers Who Have Passed Away, Together with Many Interesting and Valuable Letters Never Before Published of Washington, Jefferson, Burr, Granger, Clinton, and Others, Some of Which Throw Additional Light upon the Famous Burr Conspiracy*. St. Louis, F. H. Thomas and Company, 1878.

Billington, Ray Allen, *Westward Expansion: A History of the American Frontier*. New York, The Macmillan Company, 1949.

Billon, Frederic L., *Annals of St. Louis in Its Early Days under the French and Spanish Dominations*. St. Louis, Printed for the Author, 1886.

———, *Annals of St. Louis in Its Territorial Days from 1804 to 1821*. St. Louis, Printed for the Author, 1888.

Bingham, Caleb, *The Columbian Orator: Containing a Variety of Original and Selected Pieces; together with Rules . . .* Troy, New York, Printed and Sold by William S. Parker, 1821.

Boyton, Percy Holmes, *The Rediscovery of the Frontier*. Chicago, The University of Chicago Press, 1931.

Brackenridge, Henry Marie, *Recollections of Persons and Places in the West*. 2d ed., enlarged. Philadelphia, J. B. Lippincott and Company, 1868.

———, *Views of Louisiana; Together with a Journal of a Voyage up the Missouri River, in 1811*. Pittsburgh, Cramer, Spear and Eichbaum, 1814.

Briggs, Joshua Ely, and Ruth Floweree, *A Pioneer Missourian*. Boston, Christopher Publishing House, 1939.

Britton, Wiley, *Pioneer Life in Southwest Missouri*. Rev., enlarged ed. Kansas City, Smith-Grieves Company, 1939.

Brinton, Crane, *The Shaping of the Modern Mind*. New York, New American Library. A Mentor Book, 1953.

Bryan, William S., and Robert Rose, *A History of the Pioneer Families of Missouri, with Numerous Sketches, Anecdotes, Adventures, etc., Relating to Early Days in Missouri; Also the Lives of Daniel Boone and the Celebrated Indian Chief Black Hawk, with Numerous Biographies and Histories of Primitive Institutions*. St. Louis, Bryan, Brand and Company, 1876.

Carter, Clarence Edwin, ed., *The Territory of Louisiana-Missouri, 1803–1806*. Vol. XIII, *The Territorial Papers of the United States*. Washington, D. C., United States Government Printing Office, 1934– ———. 26 vols.

————, *The Territory of Louisiana-Missouri, 1806–1814.* Vol. XIV, *The Territorial Papers of the United States.* Washington, D.C., United States Government Printing Office, 1934– ————. 26 vols.

————, *The Territory of Louisiana-Missouri, 1815–1821.* Vol. XV, *The Territorial Papers of the United States.* Washington, D. C., United States Government Printing Office, 1934– ————. 26 vols.

Chambers, William Nisbet, *Old Bullion Benton: Senator from the New West. Thomas Hart Benton, 1782–1858.* Boston, Little Brown and Company, 1956.

Chittenden, Hiram M., and Alfred Talbot Richardson, *Life, Letters and Travels of Father Pierre-Jean De Smet, S. J., 1801–1873. Missionary Labors and Adventures Among the Wild Tribes of the North American Indians, Embracing Minute Descriptions of Their Manners, Customs, Games, Modes of Warfare and Torture, Legends, Traditions, etc., All from Personal Observations Made During Many Thousand Miles of Travel, with Sketches of the Country from St. Louis to Puget Sound and The Altrabasca Edited from the Original Unpublished Manuscript Journals and Letter Books and from His Printed Works with Historical, Geographical, Ethnological and other Notes; Also a Life of Father De Smet.* New York, Francis P. Harper, 1905. 4 vols.

Clark, Thomas D., *Frontier America: The Story of the Westward Movement.* New York, Charles Scribner's Sons, 1959.

————, *The Rampaging Frontier; Manners and Humors of Pioneer Days in the South and the Middle West.* Indianapolis, The Bobbs-Merrill Company, Inc., 1939.

Clemens, Samuel, *The Adventures of Huckleberry Finn.* New York, Harper and Brothers, 1931.

————, *The Art, Humor, and Humanity of Mark Twain.* Minnie M. Brashear and Robert Rodney, eds. Norman, University of Oklahoma Press, 1959.

Conard, Howard L., ed., *Encyclopedia of the History of Missouri, a Compendium of History and Biography for Ready Reference.* New York, The Southern History Company, 1901. 6 vols.

Dale, Edward Everett, *Frontier Ways; Sketches of Life in the Old West.* Austin, University of Texas Press, 1959.

Dale, Harrison C., *The Ashley-Smith Explorations and the Discovery of a Central Route to the Pacific, 1822–1829.* Cleveland, Arthur H. Clark, 1918.

Dalton, Reverend William J., *The Life of Father Bernard Donnelley.* Kansas City, Missouri, Grimes-Joyce Printing Company, 1921.

Darby, John F., *Personal Recollections of Many Prominent People Whom I Have Known, and of Events — Especially of Those Relating to the History of St. Louis — During the First Half of the Present Century.* St. Louis, G. I. Jones and Company, 1880.

Duncan, R. S., *A History of the Baptists in Missouri Embracing An Account of the Organization and Growth of Baptist Churches and Associations; Biographical Sketches of Ministers of the Gospel and Other Prominent Members of the Denomination: The Institutions, Periodicals, etc.* St. Louis, Scammell and Company, 1882.

Edwards, Richard, and M. Hopewell, *Edwards's Great West and Her Commercial Metropolis Embracing a General view of the West, and a Complete History of St. Louis, from the Landing of Ligueste to the Present Time.* St. Louis, Published at the office of Edwards's Monthly, 1860.

English, William Francis, *The Pioneer Lawyer and Jurist in Missouri.* University of Missouri Studies, XXI, 2. Columbia, University of Missouri, 1947.

Ewing, Robert C., *Historical Memoirs: Containing a Brief History of the Cumberland Presbyterian Church in Missouri, and Biographical Sketches of a Number of Those Ministers Who Contributed to the Organization and the Establishment of that Church, in the Country West of the Mississippi River.* Nashville, Tennessee, Cumberland Presbyterian Board of Publication, 1874.

Finney, Charles Grandison, *Lectures on the Revivals of Religion.* Boston, J. Jewett and Company, 1858.

Finney, Thomas M., *The Life and Labors of Enoch Mather Marvin, Late Bishop of the Methodist Episcopal Church, South.* St. Louis, James H. Chambers, 1880.

Flint, Timothy, *Recollections of the Last Ten Years, Passed in Occasional Residences and Journeyings in the Valley of the Mississippi, from Pittsburg and the Missouri to the Gulf of Mexico, and from Florida to the Spanish Frontier; in a Series of Letters to the Reverend James Flint, of Salem, Massachusetts.* Boston, Cummings, Hilliard, and Company, 1826.

Fordham, Elias Pym, *Personal Narrative of Travels in Virginia, Maryland, Pennsylvania, Ohio, Indiana, Kentucky; and of a Residence in the Illinois Territory: 1817–1818,* Frederick Austin Ogg, ed. Cleveland, The Arthur H. Clark Company, 1906.

Franklin, Benjamin, *The Writings of Benjamin Franklin,* Albert Henry Smyth, ed. New York, The Macmillan Company, 1905–1907. 10 vols.

Gentry, North Todd, *The Bench and Bar of Boone County, Missouri.* Columbia, Missouri, Published by the Author, 1916.

Gottschalk, Louis, ed., *Generalization in the Writing of History; A Report.* Chicago, The University of Chicago Press, 1963.

History of Howard and Cooper Counties. St. Louis, National Historical Company, 1883.

History of Saline County. St. Louis, Missouri Historical Company, 1881.

Hofstadter, Richard, *The Age of Reform.* New York, Random House. A Vintage Book, 1955.

Houck, Louis, *A History of Missouri from the Earliest Explorations and Settlements until the Admission of the State into the Union.* Chicago, R. R. Donnelley and Sons Company, 1908. 3 vols.

————, *The Spanish Regime in Missouri: A Collection of Papers and Documents Relating to Upper Louisiana Principally within the Present Limits of Missouri during the Dominion of Spain, from the Archives of the Indies at Seville, Etc., Translated from the Original Spanish into English, and Including Also Some Papers Concerning the Supposed Grant to Colonel George Morgan at the Mouth of the Ohio, Found in the Congressional Library, Edited with an Introduction and Notes, Biographical and Explanatory.* Chicago, R. R. Donnelley and Sons Company, 1909. 2 vols.

Hyde, Laurance, *Historical Review of the Judicial System of Missouri.* Kansas City, Missouri, Vernon Law Book Company, 1952.

Hyde, William, and Howard L. Conard, eds., *Encyclopedia of the History of St. Louis, a Compendium of History and Biography for Ready Reference.* St. Louis, The Southern History Company, 1899. 4 vols.

Jackson, William Rufus, *Missouri Democracy, a History of the Party and its Representative Members — Past and Present.* St. Louis, S. J. Clarke Publishing Company, Inc., 1935. 3 vols.

Jamieson, Alexander, *A Grammar of Rhetoric and Polite Literature . . . With Rules For the Study of Composition and Eloquence.* New Haven, A. H. Maltby, 1837.

Johnson, Allen, Dumas Malone, and Harris E. Starr, eds., *Dictionary of American Biography, Published under the Auspices of the American Council of Learned Societies.* Centenary edition. New York, Charles Scribner's Sons, 1946. 22 vols.

Johnson, Charles A., *The Frontier Camp Meeting: Religion's Harvest Time.* Dallas, Southern Methodist University Press, 1955.

Kirkpatrick, John E., *Timothy Flint, Pioneer, Missionary, Author, Editor, 1780–1840; the Story of His Life Among the Pioneers and Frontiersmen in the Ohio and Mississippi Valley and In New England and the South.* Cleveland, Ohio, The Arthur H. Clark Company, 1911.

Larkin, Lew, *Bingham: Fighting Artist; the Story of Missouri's Immortal Painter, Patriot, Soldier, and Statesman.* Kansas City, Missouri, Burton Publishing Company, Incorporated, 1954.

Lawson, John D., ed., *American State Trials.* Vol. II, 1914; Vol. X, 1918; Vol. XVI, 1928. St. Louis, Thomas Law Book Company, 1914–1936. 17 vols.

Lowry, Thomas Jefferson, *A Sketch of the University of the State of Missouri.* Columbia, Missouri, Herald Publishing Company, n. d.

McAnally, David R., *History of Methodism in Missouri; from the Date of Its Introduction, in 1806, down to the Present Day; with an Appendix, Containing Full and Accurate Statistical Information, etc.* Vol. I. St. Louis, Advocate Publishing House, 1881. 1 vol.

Maple, J. C., and R. P. Rider, *Missouri Baptist Biography: A Series of Life-Sketches Indicating the Growth and Prosperity of the Baptist Churches as Represented in the Lives and Labors of Eminent Men and Women in*

Missouri. Vol. II. Liberty, Missouri, Published by the Liberty Advance, 1916. 5 vols.

March, David D., *The History of Missouri.* New York, Lewis Historical Company, Inc., 1967. 4 vols.

Marvin, Enoch Mather, *The Life of Reverend William Goff Caples, of the Missouri Conference of the Methodist Episcopal Church, South.* St. Louis, Southwestern Book and Publishing Company, 1870.

Meigs, William M., *The Life of Thomas Hart Benton.* Philadelphia, J. B. Lippincott Company, 1924.

Meyers, Marvin, *The Jacksonian Persuasion: Politics and Belief.* Stanford, California, Stanford University Press, 1957.

Musick, John R., *Stories of Missouri.* New York, American Book Company, 1897.

Neuhoff, Dorothy, *The Platte Purchase.* Humanistic Series, Vol. XI, 2. Reprinted from *Washington University Studies.* St. Louis, Washington University, 1924.

Parrish, William E., *David Rice Atchison of Missouri, Border Politician.* Columbia, University of Missouri Press, 1961.

Paul Wilhelm, Duke of Württemberg, *First Journey to North America in the Years 1822 to 1824,* trans. by William G. Bek. Stuttgart and Tübingen, J. B. Cotta, 1835.

Peters, George L., *The Disciples of Christ in Missouri, Celebrating One Hundred Years of Cooperative Work.* Kansas City, Missouri, The Centennial Commission, 1937.

Robb, John S., *The Swamp Doctor's Adventures in the Southwest, Containing the Whole of the Louisiana Swamp Doctor, Streaks of Squatter Life and Far Western Scenes . . . by Madison Tensas, M.D., and "Solitaire" (John S. Robb of St. Louis, Mo.).* Philadelphia, T. B. Peterson, 1843. 2 vols.

Rothensteiner, Reverend John, *History of the Archdiocese of St. Louis in Its Various Stages of Development from A.D. 1673 to A.D. 1928.* St. Louis, Blackwell Wielandy Company, 1928. 2 vols.

Scharf, J. Thomas, *History of St. Louis City and County, from the Earliest Periods to the Present Day: Including Biographical Sketches of Representative Men.* Philadelphia, Louis H. Everts and Company, 1883. 2 vols.

Schlesinger, Arthur M., Jr., *The Age of Jackson.* Boston, Little, Brown and Company, 1945.

Shoemaker, Floyd Calvin, *Missouri and Missourians: Land of Contrasts and People of Achievements.* Chicago, The Lewis Publishing Company, 1943. 5 vols.

———, *Missouri's Struggle for Statehood, 1804–1821.* Jefferson City, Missouri, The Hugh Stephens Printing Company, 1916.

Smith, Henry Nash, *Virgin Land; The American West As Symbol and Myth.* Cambridge, Harvard University Press, 1950.

Smith, Timothy Lawrence, *Revivalism and Social Reform in Mid-Nineteenth Century America*. New York, Abingdon Press, 1957.

Smith, William B., *James Sidney Rollins: Memoir*. New York, Printed at the Devinne Press, 1891.

Smyth, Albert Henry, ed., *The Writings of Benjamin Franklin*. New York, The Macmillan Company, 1905-1907. 10 vols.

Sprague, William B., *Annals of the American Pulpit; or Commemorative Notices of Distinguished American Clergymen of Various Denominations, from the Early Settlement of the Country to the Close of the Year 1855, with Historical Introductions*. Vol. IV. New York, Robert Carter and Brothers, 1859. 12 vols.

Stevens, Walter B., *Centennial History of Missouri (The Center State) One Hundred Years in the Union, 1820-1921*. St. Louis, The S. J. Clarke Publishing Company, 1921. 6 vols.

Stewart, A. J. D., ed., *The History of the Bench and Bar of Missouri, with Reminiscences of the Prominent Lawyers of the Past, and a Record of the Law's Leaders of the Present Containing also Personal Recollections and Articles Contributed by the Most Eminent Jurists, Able Lawyers and Learned Authorities in the State*. St. Louis, The Legal Publishing Company, 1898.

Stoddard, Amos, *Sketches, Historical and Descriptive, of Louisiana*. Philadelphia, Mathew Carey, 1812.

Sweet, William Warren, *Religion on the American Frontier: The Baptists, 1783-1840, A Collection of Source Material*. Vol. I, Religion on the American Frontier Series. New York, Henry Holt and Company, 1931. 4 vols.

————, *Religion on the American Frontier: The Presbyterians, 1783-1840, A Collection of Source Materials*. Vol. II, Religion on the American Frontier Series. New York, Harper and Brothers, 1936.

————, *Religion on the American Frontier: The Methodists, A Collection of Source Materials*. Vol. IV, Religion on the American Frontier Series. Chicago, The University of Chicago Press, 1946.

————, *Revivalism in America, Its Origin, Growth, and Decline*. New York, Charles Scribner's Sons, 1944.

Switzler, William F., *Illustrated History of Missouri from 1541 to 1877*. St. Louis, C. R. Barns, 1879.

Taylor, George Rogers, ed., *The Turner Thesis Concerning the Role of the Frontier in American History*, Problems in American Civilization. Rev. ed. Boston, D. C. Heath and Company, 1955.

Tocqueville, Alexis de, *Democracy in America*, trans. by Henry Reeve, esq. 4th ed., rev. and corrected from the 8th Paris ed. New York, J. and H. G. Langley, 1841. 2 vols.

Tyler, Alice Felt, *Freedom's Ferment; Phases of American Social History From The Colonial Period to the Outbreak of the Civil War*. New York, Harper and Brothers, 1962.

Violette, Eugene Morrow, *A History of Missouri*. Reprint ed. Cape Girardeau, Missouri, Ramfre Press, 1953.

Ward, John William, *Andrew Jackson, Symbol for an Age*. New York, Oxford University Press, 1955.

Weaver, Richard M., *The Ethics of Rhetoric*. Chicago, H. Regnery Company, 1953.

Webb, Walter Prescott, *The Great Frontier*. Boston, Houghton Mifflin Company, 1952.

Weisberger, Bernard A., *They Gathered at the River, The Story of the Great Revivalists and Their Impact upon Religion in America*. Boston, Little, Brown and Company, 1958.

Wetmore, Alphonse, *Gazetteer of the State of Missouri with a Map of the State from the Office of the Surveyor-General, Including the Latest Additions and Surveys to Which Is Added an Appendix Containing Frontier Sketches, and Illustrations of Indian Character*. St. Louis, C. Keemle, 1837.

Williams, James, *Seventy-Five Years on the Border*. Kansas City, Missouri, Press of Standard Printing Company, 1912.

Wright, Louis B., *Culture on the Moving Frontier*. Bloomington, Indiana University Press, 1955.

Woodard, W. S., *Annals of Methodism in Missouri, Containing an Outline of the Ministerial Life of More Than One Thousand Preachers, and Sketches of More Than Three Hundred, Also Sketches of Charges, Churches and Laymen from the Beginning in 1806 to the Centennial Year, 1884, Containing Seventy-Eight Years of History*. Columbia, Missouri, E. W. Stephens, 1893.

Wyman, Walter DeMarquis, *The Frontier in Perspective*. Walker D. Wyman and Clifton B. Kroeber, eds. Madison, The University of Wisconsin Press, 1957.

Yealey, Francis J., *Sainte Genevieve, The Story of Missouri's Oldest Settlement*. [n. p.], The Bicentennial Historical Committee, 1935.

IV. STATE AND NATIONAL DOCUMENTS

DeBow, J. D. B., ed., *The Seventh Census of the United States 1850, Embracing a Statistical View of Each of the States and Territories, Arranged by Counties, Towns, Etc.* Washington, D. C., Robert Armstrong, public printer, 1853.

Journal of the House of Representatives of the State of Missouri, at the First Session of the First General Assembly: Begun and Held in the town of St. Louis, on Monday the 18th September, 1820. St. Louis, Printed by Edward Charless and Company, 1822.

Journal of the Missouri State Convention. Photo facsimile reprint. St. Louis, I. N. Henry and Company, 1820.

Journal of the Senate of the State of Missouri at the First Session of the First General Assembly Begun and Held in the Town of St. Louis, Monday the 18th September, 1820. Photostatic copy. St. Charles, Printed by Robert McLeod, 1822.

Laws of the State of Missouri; Revised and Digested by Authority of the General Assembly. St. Louis, Printed by E. Charless for the State, 1825. 2 vols.

Register of Debates in Congress Comprising the Leading Debates and Incidents of the First Session of the Twenty-First Congress; Together with an Appendix Containing Important State Papers and Public Documents and the Laws Enacted During the Session: with a Copious Index to the Whole. Vol. VI. Washington, D. C., Gales and Seaton, 1825–1837. 14 vols.

The Revised Statutes of Missouri; Revised and Digested by the Thirteenth General Assembly, during the Session of Eighteen Hundred and Forty-Four and Eighteen Hundred and Forty-Five; to Which are Prefixed the Constitutions of the United States and of the State of Missouri, Printed under the Superintendence of William Claude Jones, Commissioner. St. Louis, Printed for the State by J. W. Dougherty, 1845.

The Revised Statutes of the State of Missouri; Revised and Digested by the Eighth General Assembly during the Years One Thousand Eight Hundred and Thirty-Four, and One Thousand Eight Hundred and Thirty-Five, Printed and Published under the Direction of the Superintendent Appointed by the General Assembly for that Purpose. St. Louis, Printed at the Argus Office, 1835.

V. UNPUBLISHED STUDIES

Barton, Frank L., "History of the Academy in Missouri." Master's thesis, University of Missouri, Columbia, 1910.

Bates, Evelyn, "A History of the Presbyterian Church in Missouri to 1860." Master's thesis, University of Missouri, Columbia, 1939.

Gordon, Joseph F., "The Public Career of Lilburn W. Boggs." Master's thesis, University of Missouri, Columbia, 1949.

Hartley, James Robert, "The Political Career of Lewis Fields Linn." Master's thesis, University of Missouri, Columbia, 1951.

Hill, Leslie G., "The Pioneer Preacher in Missouri." Master's thesis, University of Missouri, Columbia, 1948.

Jones, Claude, "The Status of the Whig Party in Missouri from 1848–1854." Master's thesis, University of Missouri, Columbia, 1930.

Lewis, Donald Fremont, "Economic and Social Life in the French Villages of Missouri." Master's thesis, University of Missouri, Columbia, 1936.

McCandless, Perry G., "Thomas Hart Benton, His Source of Political Strength in Missouri from 1815 to 1838." Doctoral dissertation, University of Missouri, Columbia, 1953.

McClure, Clarence, "Opposition to the Reelection of Thomas Hart Benton in 1844." Master's thesis, University of Missouri, Columbia, 1913.

McCurdy, Frances Lea, "Pioneer Orators of Missouri." Doctoral dissertation, University of Missouri, Columbia, 1957.

Newhard, Leota Mabel, "The Beginnings of the Whig Party in Missouri." Master's thesis, University of Missouri, Columbia, 1928.

Schilling, Sister Mary Felicia, "The Catholic Church in Kansas City and in Southwest Missouri." Master's thesis, University of Missouri, Columbia, 1943.

Seelen, William Earl, "A Rhetorical Criticism of Thomas Hart Benton's Expunging Speech." Master's thesis, University of Missouri, Columbia, 1940.

Utz, Cornelius, "Life in Missouri, 1800–1840, as Pictured in Travellers' Accounts, Letters and Journals." Master's thesis, University of Missouri, Columbia, 1933.

West, Alma M., "The Earlier Political Career of Claiborne Fox Jackson, 1836–1851." Master's thesis, University of Missouri, Columbia, 1941.

VI. NEWSPAPERS

The following newspapers are located in the library of The State Historical Society of Missouri, Columbia.

[Boonville] *Missouri Register*, July, 1840.

Boonville Observer, March, 1844–December, 1849.

[Bowling Green] *The Salt River Journal*, November, 1839–October, 1841.

The Canton Press, August 12, 1869; September 23, 1869; January 27, 1870; August 4, 1870.

[Columbia] *Missouri Intelligencer and Boon's Lick Advertiser*, May, 1830–December 5, 1835.

[Columbia] *The Missouri Statesman*, July, 1848–December, 1852.

[Fayette] *Boon's Lick Times*, July, 1840–December, 1844.

[Fayette] *Missouri Intelligencer and Boon's Lick Advertiser*, June, 1826–April, 1830.

[Fayette] *The Western Monitor*, February, 1829–December, 1830.

[Franklin] *Missouri Intelligencer*, November, 1819–June, 1826.

[Franklin] *Missouri Intelligencer and Boon's Lick Advertiser*, April 23, 1819–October 15, 1819.

Fulton Telegraph, August, 1848–December, 1849.

Glasgow Weekly Times, October, 1848–December, 1852.

[Jackson] *Independent Patriot*, December, 1820–December, 1826.

[Jefferson City] *Daily Jefferson Inquirer*, August 25, 1860; September 8, 1860; November 3, 1860; January 19, 1861; January 26, 1861; January 28, 1861.

[Jefferson City] *The Daily Tribune*, November 28, 1893.

[Jefferson City] *Jefferson Inquirer*, January, 1843–December, 1850.

[Jefferson City] *Jeffersonian Republican*, January, 1834–March, 1843.

[Jefferson City] *Metropolitan*, October 30, 1849.

Lexington Express, July, 1844–December, 1844.

[Liberty] *The Weekly Tribune*, January, 1847–December, 1849; July 20, 1866; October 12, 1866; October 18, 1867; August 28, 1868.

[Palmyra] *The Missouri Whig*, July, 1845–June, 1846.

[St. Charles] *The Missourian*, June, 1820–October, 1822.

[St. Louis] *Louisiana Gazette*, November 30, 1809–July 18, 1812.

[St. Louis] *Missouri Gazette*, July, 1808–November 23, 1809.

[St. Louis] *Missouri Gazette*, July 15, 1815–May, 1818.

[St. Louis] *Missouri Gazette and Illinois Advertiser*, February 26, 1814–July 8, 1815.

[St. Louis] *Missouri Gazette and Illinois Advertiser*, May 8, 1818–July 3, 1818.

[St. Louis] *Missouri Gazette and Public Advertiser*, July 10, 1818–March 6, 1822.

[St. Louis] *Missouri Republican*, March 20, 1822–December 23, 1828.

[St. Louis] *Missouri Republican*, January, 1849–March, 1850, daily.

[St. Louis] *Daily Missouri Republican*, March, 1841–August, 1841; January 19, 1870.

St. Louis Beacon, June, 1829–December, 1832.

St. Louis Enquirer, December 23, 1818–March 10, 1819, photostatic copy. March 17, 1819–December 20, 1819; May 10, 1820–December 30, 1820; May 17, 1820–September, 1822.

Semi-Weekly St. Louis Enquirer, September 4, 1819–August 30, 1820.

Springfield Advertiser, May, 1844–June, 1847.

Index